Forensic Investigation of UNUSUAL FIREARMS

Ballistic and Medico-Legal Evidence

Forensic Investigation of UNUSUAL FIREARMS

Ballistic and Medico-Legal Evidence

J.K. Sinha, PhD
Former Director In-charge and Deputy Director (Ballistics)
Central Forensic Science Laboratory
Chandigarh, India

CRC Press
Taylor & Francis Group
Boca Raton London New York

CRC Press is an imprint of the
Taylor & Francis Group, an **informa** business

CRC Press
Taylor & Francis Group
6000 Broken Sound Parkway NW, Suite 300
Boca Raton, FL 33487-2742

First issued in paperback 2021

ISBN-13: 978-0-367-77868-2 (pbk)
ISBN-13: 978-1-4665-7137-2 (hbk)

Library of Congress Cataloging-in-Publication Data

Sinha, J. K.
Forensic investigation of unusual firearms : ballistic and medico-legal evidence / J.K. Sinha.
pages cm
"A CRC title."
Includes bibliographical references and index.
ISBN 978-1-4665-7137-2
1. Forensic ballistics. 2. Firearms--Identification. 3. Firearms--Markings. I. Title.

HV8077.S57 2015
363.25'62--dc23 2014021769

Visit the Taylor & Francis Web site at
http://www.taylorandfrancis.com

and the CRC Press Web site at
http://www.crcpress.com

Dedicated to my loving grandchildren,
Ananya, Ambika, and Aryan

Contents

Foreword **xiii**
Preface **xv**
Acknowledgments **xix**
About the Author **xxi**

1 Introduction to Unusual Firearms **1**

1.1 Advent of Unusual Firearms in Crime 2
1.2 Making/Manufacture of Illegal Firearms 3
1.2.1 Illegally Modified, Legal Firearms 3
1.2.2 Substandard and Copies of Branded Firearms 4
1.2.3 Homemade Firearms 7
1.3 Inappropriate Constructional Features of Unusual Firearms 7
1.3.1 Irregular Rifling 9
1.3.2 Varying Barrel Shape and Size 9
1.3.2.1 Barrel Shape 10
1.3.3 Varying Bore Dimension 10
1.3.3.1 Varying Breech Diameter 12
1.3.3.2 Varying Muzzle Diameter 12
1.3.4 Varying Barrel Lengths Irrespective of Type of Ammunition 12
1.3.5 Varying Muzzle and Breech Thickness Irrespective of Type of Ammunition 13
1.3.6 Varying Chambers: Shape and Size 13
1.3.6.1 Relative Chamber–Bore Diameter 15
1.3.6.2 Relative Chamber–Bore Alignment 15
1.3.6.3 Chamber Length 15
1.3.6.4 Irregular Bottlenecked Chamber 16
1.4 Cartridge Headspace 16
1.5 Unusual Firing Pin Arrangement 18
1.6 Trigger Pull 18
1.7 Locking Arrangement 19
1.7.1 Unusual Locking Arrangement 19

1.8 Caliber Designation of Unusual Firearms: New Nomenclatures 20
1.8.1 Bore/Caliber Designation 20
1.8.1.1 Relative Bullet–Bore Diameter Designation 20
1.8.1.2 Relative Wad–Bore Diameter Designation 21

2 Forensic Investigation of Fired Cartridges of Unusual Firearms 23

2.1 Breech Face Marks 24
2.1.1 Modified Procedures for Reproducing Breech Marks 27
2.1.1.1 Inappropriate Constructional Features 27
2.1.1.2 Tampered Firearm 28
2.1.2 Evaluation of Deceptive and Ambiguous Marks 33
2.1.2.1 Deceptive Striations on Primer 33
2.1.2.2 Deceptive Striations Due to Cartridge Tampering 36
2.1.2.3 Breech Scrape Marks and Deceptive Partial Sliding Marks 37
2.1.3 Examination of Breech and Unusual Firearms 38
2.1.3.1 Elimination by Striated Breech Comparison 40
2.2 Chamber Marks 41
2.2.1 Chamber Shape and Size 42
2.2.2 Chamber–Bore Joint Marks 43
2.2.3 Modified Procedures for Reproducing Chamber Marks 44
2.2.3.1 Chamber Marks without Firing 45
2.2.3.2 Chamber Marks by Low-Pressure Test Rounds 47
2.3 Firing Pin Marks 47
2.3.1 Evaluation of Multifiring Pin Hits 48
2.3.2 Tampered Firing Pin 51
2.3.2.1 Replaced Firing Pin 52
2.3.2.2 Firing Pin Periphery Marks 53
2.3.2.3 Firing Pin Marks without Test Firing 54
2.4 Extractor and Ejector Marks 55
2.4.1 Extractor Marks by Low-Pressure Round 56
2.4.2 Ejector Marks and Tampered Firearms 57
2.5 Summary of Modified Cartridge Identification Procedures 59

3 Forensic Investigation of Fired Bullets from Unusual Firearms 61

3.1 Inappropriate Rifled Bore Barrel Marks 63
3.1.1 Under-Bore Sized Rifled Barrels 63
3.1.1.1 Lead Bullets 63
3.1.1.2 Jacketed Bullets 64
3.1.2 Over-Bore Sized Rifled Barrels 65
3.1.2.1 Slightly Oversized Rifled Barrels 65
3.1.2.2 Excessively Oversized Rifled Bore 67
3.1.3 Inappropriate Modified Chamber 67
3.1.4 Inappropriate/Irregular Rifling 67
3.1.5 Mismatch Rifled Firearms 68
3.2 Smoothbore Firearms Using Rifled Ammunition 69
3.2.1 Smoothbore Barrel Marks Using Rifled Ammunition 70
3.2.1.1 Undersized Smoothbore Barrel Marks 70
3.2.1.2 Oversized Smoothbore Barrel Marks 71
3.2.1.3 Variable Smoothbore Barrel Marks 74
3.2.2 Class Characteristic Parameters of Unusual Firearms: New Parameters 76
3.2.2.1 Assessment of Bore Size from Barrel Marks 77
3.2.2.2 Assessment of Chamber Alignment From Barrel Marks 81
3.2.2.3 Assessment of Longitudinal Joints or Protrusions from Barrel Marks 83
3.2.3 Identification of Bullets Fired from Smoothbore Firearm 83
3.2.3.1 Undersized Smoothbore Firearms 84
3.2.3.2 Oversized Smoothbore Firearms 87
3.2.3.3 Mixed-Sized, Smoothbore Firearms 91

4 Forensic Investigation of Fired Shot Charge of Unusual Firearms 93

4.1 Dispersion of Pellets and Possible Misleading Range Determination 95
4.1.1 Type of Wad 95
4.1.1.1 Uncupped Shotgun Cartridge and Spread of Pellets 95
4.1.1.2 Cupped Shotgun Cartridge and Spread of Pellets 97

4.1.2 Barrel Dimension 97
4.1.2.1 Choke 97
4.1.2.2 Barrel Length 98
4.2 Linkage of Fired Pellets with Suspect Firearm 101
4.2.1 Barrel Marks on Fired Shot/Pellets 101
4.2.2 Reproducibility and Identification of Barrel Marks 101
4.3 Misleading Conclusion on Number of Fires from Fired Pellets 105
4.4 Pellets without Striations Appear as Unfired, Whether Fired or Not 108
4.5 Reloaded Shot Size from a Fired Shell 110
4.6 Dispersion of Wads and Reconstruction of Shooting Incidents 112
4.6.1 Wads at the Crime Scene 113
4.6.1.1 Flight of Closing Disks 114
4.6.1.2 Flight of Cushion/Sealing Wads 116
4.6.2 Unusual Firearms and Flight of Wads 118
4.7 Unusual Barrel Marks on Wads 119
4.8 Cartridge Splits and Unusual Chamber Marks on Fired Wads 120

5 Unusual Firearms and Medico-Legal Evidence 123

5.1 Shape and Size of Bullet Hole 123
5.1.1 Unrifled Bore Using Rifled Ammunition 124
5.1.1.1 Undersized, Unrifled Bore 125
5.1.1.2 Oversized, Unrifled Bore 128
5.1.1.3 Unusual Bent Bullets 128
5.1.1.4 Variable Unrifled Bore and Bullet Holes 128
5.1.2 Unusual Rifled Firearms 129
5.2 Presence or Absence of the Close-Range Phenomena 130
5.2.1 Burning 131
5.2.2 Scorching 131
5.2.3 Blackening 132
5.2.4 Powder Tattooing 132
5.2.4.1 Unusual Firearms and Powder Tattooing 133
5.2.5 Metal Vapor Smudging 133
5.2.6 Projectile Scrapings (Bullet Chips) 133
5.2.7 Gunshot Residue (GSR) Particles 135
5.2.7.1 Absence of Close-Range Phenomena 135
5.2.8 Unusual Firearms and Contact Shots 135

5.3 Abraded and Dirt Collar 135
5.3.1 Abraded Collar 138
5.3.2 Dirt Collar/Ring 138
5.3.3 Visual Examination of Firearm Injuries and Caution Needed 138
5.3.4 Blackening and Blackened Bullet Periphery 138
5.3.5 Detection of Powder Particles on the Bare Body 141
5.4 Probable Caliber of Bullet and Type of Firearm from Bullet Hole 143
5.4.1 Caliber from Bullet Hole 143
5.4.2 Determining the Type of Firearm from a Bullet Hole 144
5.4.2.1 Type of Firearm from Shape and Size of Bullet Hole and Keyhole 144
5.4.2.2 Type of Firearm from Curved Keyhole 144
5.4.2.3 Type of Firearm from Circular and Oval Holes 145
5.5 Entry Wound and Direction of Fire 146
5.6 Projectile–Tissue Interactions and the Wound Track 151
5.7 Exit Holes and Unusual Firearms 152
5.8 Wounding Effect of Fired Bullets of Unusual Firearms 154
5.8.1 Determination of Striking Velocity 155
5.8.1.1 Muzzle Velocity 155
5.8.1.2 Ballistic Coefficient 156
5.8.1.3 Remaining Velocity 157
5.8.2 Orientation/Area of Presentation of Nonspinning Bullets at Impact 158
5.8.3 Wounding Capability of Nonspinning Bullets of Unusual Firearms 158

6 Additional Reading 161

6.1 Firearm Discharge and Time of Firing 161
6.1.1 Evidence of Firing and Unusual Firearms 161
6.1.2 Time of Firing 163
6.1.2.1 Time of Firing of Firearm 164
6.1.2.2 Time of Firing of Fired Cartridge 169
6.2 Unusual Rifling Marks on Jacket Pieces and Lead Core 170

Related References and Readings 175

Index 179

Foreword

The art of manufacturing country-made and improvised firearms in home-made workshops and illicit factories is no more the domain of developing and underdeveloped countries but is now emerging its monstrous head even in the developed and western world. In the constant waging war for superiority between forensic scientists and criminals, the onslaught of peculiar operational characteristics of illegally made firearms renders even recent scientific advances ineffective. The greatest drawback with country-made firearms is that the usual determinable inferences are no longer valid and can mislead crime scene reconstruction and the evaluation process of gunshot injuries with disastrous outcomes.

Dr. J. K. Sinha's book, *Forensic Investigation of Unusual Firearms: Ballistic and Medico-Legal Evidence*, deals with varied forensic aspects of country-made and improvised firearms and is a treatise that will be highly relevant to present day investigators and law enforcement officers, defence and prosecution attorneys, the judiciary from all over the world and, of course, forensic scientists and university students.

So far there has not been a comprehensive forensic-related study of country-made firearms that could aid the forensic experts to counter the ill effects of the situation. A book on forensic aspects of country-made firearms was a long felt necessity for forensic professionals. This book fills this treacherous gap in the field. An honest attempt has been made to provide innovative solutions to the vexed issues, those deemed to be generally unsolvable. The book covers investigative, forensic and legal aspects of country-made firearms in great detail. Some interesting case studies, keynotes and cautions so experts can avoid likely misleading conclusions are very helpful. A chapter on medico-legal aspects of gunshot wounds caused by country-made and improvised firearms has been added for the benefit of medico-legal experts and forensic medicine students. Good illustrative photographs that aid in easy understanding of the text illustrate the book.

I am sure that this book will be a great companion to forensic scientists and to all who are related to the field.

Dr. M. S. Rao
Ex-Director cum Chief Forensic Scientist
Ministry of Home Affairs, Govt. of India, New Delhi, India
Honorary Advisor, Gujarat Forensic Science University
Gandhinagar, Gujarat, India

Preface

I have had the opportunity of examining more than 5,000 criminal cases as an expert of the federal (central) government of India for 34 years. I came across a wide variety of firearms—modern, obsolete, improvised, and homemade. Amongst the firearms that fascinated me most were nonbranded, substandard firearms that were different from the usual firearms both in appearance and from a forensic point of view. They were cheap, substandard firearms manufactured in clandestine factories, improvised/converted firearms, and homemade firearms. They defied known nomenclatures, classification/identification criteria, and crime scene investigative procedures. It often led to unpredictable and misleading reconstruction of the shooting incident, in identifying the type of firearm from class characteristics marks, in linking the fired bullets of smoothbore barrels, in ascertaining range and angle of fire, and the wounding effect. It was equally problematic and misleading when legally owned firearms were tampered with, modified, or improvised to evade detection.

A plausible solution to these problems of forensics was lacking in available firearm books. The working manuals of federal/state forensic laboratories in India and abroad that I had come across also lacked such details. Research publications on the topic were meager and scanty. Admittedly, not much research had been done to fully exploit the unusual firearms evidence. A vast area of possibilities was left unexplored for seemingly unattainable results. In short, usual procedures of investigation and identification known to firearm examiners were not available in cases involving illegally made, substandard firearms. Hence, being noncommittal was the safest recourse, especially in "no gun" cases. Surprisingly, a big chunk (more than 25% of the shooting incidents) were from low-cost, illegally made, nonstandard firearms, popularly known as *country-made firearms*. In the absence of adequate scientific data, a sizeable number of crimes thus remained devoid of connecting the criminal through the weapon of the offense and crime scene reconstruction. Apparently, the scenario called for a detailed forensic study of unusual firearms.

With this in mind, the problem was approached in a systematic way involving about 1,000 country-made firearms of various types that had been used in various crimes in this region of the country. Based on exhaustive experimental results and their plausible interpretation, it was possible to identify and determine the new class characteristic parameters needed to establish linkage of projectile with irregular rifled and smoothbore barrels. This was done primarily by modifying identification procedures to identify parameters for determining bullet diameter and type of unusual firearm from bullet holes, and to construct a modified ballistic table for nonspinning projectiles. My area of research and thesis centered on these case-oriented practical problems involving unusual firearms. Many research papers on the topic were published and presented in conferences and seminars in India and abroad, although many more significant findings still remained unpublished.

In the early 1990s, IBIS (Integrated Ballistic Identification System) emerged as a powerful investigative tool for zeroing in on the suspect firearm and its owner from a data bank of stored digital images of fired sample cartridges and bullets from legally owned and legally manufactured regular, branded firearms. Though short-lived due to inherent limitations well known and documented, IBIS had a great impact in the criminal world for finding ways to evade detection by this popular new investigative tool. The early success of IBIS in actual criminal cases also contributed to the advent of unusual firearms in crime. Use of illegally made, improvised, and homemade firearms obviously was the safest alternative, because these firearms and their owners remained exempt from the precincts of firearm tracing and the IBIS data bank. The resultant fallout was the worldwide flourishing trade of illegally made, substandard firearms and their frequent usage in crime.

With a view to share my experiences on less-known forensic investigation of unusual firearms, after my retirement in the 1990s, I hosted a forensic firearm web page called "Sinha's Forensic Firearm Experts Page" (www.geocities.com/j_ksinha); presently the address is www.forensicfirearminvestigation.com. It covered a few of my published and unpublished papers highlighting problems associated with ambiguous, misleading, and unusual exhibits in firearm cases, with a special reference to unusual firearms and their remedial measures. As expected, there had been overwhelming response in view of worldwide exponential increase in the use of illegally made, substandard firearms in crime. It is believed that more than 90% of crimes committed worldwide are by illegally procured or illegally made firearms. Needless to say, the professionals in the field have long felt the necessity of an exhaustive treatise on forensic investigation of unusual firearms that would essentially help in minimizing noncommittal inferences and in eliminating erroneous conclusions. It seemed to be the need of the hour and, hence, this book, which is exclusively on forensic investigation of fired cartridges, bullets, shot charge of illegally made substandard unusual firearms, and evaluation of allied medico-legal issues of forensic importance.

Highlighting the salient features of the book, Chapter 1 introduces readers to unusual firearms. Briefly, it reviews the increasing worldwide trend of illegal and illegally made firearms in crime, their potential cause, and remedial measures. It introduces new nomenclature and classification criteria. Chapter 2 discusses forensic significance of fired cartridges from unusual firearms. It suggests modified identification techniques for establishing linkages and the caution needed while evaluating ambiguous and deceptive marks on fired cartridges. Chapter 3 is devoted to less-known barrel marks by various bullet–bore combinations of illegally made rifled and smoothbore firearms. It suggests innovative, fool-proof procedures for linkage with smoothbore, unusual firearms. Chapter 4 describes barrel marks on fired shots (pellets) and explores the possibility of their reproduction for establishing linkage with the suspect firearm, especially locally made handguns. It discusses range and direction of fire from pellet dispersion and wads in "no gun" cases and the caution needed thereof. Chapter 5 (on medico-legal evidence) deals with the bullet wound/bullet hole characteristics of illegally made, substandard, rifled, and smoothbore firearms. It suggests caution on significant issues relating to direction and close range of fire in "no gun" cases. It introduces a suitable ballistic table for nonspinning bullets fired from substandard, unusual, smoothbore and rifled firearms. Chapter 6 includes case studies that evaluate the time of firing and the unusual rifling marks for identifying lead core and nonidentifying jacket pieces.

J. K. Sinha

Acknowledgments

I wish to express my sincere thanks to my professional colleagues, especially Professor R. M. Sharma, Dr. J. K. Modi, B. C. Ravindra, Dr. N. P. Waghmare, Dr. S. K. Jain and R. Suresh for their direct or indirect help and useful suggestions that have found their way into this book.

I acknowledge and express my very great appreciation for Dr. Bharat Singh, a noted autopsy surgeon and forensic medicine expert for giving his valuable time for discussions and constructive suggestions on firearm injury illustrations.

I am particularly grateful to Dr. M. S. Rao, former chief forensic scientist and honorary advisor at Gujrat Forensic Science University, for writing the Foreword for this book.

I sincerely acknowledge rights holders of journals for granting me permission to reuse partial content, figures, tables, etc. of my previously published papers.

Lastly I would like to thank my family, especially my wife, whose encouragement gave me constant strength throughout the writing of this book. My son, despite his very busy schedule, helped me in reading through my manuscript to give me feedback on the lucidity of my writing.

About the Author

J. K. Sinha earned his PhD degree in forensic science and has been associated with this field for more than half a century. An internationally known, forensic firearm consultant, he has been a firearm examiner of the Indian federal/central government for 34 years and served as director in-charge and deputy director (ballistics). He has examined more than 5,000 firearm cases and has testified in hundreds of courts as a prosecution, defense, and court witness. His testimony on significant forensic issues can be found in law journals of court judgments, and referred to as case law by practicing attorneys/lawyers in India.

Dr. Sinha has been actively engaged in university teaching and research in forensic science. He has supervised successful PhD candidates on topics related to forensic ballistics and explosives. His area of research revolved around case-oriented practical problems and development of innovative identification techniques. He has published several papers in India and abroad. He has added new dimensions in the little-known and unsolvable area of illegally made firearms; his popular web page on forensic firearm and unusual forensic ballistics (www.forensicfirearmidentification.com) ranks among the top five in almost all popular search engines, directories, and metacrawlers. Dr. Sinha had been the editor of the forensic firearm category of the open directory project of Netscape (popular web browser). Some of his published papers and unpublished work on evaluation of unusual, evidentiary clues detailed in his website are cited and referenced by many popular forensic firearm sites, online educational institutes, manuals and books on forensic firearms, and forensic medicine.

1 Introduction to Unusual Firearms

Modern era has witnessed extensive use of firearms as a weapon of offense for a variety of purposes ranging from petty crime to gang/militant warfare. Being an effective device for propelling a projectile from a considerable distance with sufficient velocity and wounding capability, it has become the weapon of choice for homicidal purposes and so also for antisocial activities, such as militancy, rigging of elections, communal riots, gang war, drugs smuggling, public demonstrations, etc. The consequential fallout is the ever-increasing demand for firearms for criminal and antisocial activities. A wide variety of firearms are readily available for military and civilian purposes. The firearms that can conveniently be carried and operated by one person are of interest in the forensic field. They include service and hunting rifles, revolvers and pistols, carbines and submachine guns, shotguns and muzzle loaders, to name a few. These firearms are commonly used in crimes. In recent years, the use of illegally produced firearms has increased exponentially worldwide. Frequent seizures of a variety of illegally made firearms and unearthing of substandard/clandestine firearm factories in various countries, which are documented, include the United States, Canada, United Kingdom, and France as well as ones in Latin American countries, South Africa, China, India, the Philippines, and other Southeast Asian countries.

Among the illegal firearms that are commonly encountered in crimes are:

- Stolen, smuggled, or illegally procured branded legal firearms
- Illegally modified legal firearms
- Copies of popular branded firearms
- Cheap, substandard firearms manufactured in clandestine factories
- Functional firearms modified from replica guns, starter pistols, toy guns, air guns, etc.
- Disguised firearms converted from items of common use, such as mobile phones, pens, key chains, walking sticks, etc.
- Homemade firearms that are easy to make from readily available materials, inexpensive, and fairly effective at short ranges

The constructional features of illegally made firearms are varied. Copies and converted replicas may look genuine and similar in external appearance. The design and general makeup of illegal firearms made at different sources make them a class apart. They are often dissimilar from legally made conventional firearms that fire similar ammunition. They differ both from a forensic point of view and in appearance, and, hence, they are designated as unusual firearms.

1.1 Advent of Unusual Firearms in Crime

It is a shocking global statistic that a vast majority of firearms that are usually encountered in crime are either illegally made or illegally procured regular firearms. Their frequent use in criminal and antisocial activities has reached an alarming proportion, especially in developing countries. The reasons for the advent of illegally made, unusual firearms in crime are varied. However, the main reason is a stringent licensing policy for legal firearms and easy availability of unusual firearms as an alternate remedy.

The majority of countries enforce stringent laws for possession of firearms. Those having liberal laws also enforce strict licensing policies for juveniles and those citizens who have past records of criminal and antisocial activities. Even domestic violence is viewed as a potential factor for refusal of a gun license. The lower strata of society, from where the bulk of violent criminal is drawn, is deprived of firearm licenses. Yet, the utility of a firearm as the greatest equalizer among the physically weak and the strong is fully realized. The consequential fallout is the flourishing trade of illegally produced or illegally procured firearms. Other reasons that promote the sale and use of illegally made firearms include:

- Even a licensee has to pay a good deal of money for acquiring a firearm. The price increases manyfold in illegal trade. Therefore, the average violent or one-time criminal prefers to spend less and go for illegally made firearms.
- Financially unsound startup gang/militant groups requiring a sizeable number and varieties of firearms prefer to go for easily available, illicit-branded firearms and/or for illegally made, unusual firearms.
- The infrastructure existing in areas of legal gun factories can conveniently be exploited in setting up clandestine workshop/factories. Skilled workers in gun factories, especially those who are disgruntled, retired, or fired, contribute to the required know-how. The old manufacturing machines, on upgrading or closure of the unit, are easily procurable without legal hassles and at a low cost. Clandestine factories are mushrooming worldwide to meet ever-increasing demand.
- It is easy to set up a home workshop for making homemade firearms from easily available materials. Making of homemade firearms is a

lucrative and profitable cottage industry in areas of great demand. This is becoming a flourishing trade worldwide because of low-cost and easily made firearms that are available on order.
- Items of common use and replicas can be made into functional guns by a converter specialist at a low cost. They are being converted on the commercial scale as well. They are cheap and easily available in illegal markets.
- Books, along with kits, are available for making pistols, carbines, and other firearms with easily available material at home without much expertise or know-how.
- Worldwide juveniles are actively engaged in making of homemade contraptions for fun and antisocial acts. Their ingenuity supersedes the gun professionals. This accounts for availability of a variety of unusual firearms and their frequent use in crimes. It is believed that even plastic tubes have been used as barrels, which go undetected under x-ray. Other than self-made, some prefer to go for easily available, cheap firearms instead of sophisticated and costly ones. Cheap substandard pistols are equally popular among juveniles in the United States. They are popularly known as "Saturday Night Specials" and "ring of fire."

1.2 Making/Manufacture of Illegal Firearms

Making and manufacturing processes of illegal firearms is no secret, but it is outside the preview of this book. There is ample literature on the subject in the form of books, journals, and web sites. This book is relevant, however, to the extent of investigative, scientific, and legal aspects of crime involving *unusual* firearms. Therefore, representative, unusual firearms, wherever needed, has been included for illustrations for easy understanding of the text. This aids in a meaningful understanding of the unusual firearms and likely misleading inferences. They are discussed in the subsequent chapters, which deal with various aspects of forensic investigation of unusual firearms.

1.2.1 Illegally Modified, Legal Firearms

Branded legal firearms are sometimes modified to fire different caliber ammunition that is easily available and cheap. Their parts are modified or replaced accordingly. The commonly modified parts for firing different caliber ammunition are chamber and bore dimensions. Sometimes, the barrel itself is replaced. Other parts may be modified or replaced, if needed. The author had the opportunity to examine such firearms. For example:

- In a criminal case, a 9 mm LLAMA auto pistol was improvised to fire 7.65 mm auto cartridges. The rifled barrel of the 9 mm pistol was replaced with a smoothbore barrel. The bore diameter of the replaced barrel was less than 7.65 mm (.29 inch). The original pistol magazine, though designed to house 9 mm auto cartridges, could also load 7.65 mm auto cartridges manually as well as through the magazine. Therefore, the magazine was not required to be replaced or modified. The pistol was used in the crime to fire 7.65 mm cartridges as a self-loader.
- In another criminal case, an obsolete .32 sporting rifle was improvised to fire .303 cartridges. The chamber was modified to fire .303 cartridges. The cartridges for the sporting rifle were not available even at high cost. It was almost obsolete. The chamber of the rifled barrel was modified to accommodate and fire easily available .303 cartridges.
- It is believed that service rifles have been modified to fire available, different caliber ammunition in the Philippines in World War II. The skilled gunmakers of Danao (province of Bohol) modified the chamber of Japanese service rifles to fire .30 rifle cartridges of the U.S. army.

Note: In "no gun" cases, neither the base markings on the fired cartridges nor the rifling marks on the fired bullets would reveal the caliber and type of firearm used—a misleading investigative aspect.

1.2.2 Substandard and Copies of Branded Firearms

With the increasing demand of low-cost firearms, copies of branded firearms are becoming popular with criminals. Copies of revolvers, pistols, and rifles of famous brands are made/manufactured on a commercial scale. There are traditional hubs where the art of making guns has been a family trade for ages and carried down generations. A few well-known in the Southeast Asian region are worth mentioning.

The cottage industry of the traditional Darra tribal area of the Pakistan–Afghanistan border is a well-known hub for making copies of famous brand pistols, revolvers, and rifles including assault rifles and submachine guns (SMGs). It is believed that one can get a copy of branded firearms made to order of any make and model. It has a worldwide gray market, especially in neighboring countries.

The author had the opportunity of examining duplicate copies of Webley and Scott revolvers made by tribes of the Darra region. They are single- as well as double-action revolvers. Their barrels are rifled. Usually there are no proof marks. The monogram "Webley," "Made in England," and .32 MKII/MKIV serial number or alike are invariably punched on the body. Though

Figure 1.1 Copy of a .32 Webley Scott revolver.

their external appearance generally resembles the original ones, their dimensions are dissimilar compared to the specified dimension of their counterpart models of the Webley and Scott revolvers (Figure 1.1). A comparison of monogram, writing, and dimension with regular genuine revolvers clearly differentiates between the two.

Munger is a traditional hub for the indigenous gunmaking industry in India. The skilled illegal gunmakers of Munger are famous for making copies of branded firearms. Known for making single-shot, crude, homemade pistols, popularly known as *Katta*. They have now switched over to commercial scale manufacturing of copies of popular western pistols/revolvers, such as the Webley and Scott, Beretta, Smith and Wesson, Colt, Ruger, etc. The make of the branded firearm is usually punched on the pistols/revolvers, such as Made in USA, Made in China, Made in Italy, etc. Serial numbers also are usually mentioned, but they are very poorly written. Handguns, rifles, and SMGs are in great demand among criminals, terrorists, and antisocial activists of the country and neighboring countries like Nepal and Bangladesh (Figure 1.2(a)–(c)).

Danao City on the island of Cebu is a traditional hub in the Philippines that is engaged in the making of illegal firearms. It has been a family trade for ages, and the area is known for homemade firearms popularly known as *Paltik*. Copies of popular firearms are now made on a commercial scale in clandestine and established factories to meet the ever-increasing demand of criminal gangs, rebels, and separatists.

In view of increasing demand of cheap firearms, worldwide clandestine factories are engaged in the manufacture of copies of branded firearms whose ammunition is easily available. In India, as well, several clandestine factories have started making illegal firearms to meet the growing demand of ever-increasing criminals, gangs, and militant groups in the country.

(a)

(b)

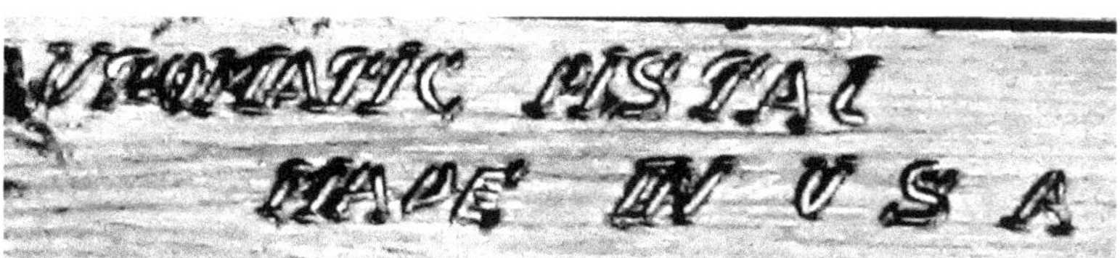

(c)

Figure 1.2 Illegally made (a) auto pistol (b) revolver (c) misleading punched mark.

1.2.3 Homemade Firearms

Homemade firearms are characterized by certain features that have set them apart and put them in a class of their own.

1. They are often crude productions from easily available materials, which differ from one firearm to the other. Even water pipes, coffee percolators, and steering wheel tubes are used.
2. They are often made to order by local blacksmiths, ironmongers, or by clandestine factories.
3. The overriding determinant for the type of the firearm to be manufactured is the availability of the ammunition and convenient concealment of the weapon.
4. They do not conform to specified dimensions of corresponding branded firearms; hence, both aim and range suffer.
5. They are usually short barreled, irrespective of the type of ammunition used.
6. They are usually smoothbore, but designed to fire easily available pistol, revolver, and rifle cartridges besides shotgun cartridges.
7. They are dangerous, and may injure the shooter him/herself.

Homemade firearms are usually single shot, short barreled firearms. They also may be double barreled and revolvers (Figure 1.3(a)(b)).

1.3 Inappropriate Constructional Features of Unusual Firearms

It is the inappropriate constructional features that differentiate legally and illegally made/manufactured firearms. Even same caliber firearms show extreme dimensional variations from their counterpart branded firearms and also amongst themselves that are made at different sources. This matters most in arriving at significant forensic inferences. For an easy and clear understanding of the text to follow, it is necessary to discuss the constructional features of unusual firearms that influence significantly the evaluation of evidentiary clues and in reconstructing the shooting incident. The constructional features of unusual firearms that need detailed discussions include rifling characteristics, chamber and barrel dimension, cartridge head space, and firing and locking arrangements. The constructional features of homemade firearms are so varied that they embrace all possible extreme variations. They also are demonstrable through illustrative photographs, which are usually not possible with factory-made substandard, unusual firearms. Therefore, for clarity and a meaningful understanding, the illustrations relate to homemade firearms, wherever needed.

(a)

(b)

(c)

Figure 1.3 Homemade (a) 12-bore, double-barrel pistol and (b) single-shot .38 pistol (c) revolver.

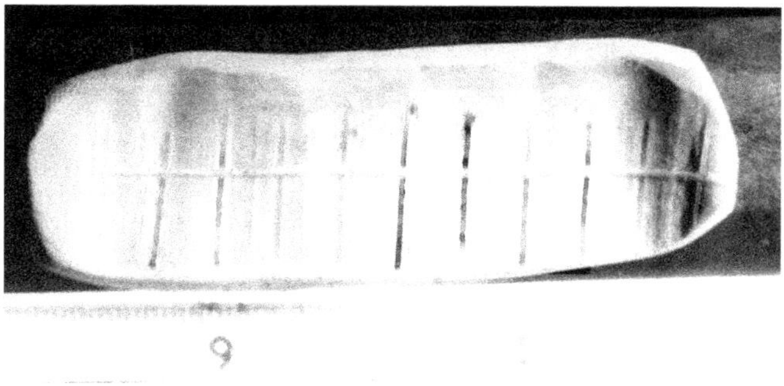

Figure 1.4 Varying land/groove widths and angle of slant on bullet fired by irregular rifling.

1.3.1 Irregular Rifling

Rifling is the most important constructional feature of a rifled firearm. The projectiles that are fired from rifled firearms are cylindro-conical. They are spin-stabilized projectiles. Spin is provided by spiral grooves that are cut longitudinally inside the barrel having uniform pitch, known as rifling. It needs sophisticated equipment to provide precise rifling dimensions. It increases the cost of production exponentially. To keep the cost low, proper rifling is seldom provided in illegally made firearms. The grooves, instead of spiral may be straight. The groove widths may vary in the same rifled barrel; so, also, does the angle of rifling vary from one groove to the other. For a meaningful illustration of inappropriate rifling, a bullet fired from an illegally made rifled pistol was rolled over plasticine, its imprinted demarcated lands and grooves showing clearly variable width and angle of slant (Figure 1.4).

It is apparent that despite a provision of rifling, the bullet does not achieve proper spin. This affects the ballistics of the emergent bullet. The need for proper rifling is often offset because of effective wounding capabilities at short ranges, an ideal low-cost companion of criminals for offense or defense. In fact, it is the external craftsmanship of illegally made guns that is taken care of because the same fetches more money at a low cost of production.

1.3.2 Varying Barrel Shape and Size

Barrels of branded firearms are made from alloy steel of high tensile strength and elasticity. Contrarily, the barrels of illegally made firearms are usually made from cheap and easily available materials and, hence, the desired tensile strength and elasticity is seldom achieved. The barrels of substandard pistols are invariably made from cheap alloy steel. However, the need is often offset because illegally made firearms invariably develop low pressure compared to those of their branded counterparts.

Barrels designed to fire same/similar specific ammunition vary in shape and size. Their bore and chamber dimensions also vary considerably. The likely variations are enumerated below.

1.3.2.1 Barrel Shape

Unlike regular rifled firearms, the barrel shape may not necessarily depend on the type of ammunition used, especially if it is a homemade firearm. The popular shapes are true cylindrical, tapered, or multigradient.

1. True cylindrical: Usually found in improvised and homemade firearms. It has added advantages:
   a. The rear end supports the rim of the cartridge and, hence, is suitable for rimmed and semirimmed cartridges.
   b. Additional provision for chamber or leed is not needed.
   c. It can easily be made/manufactured.
   d. Readymade, commonly used steel or other metal tubing is often found suitable to load and fire easily available ammunition without making modifications. Water pipes, coffee percolator parts, car steering tube parts, etc. are often used for the purpose.
2. Tapered: Usually found in homemade firearms. The tapering near the muzzle acts as a choke for firing shotgun cartridges, though it is not specially designed for that purpose. They also may be used for replacing the original barrel for firing intended rifled or shotgun cartridges.
3. Irregular shape having one or more gradient at the rear: They are usually found in homemade firearms for firing bottle-necked cartridges (Figure 1.5(a)–(c)).

1.3.3 Varying Bore Dimension

The bore diameter of a firearm is nominal, but specific, whether it is rifled or smoothbore. However, this is not true for illegally made unusual firearms.

1. The bore may be undersized, oversized, or both.
   a. The bore is usually oversized in true cylindrical barrels.
   b. The bore is undersized near the muzzle in tapered barrels and oversized at the rear.
   c. The bore diameter is not necessarily uniform from breech to muzzle except for true cylindrical barrels.
2. The bore diameter may be different for firearms designed to fire the same specific ammunition.
3. Bore diameter may be the same for firearms meant to fire different calibers ammunition.

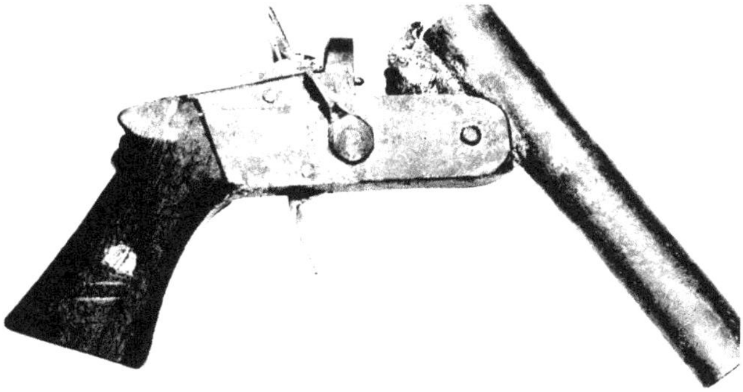

(a)

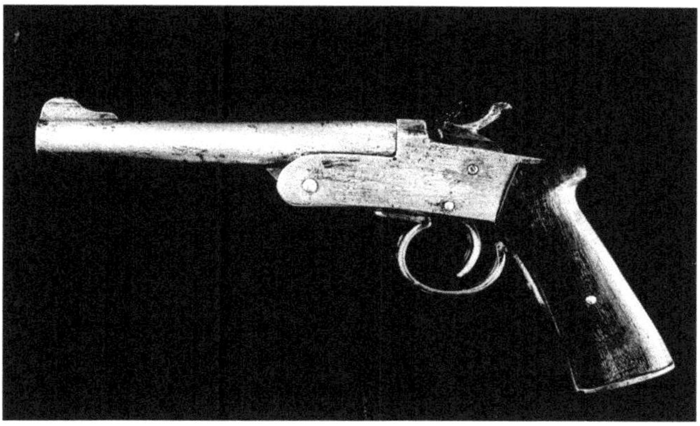

(b)

(c)

Figure 1.5 Homemade (a) 12-bore cylindrical barrel, (b) .303 tapered barrel, and (c) .303 multiple gradient barrel.

Bore diameter of illegally made firearms, especially homemade firearms, can be conveniently measured only near breech or muzzle.

1.3.3.1 Varying Breech Diameter

Breech diameter depends upon the type of the housing arrangement of the cartridge.

1. Breech diameter is less than the rim diameter, if a recess is made for housing the rim of the cartridge.
2. Breech diameter corresponds to the rim diameter of the cartridge, if provision for housing the rim is not made inside the barrel. The rim rests on the outer edge of the chamber. This is usually observed in true cylindrical barrels.

1.3.3.2 Varying Muzzle Diameter

Muzzle diameter of unusual firearms invariably does not correspond to the approximate diameter of the bullet/projectile to be fired.

1. Higher caliber firearms may have smaller muzzle diameters compared to smaller bore firearms.
2. Firearms designed to fire same caliber ammunition may have different muzzle diameters (Figure 1.6).

Note: Movement of the projectile is significantly influenced by the bore dimension. This results in varying barrel marks on fired bullets.

1.3.4 Varying Barrel Lengths Irrespective of Type of Ammunition

The length of the barrel depends on the type of ammunition used. Shotguns and rifles have long barrels, whereas pistols and revolvers have short barrels. However, illegally made, unusual firearms are usually short barreled

Figure 1.6 Different muzzle diameters of three .315 homemade pistols.

irrespective of the type of ammunition used. Their barrel lengths are usually more than two inches long excluding the chamber and vary between five to six inches. It aids in concealment. Homemade firearms designed to fire .22/.32/.38/.45 revolver and 9 mm auto handgun cartridges are short barreled. Their barrel lengths are usually three to four inches. The barrel lengths of commonly used sawed off shotguns are also far less compared to usual long-barreled shotguns. Long-barreled, illegally made firearms designed to fire shotgun or rifle cartridges are uncommon.

1.3.5 Varying Muzzle and Breech Thickness Irrespective of Type of Ammunition

Wall thickness is an important aspect in the manufacture of the barrel of a firearm. The barrel is thickest at the rear to withstand high pressure during firing. The higher the exerted pressure, the greater is the wall thickness. The barrel thickness of handguns and shotguns is less than those of high-powered rifles. However, these criteria are not adhered to in the manufacture of illegally made firearms, especially homemade firearms. A wide variation exists.

1. Different barrel thickness for firearms designed to fire same caliber ammunition
2. Similar barrel thickness for firearms designed to fire different caliber ammunition
3. Variable thickness around breech and/or muzzle
4. Irregular thickness from chamber to muzzle
5. Lesser thickness in high-velocity firearms than low-velocity firearms (Figures 1.7(a)(b))

The difference in between the breech and the muzzle is:

1. Highly significant if additional attachment is fitted at the breech end, internally or externally
2. Insignificant if chamber forms part of the barrel.
3. More thickness in continuously tapered barrel compared to other barrels.

Note: Less thickness may result in bursting of the barrel by high velocity cartridges.

1.3.6 Varying Chambers: Shape and Size

Provision for proper chamber and leed is seldom made in cheap, illegally made firearms especially homemade firearms because it is difficult to provide

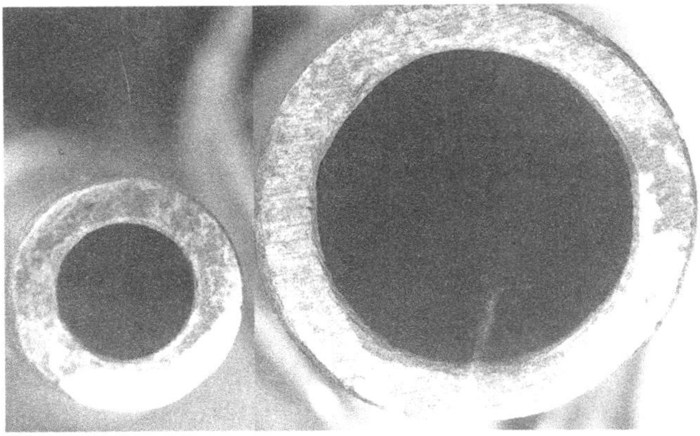

(a)

(b)

Figure 1.7 Homemade muzzle thickness: (a) .303 pistol .11 inch and 12-bore pistol .14 inch, and (b) 12-bore pistol maximum .07 inch and minimum .05 inch.

proper gradient at appropriate positions without utilizing high-precision implements. Therefore, a wide variety of chamber shape and size is generally found in unusual firearms. Their dimensions are so varying that sometimes the same firearm can accommodate and fire different caliber ammunition (Figure 1.8).

Note: The chamber of homemade firearms is invariably capable of loading and firing different caliber ammunition. The chamber shape and size may be used as a class characteristic parameter.

Figure 1.8 Three different caliber cartridges, conveniently loaded and fired, from the same firearm.

1.3.6.1 Relative Chamber–Bore Diameter

Relative chamber–bore diameter varies with the type of the barrel.

1. Chamber and bore diameters are the same in true cylindrical barrels; no demarcation exists.
2. Chamber diameter in a tapered barrel is more than bore diameter; demarcation may or may not exist.

1.3.6.2 Relative Chamber–Bore Alignment

Bullets loaded in the chamber are invariably noncoaxial with the axis of the bore in majority of unusual firearms whether rifled or smoothbore, especially in homemade firearms. It may be inclined toward the right or left to the axis of the bore. Sometimes, the chamber is loose or oversized. The cartridge sits loosely in oversized chambers. Loose chambers are neither aligned nor misaligned.

Note: The varying positioning of loaded cartridge inside the loose chamber results into (a) varying chamber marks and (b) varying bullet–barrel contacts from one round to the other.

1.3.6.3 Chamber Length

The length of the chamber is an important constructional feature of firearms especially in shotguns. A three-inch shotgun cartridge cannot be loaded in a shotgun chambered for two and one-half-inch cartridges. The

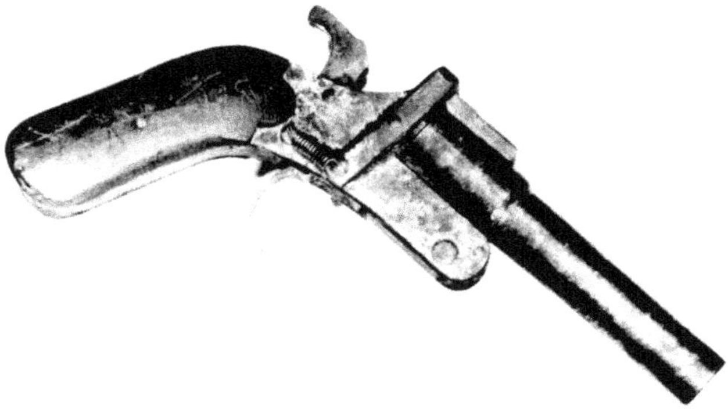

Figure 1.9 Deceptive gradient on barrel indicating chamber length.

chamber length is written on the barrel of shotguns. It may be necessary to know the chamber length in substandard firearms for firing appropriate cartridge length. Usually, it cannot be determined from the shape and size of its chamber. It can sometimes be ascertained for parallel walled cartridges having specific provision for the chamber. It can also be determined from the position of the gradient on the outer surface of the barrel connecting the chamber and the bore. However, gradients on the outer surface are often misleading (Figure 1.9).

Additional attachment inside or outside the barrel at the breech end is deceptive. It does not indicate the chamber length (Figure 1.10(a)(b)).

1.3.6.4 Irregular Bottlenecked Chamber

An irregular bottlenecked chamber is very often found in homemade and improvised firearms. This provides class characteristic as well as individual characteristic that are helpful in establishing linkage with crudely made unusual firearms.

1.4 Cartridge Headspace

Associated with the arrangement of locking and unlocking of the barrel, a firearm must have a proper cartridge headspace. However, in unusual firearms, proper headspace may not be provided. The cartridge headspace (CHS) may be very high or very low. In some firearms, there is hardly any headspace. The cartridge headspace in crudely finished, homemade firearms is usually on the higher side (Figure 1.11).

(a)

(b)

Figure 1.10 Deceptive chamber length: (a) additional outer attachment and (b) inner attachment.

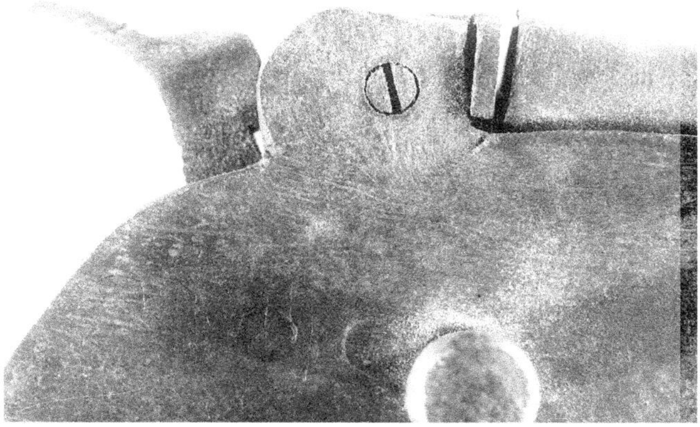

Figure 1.11 Excessive cartridge headspace, 12-bore homemade pistol.

1.5 Unusual Firing Pin Arrangement

Cocking and firing operations are usually achieved by hammer and trigger actuated by a spring, such as those of branded, hammered firearms. A rearward movement of the hammer compresses the main spring and the trigger is engaged in the rear position. On pressing the trigger, the hammer disengages and the spring-driven firing pin or the integral firing pin moves forward to hit the percussion cap resulting in the firing of the cartridge.

In a criminal case, the firing pin was a detachable part tied to a string, which could be inserted in the spring-driven firing pin hole as and when required.

Note: With the change in the detachable firing pin, the firing pin marks would change, even though fired from the same firearm. Caution is needed while forming an opinion.

1.6 Trigger Pull

The trigger pull is an important safety feature. The lighter the trigger pull, the more prone the firearm is to accidental discharge. Very low trigger pull firearms are prone to accidental discharge. This aspect is well taken care of in the manufacture of regular standard, factory-made firearms. The trigger pull varies with the type of the firearm. It may be as high as 16 to 20 pounds in revolvers and as low as 3 to 4 pounds in pistols. Contrarily, the trigger pull of illegally made firearms may vary widely from one firearm to the other irrespective of the type of ammunition used. This is especially so in homemade firearms

1. It may be as low as 1 to 2 pounds for firearms designed to fire revolver cartridges compared to the usual 16 to 20 pounds.
2. It may be as high as 25 pounds for firearms designed to fire shotgun or rifle cartridges compared to the usual 3 to 5 pounds.
3. Firearms designed to fire the same ammunition may vary widely. The trigger pull of 12-bore homemade pistols usually varies from 2 to 20 pounds compared to the usual 3 to 5 pounds in branded shotguns.
4. The trigger pull of homemade firearms is usually on the higher side.

1.7 Locking Arrangement

The provision of locking the barrel is always made whether the firearm is a regular branded or illegally made, substandard, improvised or homemade weapon. The operation of locking and unlocking of the barrel in homemade firearms may vary from one firearm to the next when firing the same ammunition. They are usually actuated by a lever. The shape, size, and location of the actuating lever vary from firearm to firearm. It may be on either side of the body, on top of the body, in front of or behind the trigger, or on the trigger guard itself. The actuating spring is often weak, which makes the firearm prone to opening of the breech during firing. In such cases, the breech may partially or wholly open before the projectile leaves the barrel. In doing so, the barrel is tilted downward, thereby changing the direction of the emergent bullet. One needs to be cautious while forming an opinion on the direction of fire in cases involving homemade firearms.

1.7.1 Unusual Locking Arrangement

Sometimes, the operation of locking and unlocking is achieved by the hole and nail arrangement. There are three small holes of similar dimension. There is one hole on either side of the body, and the third on the lug attached to the bottom of the body. To lock the breech, a nail is provided that is tied to a string attached to the firearm. All three holes align when the barrel is brought in contact with the breech. The nail inserted in the aligned holes locks the breech. It is opened when the nail is taken out. The barrel is manually hinged downward for extracting the fired cartridge and loading of a fresh cartridge. The barrel is hinged downward during firing if the nail is not inserted. This, in turn, changes the direction of the fire downwardly (Figure 1.12).

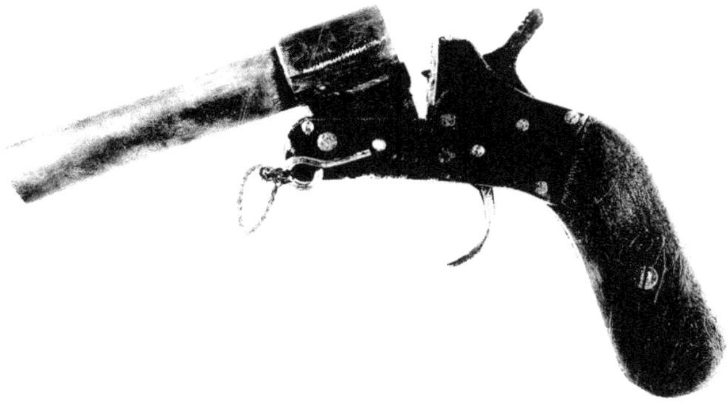

Figure 1.12 Unusual locking by hole and nail arrangement.

1.8 Caliber Designation of Unusual Firearms: New Nomenclatures

The constructional features of illegally made firearms are so different from legally manufactured firearms that they defy usual nomenclatures and classification systems. A new classification system has been adopted for designating unusual firearms that are illegally made or manufactured.

1.8.1 Bore/Caliber Designation

Illegally made, substandard firearms cannot be designated by their bore diameters. They do not necessarily correspond to the specified bore dimensions of corresponding legally manufactured branded firearms. They can conveniently be designated by the caliber/bore of the ammunition they are designed to load and fire irrespective of their bore whether rifled or smooth. The bore dimensions of similarly designated firearms are not necessarily the same and vary widely from one firearm to the other. There may be appreciable variation in the bore size from breech to muzzle in the same firearm and, hence, designating the caliber from the bore size may be misleading. Instead of making absolute measurements of bore size, a practical approach is adopted to classify similarly designated, unusual firearms. Only the relative projectile–bore diameter, i.e., relative bullet–bore diameter for rifled firearms and relative wad–bore diameter for shotgun cartridges is measured/assessed to ascertain whether under, over, or variable.

1.8.1.1 Relative Bullet–Bore Diameter Designation

Assessment of relative bullet–bore diameter can conveniently be made by dropping an unfired/fired bullet from both breech and muzzle of the barrel.

1. If the bullet passes through the bore without obstruction, then the firearm is designated as an overbore firearm.
2. If the bullet, on dropping from breech or muzzle, is stuck near the chamber and muzzle ends except for the ogival portion, then the firearm is designated as an underbore firearm.
3. If the bullet moves freely but partly, on dropping from breech or muzzle and gets stuck, then the bore is variable, i.e., oversized as well as undersized, and the firearm is designated as a variable or mixed-bore firearm.

1.8.1.2 Relative Wad–Bore Diameter Designation

Assessment of relative wad–bore diameter can conveniently be made by dropping an unfired air cushion/plastic/felt wad or the like meant for sealing the bore from both breech and muzzle of the barrel.

1. If the wad passes through the bore without obstruction, then the firearm is designated as an overbore firearm.
2. If the wad is stuck near the chamber as well as muzzle, then the firearm is designated as an underbore firearm.
3. If the wad moves freely but partly and gets stuck on dropping from breech or muzzle, then bore is variable, i.e., oversized as well as undersized, and the firearm is designated as a variable or mixed-bore firearm.

The subclassification of unusual firearms on the basis of relative bullet–bore diameter or wad–bore diameter is practical, convenient, and very useful in evaluating problems of forensic interest. An oversize bore .303 country-made pistol refers to:

1. A short-barreled, illegally made firearm designed to fire .303 rifle cartridges.
2. Its bore diameter from breech to muzzle is more than .303 bullet diameter.
3. Its bore diameter may or may not be uniform throughout the bore.

An undersized 12-bore shotgun pistol refers to:

1. A short-barreled, substandard firearm designed to fire 12-bore shotgun cartridges.
2. Its breech and muzzle diameter are less than a 12-bore sealing wad diameter.

Likewise, a mixed (variable) 16-bore pistol refers to both under- and over-bore dimension compared to sealing 16-bore wads.

2 Forensic Investigation of Fired Cartridges of Unusual Firearms

Identification of fired cartridges is an important aspect of forensic investigation in shooting incidents. The fired cartridge bears surface profiles of the parts of the firearm that came in contact during the firing process. The cycle of the firing process is well known. When the trigger is pressed, the firing pin hits the primer of the cartridge. The priming mixture is crushed and a flame is produced. The flame ignites the propellant charge inside the cartridge. The ignited propellant rapidly converts into gases and develops a very high temperature and pressure inside the chamber. The cartridge case expands in the chamber and touches the walls, which in turn seals the backward escape of gasses. The forward moving gas propels the projectile out of the muzzle and the cartridge case is pushed backward against the breech face of the firearm. Finally, the fired cartridge is unloaded to make room for a fresh cartridge in the chamber. The cartridge case is unloaded manually or by the extractor and ejector of the firearm. Thus, the prominent parts of the firearm that come in contact with the cartridge include the chamber that houses the cartridge, the breech face that supports the cartridge, the firing pin that hits the cartridge (primer), and, finally, the extractor and ejector that unloads the fired cartridge. During the process, the fired cartridge records the toolmarks' profile of the firing pin, breech, chamber, extractor, and ejector of the firearm. These toolmarks are created during the manufacturing process of the firearm.

The finished parts of a firearm undergo various manufacturing and finishing processes. Details of the manufacturing process of firearms are well documented and are outside the preview of this book. During the manufacturing process, a randomly distributed tool pattern is imprinted on the surface of the finished parts of the firearm. The resultant surface profile of the finished parts of the firearm is not duplicated in another firearm even of the same make, lot, and batch and, hence, it is characteristic and individualistic. This forms the basis of identifying fired cartridges in respect of the questioned firearm. Imperfections produced accidently by use, corrosion, erosion, and damage also are unique and individualistic. In addition to individual characteristic marks, there exist class characteristic marks that depend on the specified dimensions of the firearm manufacturer. The dimensional specifications of the firearm vary from one manufacturer to the other and from one model to the other of the same make. This forms the basis of identifying the type, make, and the model of the firearm from the fired cartridge when the questioned firearm is not available. The identifying toolmarks that are of forensic significance are the marks of the firing pin, breech, chamber, extractor, and the ejector. Sometimes, the cartridge carries scratch marks that are created during the loading operation in automatic, self-loader, and repeater firearms having provision for accommodating a number of cartridges. Their utility is limited because they can be produced by loading and unloading a live cartridge, without being fired. The usual procedure of cartridge identification is to fire test cartridges from the suspect firearm for imprinting of characteristic marks of the identifying parts of the firearm. The class and individual characteristic marks on the test and the evidence cartridges are examined and compared under a comparison microscope. Whereas, similar marks establish linkage, dissimilar marks eliminate the suspect firearm. This procedure is routinely followed in forensic laboratories worldwide.

It poses a problem if the involved firearm is substandard, improvised, homemade, or has been tampered with. The constructional features of firearms that are illegally manufactured or made at different sources are so different that even the same caliber firearms show extreme variation in their bore diameter, chamber shape and size, cartridge headspace, barrel length, etc. They defy known classification and identification criteria. Inappropriate constructional features and improper action mechanism of illegally made firearms influence the nature of marks that are imprinted on fired cartridges. With the worldwide increasing trend of tampering, and resorting to illegally made substandard, improvised, and homemade firearms in crime, one often comes across unusual, ambiguous, and deceptive marks of chamber, breech, firing pin, extractor, or ejector on seized fired cartridges. A thorough probe is needed after obtaining identifying marks on test cartridges. However, weak construction material of a majority of illegally made firearms, especially improvised and homemade, makes them unsuitable for firing test cartridges. It becomes difficult to obtain comparable breech and chamber marks that are usually recorded by firing high-pressure test rounds. Tampered firearms that are made nonfunctional or unserviceable are unsuitable for firing even normal load cartridges. In such cases, the usual procedure of identifying fired cartridges is inapplicable and calls for adopting a modified procedure for reproduction of characteristic marks either without firing or by low pressure test rounds. They need a detailed discussion. Plausible solutions to case-oriented practical problems in minimizing noncommittal inferences, and in eliminating erroneous conclusions, are discussed below.

2.1 Breech Face Marks

The breech face of a firearm bears minute surface irregularities that are created during manufacturing and finishing processes. These are in the form of

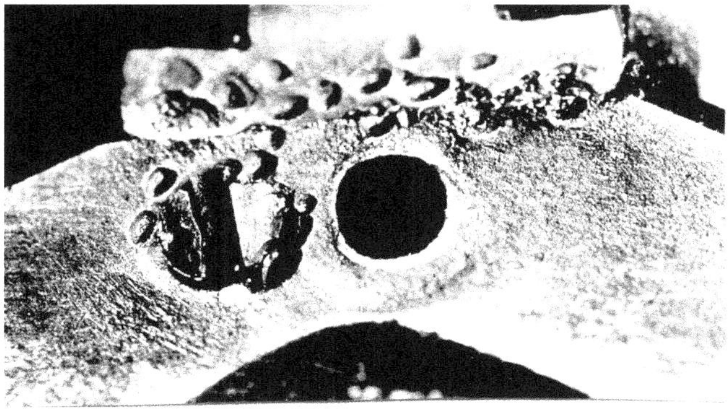

Figure 2.1 Breech marks on a crudely finished .32 revolver.

lines, curves, dots, and irregular shapes of varied dimension. Irregular elevations and depressions are usually very prominent in substandard and crudely finished firearms (Figure 2.1).

The cartridge, on firing, is violently pushed against the breech of the firearm. In doing so, the base of the cartridge meets the breech face. This results in the imprinting of the surface irregularities of the breech on the base of the cartridge. Static imprints of surface irregularities of breech are termed as *static breech marks*, commonly known as breech marks. The clarity of the breech impressions depends on the force with which the cartridge is pushed against the breech. The higher the pressure and the softer the metals of the base, the clearer are the imprints of the breech marks. Firearms that develop comparatively less pressure usually do not imprint breech marks on fired cartridges. If the cartridge does not retract even after firing and remains in contact with the breech face, then unloading of the fired cartridge leads to scraping due to sliding contact with the irregular protrusions. They create linear striations and are called *sliding breech marks* or breech scrape marks. Static and sliding breech marks are often highly characteristic and individualistic. They are utilized to identify fired cartridges with the questioned firearm (Figure 2.2).

The breech marks on the evidence cartridge, if characteristic, are obtained on test cartridges for examination and comparison. A problem is encountered if comparable breech marks are not obtained on test cartridges. This is especially so if very fine striations of the breech are to be imprinted. Furthermore, the reproduction of the entire breech is not ensured due to uncontrollable factors. Under any of these circumstances, firing of a number of test cartridges cannot be prevented. As many as 20 rounds were fired in a criminal case to obtain breech marks on test cartridges. Even then, though rarely, one may yet not be able to obtain breech marks after a good number of firings. Thus, the number of test rounds that are required to produce

(a)

(b)

Figure 2.2 (a) Static breech marks; (b) sliding breech marks.

comparable breech marks is unpredictable. If the required breech marks are not imprinted even after firing of five or six test rounds, it is then desirable to modify the procedure for reproduction of comparable breech marks.

2.1.1 Modified Procedures for Reproducing Breech Marks

One of the methods usually adopted to imprint breech marks is to fire oiled test rounds. This enhances the backward impact thereby imprinting a clearer impression of the breech. However, oiled rounds may not always serve the purpose. A heavy load cartridge that develops comparatively higher pressure is the other alternative. This enhances the backward striking force considerably, resulting in the recording of the breech marks that would not be otherwise obtainable by firing of usual normal load and oiled rounds. However, it is risky to fire heavy load and oiled rounds from unusual firearms having weak construction material and an inappropriate action mechanism. It becomes essential, in a majority of the cases involving substandard, improvised, or homemade firearms, to adopt modified procedures for obtaining breech marks; the same is true if the questioned firearm is tampered with and made nonfunctional or unserviceable. Thus, depending on the condition and type of the seized firearm, the procedure for imprinting and comparison of breech marks may need suitable modification for establishing linkage or elimination. However, before adopting a modified procedure for reproducing breech marks, it is advisable to examine the breech of the firearm wherever possible. It often proves helpful in the elimination of the suspect firearm. The marks on the breech face of the firearm are examined by a low-power magnifier or with the naked eye.

2.1.1.1 Inappropriate Constructional Features

2.1.1.1.1 Misaligned Revolving Cylinder Revolvers that are manufactured legally by conforming to proper specifications and quality control have their chambers in alignment with the bore. The axis of each chamber coincides with the axis of the bore. However, this is usually not found in homemade, improvised, and copies of branded revolvers that are manufactured in substandard and clandestine firearm factories. The chambers may not be properly aligned. If any of the chambers are significantly misaligned, then part of the breech that comes in contact with the base of the cartridge also shifts accordingly. This results in variable breech marks from one chamber to the next of the same revolver. Hence, firing of test cartridges from the misaligned chamber may not be helpful and vice versa. It may lead to negative or indefinite opinion if the marks, though characteristic, are considered extraneous. A caution is needed while evaluating the breech marks of revolvers having misaligned chambers.

In a criminal case, a .32 Webley & Scott revolver was recovered from the suspect. It was a poor copy and was manufactured by locals of Darra, Afghanistan. Test cartridges were fired from the revolver for identifying the evidence cartridge found at the crime scene. On examining the test and evidence cartridges, it was observed that:

- the firing pin marks on the evidence and test cartridges were similar;
- the firing pin hit on the evidence cartridge was near the periphery of the primer and was bulged;
- the breech marks on the evidence cartridge were near the periphery of the primer, but the same were not imprinted on any of the test cartridges.

Breech marks could not be reproduced despite oiled test rounds and, thus, comparison of breech marks could not be made. Under the circumstances, it had to be ascertained whether those marks were imprinted by the breech of the revolver or were extraneous marks. The breech of the revolver was examined under a low-power magnifier to locate available breech marks. However, such marks were not available at the relevant portion around the firing pin hole, but a screw was found fitted on the breech. The screw was fairly far away from the firing pin hole. A careful examination of the screw revealed that the breech marks in the form of an arc of a circle could be due to a part of the screw that was fitted on the breech. The screw being away from the firing pin hole, its part impression on the primer was possible by an appreciable shift of the firing pin hit. These observations indicated that the evidence cartridge was fired from a misaligned chamber that had resulted in considerable shifting of the firing pin hit. It was possible that the chamber was not properly aligned. The alignment of the chambers of the revolver, therefore, was examined. The interdistances between the holes on the cylinder were uneven. Two of the chambers were indeed misaligned.

Test cartridges were fired from excessively misaligned chambers. As expected, the firing pin hit was shifted to the periphery of the primer. A part of the screw also was imprinted on its bulged portion. The partial screw impressions on the test and evidence cartridges were similar, thereby, establishing a common source (Figure 2.3).

Note: Breech marks vary with the chamber–bore alignment of illegally made, substandard revolvers. It is essential to fire test cartridges from the relevant aligned or misaligned chamber to arrive at a right conclusion.

Caution: Direct examination of the breech of substandard revolvers having misaligned chambers may be misleading.

2.1.1.2 Tampered Firearm

Criminals often attempt to destroy evidentiary clues as far as practicable. One of the important clues is the firearm itself that was used in the crime.

Figure 2.3 Cartridges fired from misaligned chambers.

The firearm, unless seized during the commission of a crime, remains in the possession of the accused until it is recovered by the enforcement agencies. The assailant usually has sufficient time to destroy toolmarks of the firearm that are utilized to link the weapon with the evidence cartridge. Thus, to prevent the possibility of linking the crime to the firearm, criminals often tamper with the evidence-bearing parts of the firearm, especially the firing pin and the breech. The tampered firearm may be made nonfunctional by damaging the firing mechanism, locking arrangements, and, sometimes, even the barrels. It then becomes difficult to fire cartridges even for test purposes. In such cases, it is advisable to modify the procedure for reproduction of the breech marks.

2.1.1.2.1 Low-Pressure Test Rounds In criminal cases, one often comes across illegally made, substandard, and tampered firearms that are unsuitable for firing heavy load, oiled, or even normal load cartridges because of possible risk of bursting of the barrel. In such cases, a modified technique of imprinting of breech marks is adopted that essentially prevents the necessity of development of high pressure during firing.

It is apparent that the probability of recording of breech marks increases with the increase in the rearward striking force acting on the breech. In addition to increased pressure, the rearward impact also increases with the increase in the cartridge headspace. Firearms that have a high cartridge headspace require less pressure for imprinting of breech marks. In cases of excessively high cartridge headspace, even a very low pressure is usually sufficient to produce breech marks. The pressure developed by removing the projectile or the shot charge has been found sufficient to record breech impressions on the primer. The low pressure, though not sufficient to move the cartridge backward despite excessive cartridge headspace, is usually adequate to unseat the push fit cap and move it rearward. The cap is pushed rearward to the extent of available cartridge headspace. The cap bulges and strikes the breech. This striking force is usually sufficient to imprint breech marks on the primer.

This procedure of imprinting of breech marks can conveniently be adopted by providing requisite headspace wherever feasible. It also minimizes the possible risk of bursting of the weak barrel of substandard firearms having inappropriate constructional features and action mechanisms.

A high cartridge headspace is neither expected nor found in legally manufactured, branded firearms. However, the majority of illegally made, substandard firearms, especially homemade firearms, usually have high cartridge headspace, which may or may not be excessive. In such cases, the primer may bulge and imprint breech marks even by firing cartridges without projectiles. In cases of abnormally high cartridge headspace, the bulged primer may record breech marks without propellant and the projectile.

The seized firearm in a shooting incident was a 7.65 mm LLAMA self-loading pistol. Its firing mechanism was in proper working order, but the locking mechanism was damaged and broken. Even a slight downward tilt of the pistol resulted in the movement of the barrel inside the slide. The barrel could not be locked even in the cocked position. The pistol was unserviceable despite its proper firing mechanism. The evidence cartridge, received in this case, did not carry identifiable firing pin marks. The only characteristic marks imprinted on the primer were those of the breech. Therefore, breech marks had to be obtained on test cartridges for comparison. However, the tampered pistol was unsuitable for firing test cartridges. Hence, the usual procedure of obtaining breech marks by firing test cartridges could not be employed. Under the circumstances, the procedure of imprinting of breech marks by providing requisite high cartridge headspace was adopted, which was possible in the instant case.

For test purposes, live 7.65 mm cartridges were emptied by removing the bullet. The test cartridge, without a bullet, was put inside the chamber of the barrel. The moving barrel was kept at a suitable position such that the primer of the loaded cartridge was fairly away from the breech face. This provided an effective high cartridge headspace. Keeping the barrel in position by hand, the external hammer was cocked and fired. As expected, the primer was pushed rearward with a force that was sufficient to imprint a breech on the bulged primer. The linkage of the cartridges was thus established without resorting to normal or high-pressure test rounds. This would not have been possible otherwise (Figure 2.4).

In another criminal case of tampering, the barrel of a seized 12-bore SBBL (single barrel breech loading) gun was bent. Though the firing mechanism was in working order, it was not possible to fire normal load test cartridges. Under the circumstances, the best suited procedure for obtaining breech marks was to provide a significantly high cartridge headspace during test firing. A live 12-bore cartridge was emptied after removing the whole shot charge that included wads, propellant, and pellets. The barrel was hinged downward and the live emptied cartridge was loaded in the chamber.

Figure 2.4 Bulged primer on cartridges fired without bullet.

While closing the barrel, a cardboard filler (piece) of about 8 mm thick was placed between the rear end of the barrel and the uppermost portion of the breech. The cardboard filler provided necessary high cartridge headspace. The gun was cocked and fired. As expected, the primer of the emptied cartridge bulged and breech marks were imprinted. The breech marks on the bulged primer were sufficient to establish linkage of the evidence cartridge to the tampered (bent barrel) 12-bore SBBL gun (Figure 2.5).

Note: Breech marks can be imprinted by providing high cartridge headspace in tampered as well as legally manufactured branded firearms.

2.1.1.2.2 Breech Impressions without Firing Firearms are often made nonfunctional and unserviceable by tampering. In such cases, the usual procedure of identifying breech marks by firing test cartridges cannot be adopted. It becomes necessary to use a suitable procedure that prevents the necessity of firing. A suitable surface, softer than the metal of the primer and the base of the cartridge, is chosen for obtaining breech marks without firing. A thin lead piece, preferably a flattened buckshot, is chosen for the purpose. Lead, being soft, is expected to imprint breech marks by the application of comparatively far less pressure than usually developed on firing. The thin flat lead piece is kept in contact with the breech of the firearm and is struck by a very lightweight hammer. The force applied by a single hammer strike is usually sufficient for imprinting comparable breech marks. However, a number of test specimens may have to be obtained for comparison. Breech marks on the test lead specimens are compared with those available on the evidence cartridge for establishing linkage.

In another criminal case, the firearm was tampered with after committing the crime. It was a 12-bore double barrel breech loading (DBBL) gun. The left firing pin was removed. The right firing pin was cut and shortened to make the protrusion ineffective for firing. Thus, the gun was made unserviceable. The evidence cartridge, recovered from the crime scene, had characteristic firing pin and breech marks. The firing pin marks were of no

(a) (b)

Figure 2.5 (a) Bent barrel of 12-bore SBBL gun; (b) bulged primer by cardboard filler.

forensic significance because the lone, right firing pin of the DBBL gun was cut. The only useful identifying marks were of the breech marks. However, it was not possible to obtain marks of the breech of the unserviceable gun by firing. Under the circumstances, test breech marks had to be obtained without firing. Lead specimens were kept on the right and left breech face of the firearm and lightly hammered to obtain test breech impressions. As expected, comparable breech marks were obtained on lead specimens. The breech marks on the test lead pieces were compared with those available on the evidence cartridge and the linkage was established with the left breech of the gun (Figure 2.6).

Thus, the attempt to destroy the valuable evidence by the accused was foiled. Besides establishing the gun–cartridge linkage, the act of tampering provided valuable evidence to corroborate the guilt of the accused. The defense plea of doubtful recovery of the evidence cartridge also is not tenable in such cases.

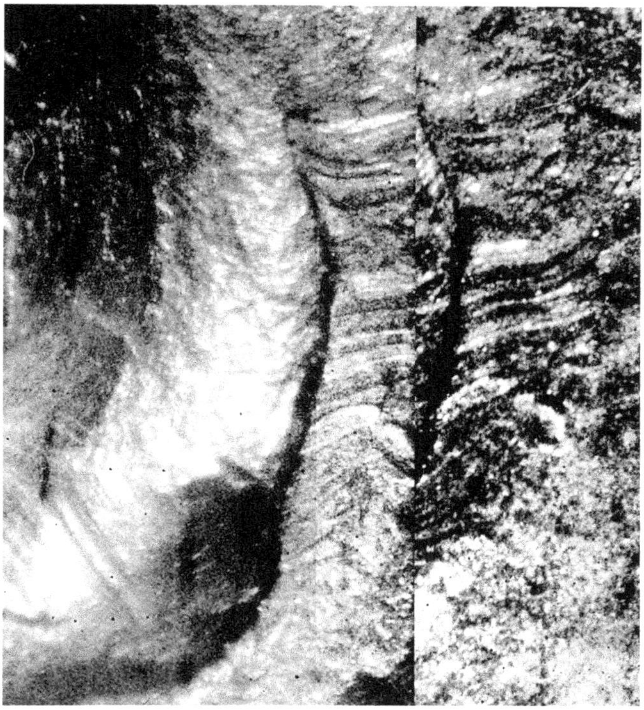

Figure 2.6 Similar breech marks on lead piece and evidence cartridge.

2.1.2.2.3 Partly Tampered Gun and Breech Edge Marks The tampering of the breech by filing is very common. However, the inner periphery of the breech at the edges often remains untouched while tampering by usual filing. These marks prove helpful in identifying the tampered firearm when other available marks do not provide requisite data to come to a conclusion. The inner periphery of the breech bears characteristic irregularities at the edges around the firing pin hole. The inner breech edges of substandard, unusual firearms are usually highly characteristic and individualistic. These marks provide an additional identifying tool to link the evidence cartridge with the tampered or illegally made, substandard firearms (Figure 2.7).

2.1.2 Evaluation of Deceptive and Ambiguous Marks

2.1.2.1 Deceptive Striations on Primer

One often comes across extraneous marks on the base of unfired cartridges. These marks are in the form of dents, curves, striations, etc. They are often produced by rough handling of live cartridges. Sometime, significant extraneous marks are produced by a primer seating punch or something similar during manufacturing processes of the cartridge. Though rare, they may

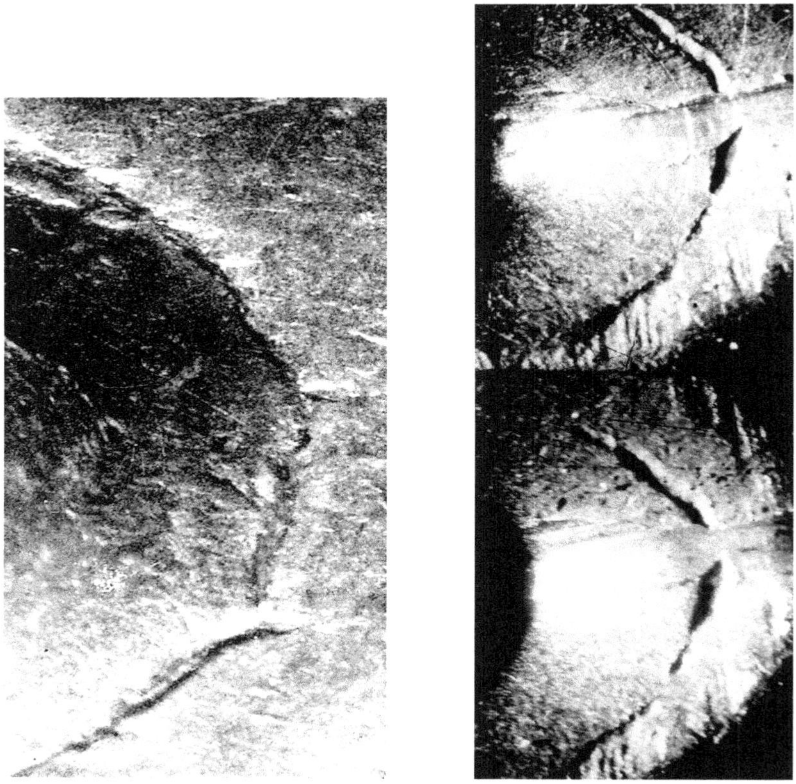

Figure 2.7 Breech edge marks.

provide a comparable match on unfired primers. It may be misleading to unwary examiners if characteristic striations of the punch, etc. are available on the evidence cartridge.

In a criminal case, characteristic parallel striations were observed on the evidence cartridge. The parallel striations were all around the firing pin impressions. The firing pin impression also bore similar striations both at the bottom and on the sides (Figure 2.8).

The following observations were made and results interpreted on examining the test cartridges fired through the suspect self-loading rifle. Thereafter, comparisons were made with the evidence cartridge.

1. The firing pin and the ejector marks on the evidence and test cartridges were found to be similar in their individual characteristics indicating a common source of origin, thereby establishing the linkage of the evidence cartridge with the suspect firearm.
2. The characteristic linear striations present on the evidence cartridge were not present on the test cartridges indicating elimination of the

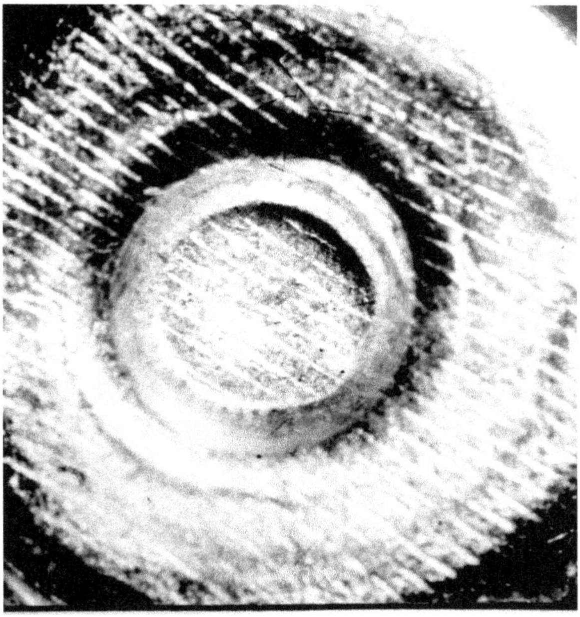

Figure 2.8 Deceptive striations inside and around the firing pin indentation.

evidence cartridge in respect of the suspect firearm. Elimination was further strengthened by examining the firing pin and the breech face of the suspect firearm. This revealed absence of similar striations on them. These observations led to ambiguity and contradictory conclusions. It was necessary to ascertain the source that created the disputed striations on the evidence cartridge. The striations inside the firing pin and on the rest of the primer were examined simultaneously to ascertain whether the striations were produced because of firing or otherwise.

a. The parallel striations on the primer revealed continuity even when they were passing through the firing pin indentation. It was not possible by firing of the cartridge because, in such a case, the gap between the peripheries of the firing pin and its hole would have exhibited discontinuity of lines between the breech and firing pin striations even if they happened to be in the same straight line. Presence of striations over the entire surface of the indentation, including slope, clearly indicated that they were neither a breech scrape nor a firing pin scrape. It was ruled out that these striations were produced during firing.
b. The possibility of creating these striations by filing the cartridge after firing also was probed. Tampering of the cartridge after firing by filing or rubbing against a rough surface would not produce such continuous striations, especially inside the indentation,

because the firing pin indentation was at a lower level. Thus, the possibility of producing these continuous striations after firing was ruled out as well.

The only plausible alternative deduction was that these striations existed on the base of the live cartridge. They could have been produced either at the time of manufacture or during handling and storage. Such striations indeed were possible by the primer seating punch during cartridge manufacture and rough handling or storage after manufacture. Being extraneous, these striations could safely be ignored while considering the linkage of the evidence cartridge with the firearm based on similar firing pin and ejector marks.

After the publication of this case, the firearm unit of the police department of Baltimore, Maryland, informed the author that they also discovered matching striations on unfired primers of Winchestor .38 special cartridges, which remained prevalent even after firing. Matching marks were observed on primers contained in 158 grain lead, round nose cartridges, head stamped W_W, lot numbers NST6A and E107300. The Winchester Company also confirmed that the marks were apparently made by a primer seating punch. According to the company, "This would be an isolated situation as normally our punches are produced to a smoothness that would not produce mating markings on the primer."

Note: One should invariably scrutinize live cartridges before test firing to determine whether they carry significant marks that are likely to interfere with identification.

Caution: A caution is needed if other identifiable marks are not available. Matching extraneous marks may be misleading if evidence and test cartridges are from the same lot. Dissimilar marks from different lots and different makes, if characteristic, also may be misleading.

2.1.2.2 Deceptive Striations Due to Cartridge Tampering

Tampering of fired cartridges is rare. The author came across a criminal case in which the fired cartridge was tampered with after the crime was committed. The evidence cartridge had characteristic striations on its base. The primer did not carry striations. Similar striations were neither observed on any of the test cartridges nor on the breech of the questioned firearm. However, firing pin marks on the evidence and test cartridges were found similar. Though, linkage of the questioned gun could be established alone on similar firing pin marks, the presence of characteristic striations on the base of the evidence cartridge was ambiguous.

The firing pin indentation on the base of the evidence cartridge was at a much lower level than the striations. The only plausible reason for such

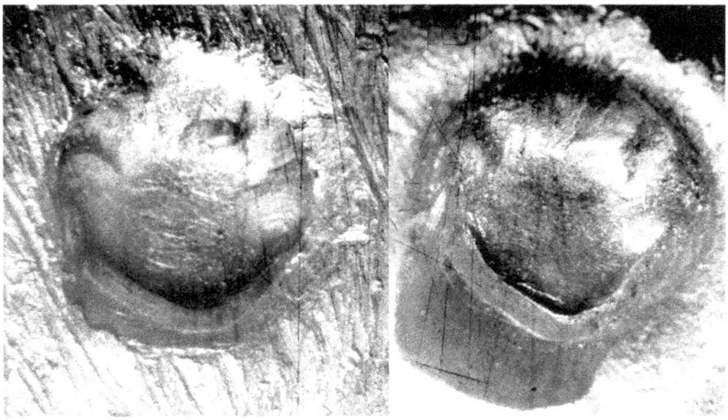

Figure 2.9 Tampered fired cartridge.

striations was tampering of the cartridge by filing or rubbing against a rough surface after firing. This was obvious, as the primer, which was at a lower level, did not carry continuous striations (Figure 2.9).

2.1.2.3 *Breech Scrape Marks and Deceptive Partial Sliding Marks*

Breech scrape marks are often utilized as an additional tool for identifying fired cartridges. These marks are imprinted on cartridges that do not retract after firing. Unloading of the cartridge makes sliding contacts with the minute protrusions of the breech. This results in imprinting of the breech scrape marks. These scrape marks are linear striations and they are parallel to the firing pin scrape. Sliding marks are often individualistic and may be utilized for identification, especially if other identifying marks are not available.

Caution

1. Breech scrape marks may be produced by mere loading and unloading of a live cartridge due to a low cartridge headspace, which is not rare in illegally manufactured, substandard firearms, especially homemade firearms.
2. Breech scrape marks are not comparable directly with the marks available on the breech of the firearm and, hence, the source that created the breech scrape marks cannot be viewed.

2.1.2.3.1 Partial Sliding Marks The phenomenon of partial sliding marks is uncommon and often misleading. These are imprinted by partial breech–cartridge contacts before or after firing. This is usually possible if the space between the breech and the rear end of the barrel, in its locked position, is significantly uneven due to an inappropriate constructional feature. Expansions of deep dents of the breech provide noticeable, uneven breech–cartridge contacts during firing. Different parts of the base of the cartridge that remain in close contact with the breech face before or after firing provide preferential scraping surfaces. An unlocking operation results in the scraping of the fired cartridges corresponding to their points of sliding contacts located at different parts of the base. A thorough probe is needed while evaluating partial sliding scrape marks to eliminate ambiguity and to establish the source that can positively be attributed to the suspect firearm and no other.

In a criminal case, the breech marks on the evidence cartridge were distributed all around the base in small patches in the form of linear striations and curves. At right angles to each patch were parallel striations. Similar patches were observed on the test cartridges. It also was noted that parallel striations were not found on any of the patches at a right angle.

The breech of the questioned gun was examined to ascertain the source that created right angle striations exclusively on the scattered patches. The seized gun was a 12-bore SBBL gun manufactured by a local licensed gun manufacturer called Small Arms Company in India. Direct examination of the breech revealed the presence of scattered indented patches of lines and curves. Almost all patches were very deeply indented, but there were no striations at right angles on any of the patches. Therefore, it could safely be concluded that right-angle striations on the patches were not static breech marks. Their direction, on examination, was found parallel to the firing pin scrape, which clearly indicated that they were breech scrape marks and were created separately on each patch. High-pressure oiled test rounds revealed apparent uneven contacts. It was observed that deeply indented patches on the breech developed extensive swollen patches on the fired cartridge. The scattered, raised swollen patches provided requisite sliding contacts while extracting the fired cartridge by hinging the barrel. The base of the cartridge was scraped by sliding contacts on the scattered raised portions and produced striations at right angles to the swollen patches. The direction of the right-angle striations on the evidence cartridge being parallel to the direction of the firing pin scrape confirmed that both static and sliding breech marks were imprinted on the evidence cartridge (Figure 2.10).

2.1.3 Examination of Breech and Unusual Firearms

Examination of the breech of the firearm is not considered necessary for identifying fired cartridges. The usual procedure of firing test cartridges provides the necessary identifiable marks. However, it may not always be true. The criminal cases, cited in the preceding paragraphs, clearly reveal the utility of direct examination of the breech of the firearm. It often proves helpful in arriving at a right conclusion. It also minimizes ambiguity that is commonly encountered in cases involving substandard unusual firearms.

The breech of the firearm imprints its negative profile on the fired cartridge and, thus, their comparison involves a positive–negative comparison.

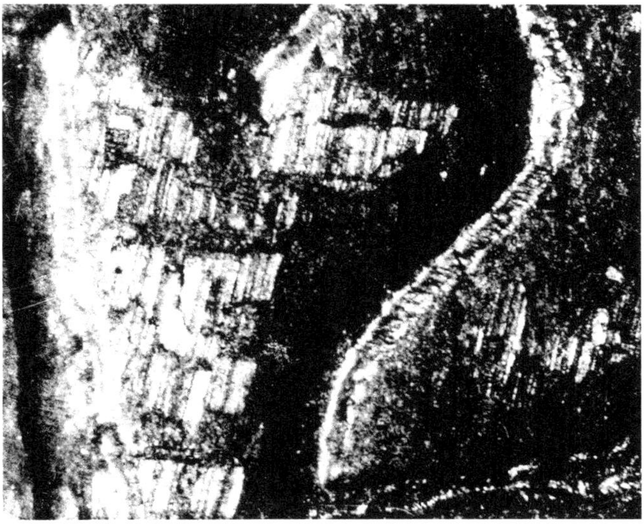

Figure 2.10 Static and partial sliding breech marks.

Sinha et al. studied the complexities of the evaluation processes of positive–negative comparison. For an objective assessment of the problems associated with a positive–negative comparison, the entire breech has to be placed on one of the stages of the comparison microscope and its fired cartridge on the other. A bolt action rifle can be chosen for the study because the bolt head can easily be dismantled and placed on the stage of the comparison microscope. The entire breech face can be examined and compared with the corresponding marks on the fired cartridge. The bolt head of a .315 sporting rifle was chosen for the study. The bolt head was placed on one of the stages of the comparison microscope and its fired cartridge on the other. Examination and comparison of breech marks revealed that the impressions on the fired cartridge appear as an image of the breech of the firearm as viewed in a mirror. Convergent striation on one appears as divergent on the other. Elevations and depressions appear as corresponding depressions and elevations. Black impressions appear as white and vice versa. Apparently, the marks on the two are not in the same phase as the cartridge–cartridge comparison. The phase difference between the two is obviously 180 degrees. Therefore, for a meaningful interpretation of similar and dissimilar breech marks, the marks on the two are adjusted such that impressions on the extreme left of the cartridge are compared with the impressions on the extreme right of the breech face. The corresponding impressions are adjusted so that they are approximately at the same distance from the demarcation line on either side, as though viewed in a mirror. The striations that are converging toward the demarcation line correspond to the striations diverging away from the demarcation line. In case of parallel striations, the orientation becomes difficult because the striations

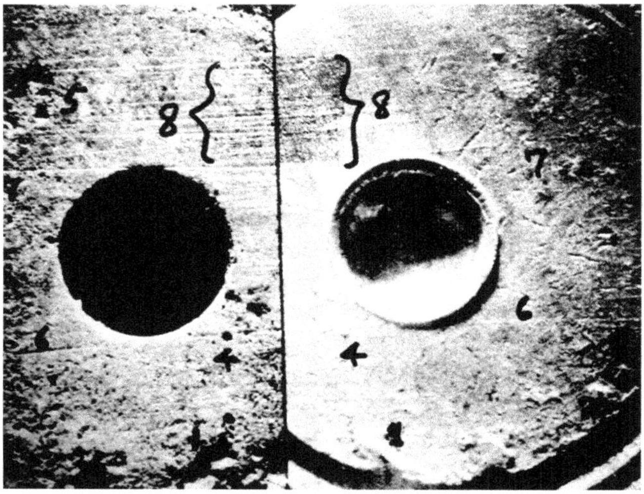

Figure 2.11 Breech–cartridge comparison.

remain parallel with a change in phase difference. In such cases, a nonstriated characteristic mark is taken as reference point for ascertaining proper phase. In the absence of characteristic reference marks, parallel striations are examined and compared by making a 180- and zero-degree phase difference. Whereas matching of parallel striations establishes linkage, a negative opinion is formed only when they do not tally in both the phases. This is necessary because a match may not be achieved even though the striations are from the same breech, if the phase difference is not proper. Due caution is needed while evaluating parallel striations in a breech–cartridge comparison. The breech–cartridge comparison has an added advantage in that corresponding impressions and striations can be viewed simultaneously, which is not possible in a cartridge–cartridge comparison (Figure 2.11).

Note: It doesn't need to be emphasized that direct breech comparison is not intended for routine analysis. It may prove helpful, however, when the usual methods of reproduction of marks do not yield satisfactory results.

2.1.3.1 Elimination by Striated Breech Comparison

The breech of a firearm usually carries parallel striations created by various manufacturing processes and finishing tools. Striations are parallel, inclined, or intermixed. The direction of parallel striations, if significant, may be utilized as a class characteristic parameter. If their directions are distinctly different, then it is usually possible to eliminate on the basis of striated breech marks. However, elimination can be considered plausible only if it is established that the striated breech impressions are due to static breech marks and not due to breech scrape. The firing pin scrape provides a valuable reference in a hinged barrel. The pin is at a six o'clock position in relation to the hole through which the firing pin protrudes. The relative position and nature of striations whether static or sliding can be accessed from the firing pin scrape. If the firing pin scrape is not present on the evidence cartridge then elimination on the basis of striated breech alone becomes difficult.

In a criminal case, firing pin marks on the evidence cartridge were not identifiable. The only identifiable marks were those of the breech. The marks were in the form of linear striations parallel to the firing pin scrape. Test breech marks could not be obtained despite oiled rounds. The breech of the questioned firearm, therefore, was examined. It was a top break, 12-bore SBBL gun. The breech of the gun also had characteristic linear striations, but they were inclined to the direction of firing pin scrape. This ruled out the possibility of imprinting of striations by the breech of the questioned gun resulting in its elimination.

2.2 Chamber Marks

The chamber is another important part of the firearm that imprints its surface irregularities on development of pressure. The surface imperfections of the chamber are conspicuous in poorly finished and illegally made substandard firearms. These imperfections are very rough and irregular in locally made, improvised, and homemade firearms. These marks are imprinted on the walls of the cartridge when it expands and pushes against the inner surface of the chamber on firing. The static imprints of surface imperfections of the chamber are termed as static chamber marks, commonly known as *chamber marks*. Cartridges fired from substandard and unusual firearms often record a clear imprint of the chamber on their walls. They are usually visible to the naked eye. Therefore, the examination and subsequent comparisons can be made by an unaided eye or under low magnification. In some cases, it is also possible to know the source causing the marks by a visual examination of the chamber of short-barreled firearms.

There also exists dynamic or sliding chamber marks besides static chamber marks. They are often found on metallic cartridges fired from an undersized chamber diameter. The cartridge, on expansion, becomes a tight fit in the undersized chamber. If it does not retract and remains a tight fit after the usual contraction, the fired cartridge cannot be taken out easily. The extraction of such a cartridge results in the formation of linear striations due to sliding contacts with the irregular protrusions on the inner walls of the chamber. These linear striations are known as *sliding chamber marks* and can be examined and compared under sufficiently high magnification like other striation matching for establishing linkages. However, sliding chamber marks can be imprinted merely by loading and unloading of live cartridges

(a)

Figure 2.12 (a) Static chamber marks; (b) sliding chamber marks. *(continued)*

in firearms having excessive undersized chambers. In such cases, sliding chamber marks establish merely loading of the cartridge in the chamber. They do not serve as a means to identifying the fired cartridge in respect to the firearm. Therefore, sliding chamber marks can be utilized for establishing linkages only if produced after the development of pressure as a result of firing. This cannot be established otherwise (Figure 2.12).

The utility of chamber marks is well recognized in cases involving illegally manufactured, substandard firearms having inappropriate constructional features.

2.2.1 Chamber Shape and Size

Inappropriate features that are used to construct the illegally made, substandard firearms influence the position and nature of chamber marks on the fired cartridge. This is especially so if it is a bottlenecked cartridge. Precision tools and instruments are seldom used to manufacture these firearms, without which it is difficult to create the correct shoulder length, shoulder gradient, and other features to accommodate bottlenecked cartridges. The shape and size of the chamber for bottlenecked cartridges are invariably inappropriate in locally made, improvised, and homemade firearms. As a result, one finds appreciable variations in bottlenecked chamber dimensions of same

(b)

Figure 2.12 *(continued)* (a) Static chamber marks; (b) sliding chamber marks.

caliber substandard firearms manufactured illegally at different sources, especially those that are homemade. Cartridges fired through these firearms, on expansion, tend to take the shape and size of the chamber. Variation in expansion of fired cartridges near the bottlenecked portion corresponds to the shape and size of the chamber. The nature of expansion usually shows distinct variations that can lead to elimination in most of the cases, even by the unaided eye (Figure 2.13). However, chamber dimensions of substandard firearms intended to be used for parallel walled cartridges generally do not show characteristic variations that can be utilized for identification.

2.2.2 Chamber–Bore Joint Marks

In addition to the usual chamber marks, there exist other types of static chamber marks, which are the marks of the chamber–bore joint. These marks are imprinted by incorrect chamber length. The chamber–bore joint marks are recorded on the fired cartridges if the length of the chamber of the firearm

Figure 2.13 Variable bottle-necked chamber shape and size of .303 homemade pistols.

is less than the length of the loaded cartridge case. They often are present on bottleneck cartridges fired from illegally made, substandard firearms, especially homemade ones. The fired cartridge develops shoulder–neck formation corresponding to the chamber–bore joint of the firearm. Therefore, the shoulder–neck joint on fired and unfired cartridges may or may not coincide. The surface irregularities of the joint are imprinted all around the circumference at the fired shoulder junction. This provides a widely distributed, identifiable area. Linkages are established by examining and comparing joint marks around the circumference or by a portion thereof depending upon the extent/nature of marks. Other joints also imprint marks on the fired cartridge. Unlike the usual chamber marks, the chamber–bore joint marks are often not visible and are overlooked. They require special attention for detection and adequate magnification for evaluation (Figure 2.14).

2.2.3 Modified Procedures for Reproducing Chamber Marks

A high pressure is normally required to imprint chamber marks. A number of test rounds, preferably oiled, are often fired to obtain proper chamber marks for comparison. However, firing of a number of rounds from improvised and homemade firearms is avoided as far as practicable due to weak constructional material. In such cases, it becomes necessary to modify the procedure

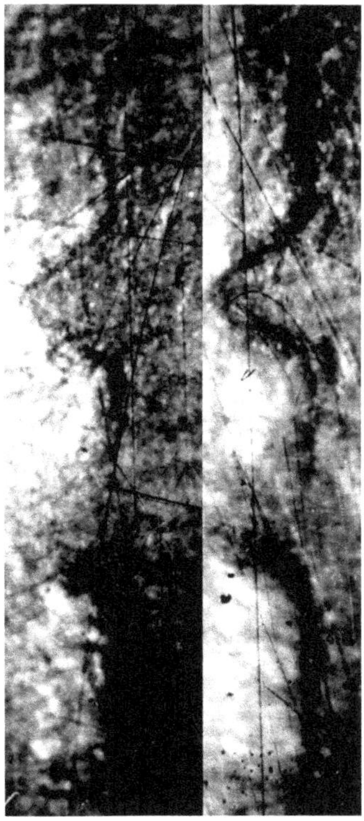

Figure 2.14 Similar chamber–bore joint marks.

that essentially obviates the necessity of firing high-pressure test rounds. It would be desirable to obtain chamber marks by low-pressure test rounds. In case of nonfunctional, tampered firearms, it may be necessary to obtain chamber marks without resorting to even test firing. Procedures for obtaining chamber marks are accordingly modified.

2.2.3.1 Chamber Marks without Firing

It is not possible to fire test cartridges from a tampered firearm that has been made nonfunctional and unserviceable. In such cases, the procedure has to be modified to obtain chamber marks without test firing. In the past, sulfur and wood metal cast of the chamber have been utilized for the purpose. The process of preparing casts, besides being cumbersome, may not provide the necessary minute details. It also is futile to obtain entire chamber marks because characteristic marks often occupy only a very small part of the chamber, especially if it is in the form of curves, lines, longitudinal joints, and regular or irregular shapes of varied dimensions. They can usually be located inside short-barreled, improvised, homemade, and crudely manufactured, substandard firearms. They can be viewed by the naked eye. If located, only the relevant portion needs to be chosen for preparing a suitable cast. Plasticine, an easily available and malleable material, is chosen as the suitable casting material. Being very soft, it is capable of imprinting minute details of surface irregularities even by applying hand pressure. Plasticine is first placed over a small glass rod and, thereafter, pressed over the relevant portion of the chamber. The impression of minute surface irregularities is recorded on the plasticine. Even longitudinal joints, commonly found inside crudely manufactured, short-barreled firearms, can be imprinted without firing. Impressions on plasticine can be obtained repeatedly for test purposes. Test impressions are compared with the impressions on the evidence cartridge for establishing linkages. Besides longitudinal joints, small portions bearing characteristic shapes also can be located inside the chamber of short-barreled firearms. They easily can be imprinted as well on plasticine, provided the mark-bearing portion is not too wide radially. This procedure of imprinting chamber marks is simple, quick, and foolproof. Even minute details can be imprinted easily that otherwise cannot be ensured by firing high-pressure test rounds (Figure 2.15).

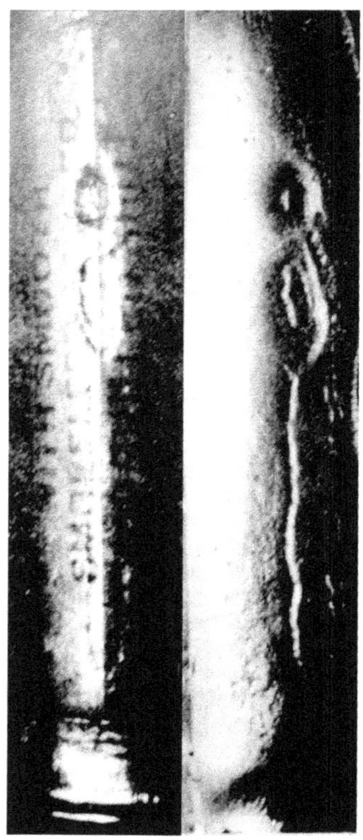

Figure 2.15 Similar joint marks on evidence cartridge and plasticine.

2.2.3.2 *Chamber Marks by Low-Pressure Test Rounds*

The chamber–bore joint provides identifiable marks for establishing the linkage of fired cartridges with the suspect firearm designed to fire bottlenecked cartridges. These marks are distributed all around the circumference at the joint junction making it difficult to view the entire joint marks. It also is difficult to apply uniform pressure all around the circumference to lift the required marks on plasticine. Therefore, the only alternative to obtaining required marks is to fire test cartridges. Needless to say, the firing of high-velocity rifle cartridges involves risk of bursting of the barrels as they are invariably weak in cheap, substandard, unusual firearms, especially homemade ones. This calls for adopting a modified procedure of reproducing chamber joint marks by firing low-pressure test rounds. It has been found that a localized low pressure near the neck of the bottlenecked cartridge is sufficient to produce chamber joint marks. Exhaustive experiments have revealed that localized pressure near the neck can easily be developed by removing the bullet and filling in the part of the empty space of the cartridge with tightly packed, small lead pellets and a cardboard piece at the top. On firing, localized pressure continues to act near the mouth until the unseating of the pellets inside the chamber. Expansion takes place only near the mouth. This invariably results in the imprinting of the chamber–bore joint marks including other circumferential marks near the mouth. This procedure avoids the necessity of firing high-velocity, bottlenecked cartridges for test purposes. Even the firing of a reduced propellant charge may not be necessary. This procedure has been found very useful when evaluating the chamber end marks in cases involving homemade and improvised firearms chambered for high-velocity bottlenecked cartridges.

2.3 Firing Pin Marks

The firing pin is the most important identifying part of the firearm. It is the firing pin hit that fires the cartridge and, hence, every fired cartridge must bear firing pin impressions. The firing pin also carries characteristic surface imperfections. Therefore, similar firing pin impressions on evidence and test cartridges signify that the evidence cartridge has been fired from the suspect firearm and no other. The importance of firing pin impressions is well recognized and is helpful in linking the crime with the weapon. In addition to the indentation of the firing pin, the primer also may be scraped and create firing pin scrape marks. It is due to the sliding contact of the protruding firing pin over the primer. This occurs when the tip of the firing pin remains protruded and makes contact with the primer and beyond while unloading the cartridge. The position of the scrape marks, therefore, depends upon the unloading operation of the cartridge. In top break, hammerless shotguns, the scrape is produced at the six o'clock position when the barrel is hinged downward to open the breech. In self-loaders and repeaters, a firing pin scrape, though uncommon if produced, is usually near the ejector mark position. The scrape marks bear linear striations and are often highly characteristic. They offer valuable data for arriving at significant forensic conclusions. However, one has to be careful while forming an opinion on firing pin scrape marks alone.

The marks may be produced by misfired cartridges as well. The incidence of misfiring of cartridges is significantly influenced by ineffective firing pin protrusions due to high cartridge headspace, weak actuating firing pin spring, pointed firing pin, etc. These inappropriate constructional features and improper action mechanism are usually found in substandard and tampered firearms. The possibility of missed hits is evidently more in such cases. The malfunction of live cartridges is equally an important factor for misfiring of cartridges. With an increase in the worldwide usage of illegally made, substandard firearms, and deliberate attempts of the accused to tamper with the evidentiary clues, one often comes across multifiring pin hits, tampered or replaced firing pins, perforated and blown caps, and broken or destroyed guns. The complexities in evaluating these marks need detailed discussion.

2.3.1 Evaluation of Multifiring Pin Hits

Multifiring pin hits are due to misfires. They pose varied problems and call for the evaluation of each firingpin hit for arriving at significant forensic conclusions on a scientific basis. The firing pin hit that results in misfires usually imprints comparatively less clear impressions than those produced by hits that fires the cartridge. However, the clarity of marks cannot be taken as the only criteria to distinguish between a fired and a misfired firing pin impression. If the firing pin has a characteristic surface pattern, one may find a very clear firing pin impression even on a missed cartridge. Alternatively, if the surface pattern is not very characteristic, then the firing pin marks on the fired cartridge may not be clear and identifiable despite high-pressure, full-charge fire. Therefore, one cannot rule out the possibility of one over the other from the clarity of marks alone, as to which of the firing pin hits was responsible for firing the cartridge. Evidently, comparison of marks caused by any one of the hits with the firing pin marks of the firearm, whether similar or not, is insufficient to permit identification. If identifying marks other than firing pin marks, such as breech marks, chamber marks, etc., are not available, one has to depend solely on firing pin marks. Therefore, it becomes essential to evaluate all firing pin hits whether similar or not. The inference depends upon the number and nature of firing pin marks available on the evidence cartridge. It needs a thorough probe for a correct and guarded opinion.

1. Similar firing pin hit impressions:
    a. If all firing pin impressions including those due to misfires are separately identified as having been caused by the firing pin of the suspect firearm, then a positive opinion can safely be furnished that the evidence cartridge had been fired from the suspect firearm and no other.
2. Separated dissimilar firing pin impressions:
    a. If two or more distinctly different firing pin impressions are available on the evidence cartridge, then it clearly indicates that they cannot be due to the firing pin of the suspect firearm alone. Evidently, more than one firing pin has hit the primer. In the absence of identification of the particular hit that resulted in firing of the cartridge, its linkage with the suspect firearm cannot be established, though identifiable firing pin hit(s) of the suspect firearm are available. It merely suggests the involvement of the firearm for misfiring or for firing of the cartridge. In such a case, the only opinion that can safely be furnished is that the evidence cartridge bears the firing pin marks of the suspect firearm, but it is not possible to offer an opinion on whether the evidence cartridge had been fired from the suspect firearm or not.
    b. If none of the distinctly different firing pin impressions tallies with the firing pin impressions of the suspect firearm, then one can safely infer that the evidence cartridge had not been fired from the suspect firearm.
    c. If any of the firing pin hits is not identifiable then, too, a positive opinion cannot be given even if other available firing pin impressions are highly characteristic and tally with the firing pin impressions of the questioned firearm. In such a case, the only opinion that can be safely provided is that the evidence cartridge bears the firing pin marks of the suspect firearm.
3. Multifiring pin hits and other identifiable marks:
    a. The identification of each multifiring pin hit may not be necessary if other identifying marks are available and comparable.

In a criminal case, the evidence cartridge was a 12-bore fired cartridge case. It contained breech marks in addition to two distinctly separated firing pin marks. One of the firing pin marks and the breech marks tallied with the firing pin and breech marks of the questioned gun. Identifiable breech marks on the evidence cartridge led to the positive conclusion that the evidence

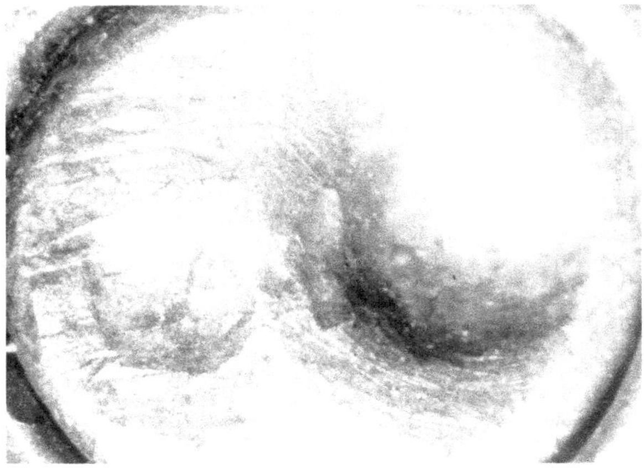

Figure 2.16 Two distinctly separated firing pin marks and breech marks.

cartridge had been fired from the gun in question. The dissimilar marks were evidently due to a misfire firing pin hit (Figure 2.16).

4. Unusual double firing pin impressions:
   Unusual double firing pin impressions by a single trigger pull of a 12-bore, external hammered SBBL gun has been observed in a criminal case. The firing pin had excessive play causing occasional partial rearward and sideways shift resulting in two firing pin hits, before and after the shift. The relative position of the two firing pin hits varied from round to round, depending on the extent of shift. Test firing revealed unusual variations:
   a. Two partly superimposed clear and identifiable firing pin impressions, indicating appreciable shift;
   b. Two almost superimposed firing pin impressions indicating negligible shift; and
   c. Only one firing pin impression indicating absence of second hit after the shift. Variation in the resultant firing pin impressions from round to round may be misleading. The clearly demarcated two firing pin impressions, partly superimposed, may be confusing as if two attempts have been made to fire the cartridge. If the firing pin movement has excessive play, then instead of moving rearward after firing, it may have partial rearward and sideways shift (Figure 2.17).
5. Multifiring pin scrapes and DBBL shotguns:
   Firing pin scrape marks usually carry characteristic striations that can establish the linkage of the evidence cartridge with the questioned firearm. In case of a double-barreled gun, linkage of the firearm from the fired cartridge can be opined even if there is more than

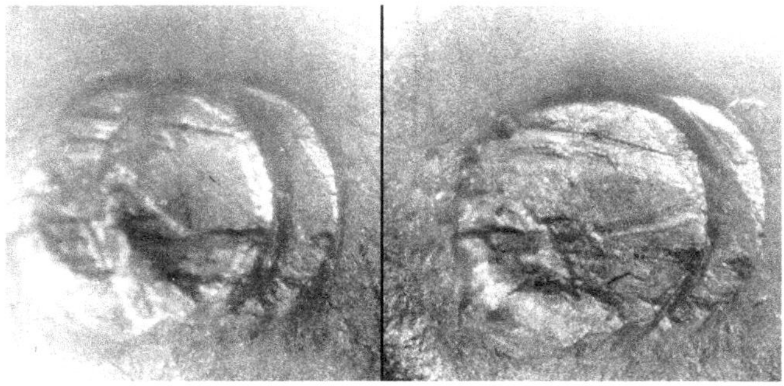

Figure 2.17 Partly superimposed firing pin marks by a single hit.

one firing pin or firing pin scrape mark, provided they are identifiable and pertain to the right and/or left barrels of the DBBL gun. Though the opinion on linkage is not specific in terms of right or left barrel, the firing of the cartridge through the gun is positively established.

In a criminal case, the evidence cartridge had one firing pin impression, but had two distinct firing pin scrapes that formed an obtuse angle. The firing pin marks partly tallied to the right and partly to the left firing pin of the questioned DBBL gun. The available mixed firing pin marks were insufficient to establish linkage. The other identifying marks available on the evidence cartridge were two firing pin scrapes. They were identified as left and right firing pin scrapes of the questioned DBBL gun. Presence of left as well as right firing pin scrapes led to the conclusion to the extent that an attempt to fire the evidence cartridge was made by loading the cartridge in both the barrels one after the other. Evidently, one of the firing pin hits had resulted in a misfire and the other had fired the cartridge. There were no other identifying marks to establish the barrel of the DBBL gun through which the evidence cartridge was fired. Therefore, the only possible opinion that could have been deduced was that the evidence cartridge had been fired from the questioned DBBL gun without specifying the barrel (right or left) through which the cartridge was fired.

Linkage of fired cartridges having different firing pin or firing pin scrape marks becomes a difficult task if the suspect firearm is a single-barreled firearm.

2.3.2 Tampered Firing Pin

Tampering with firearm is becoming the preferred method to evade detection. The firing pin is the most commonly tampered part of the firearm. It is usually carried out by filing or cutting the firing pin nose. Sometimes, the firing pin may be replaced. Dissimilar firing pin marks may be misleading to the unwary examiners, especially if other identifying marks are not available. A negative opinion on dissimilar firing pin marks would evidently be wrong. The defense attorney takes full advantage of the negative opinion to eliminate the accused gun on a scientific basis. It acts as strong corroborative evidence to plead innocence and noninvolvement of the gun in the commission of a crime. However, the evidence cartridge can positively be identified, despite dissimilar firing pins, only if other identifiable marks produced by the development of pressure are available or marks from a part of the firing pin that remained untampered are available and identifiable.

2.3.2.1 Replaced Firing Pin

The firing pin may be replaced instead of being tampered with. In such cases, the firing pin evidence becomes redundant. In the absence of other identifying marks, forming of opinion on linkage with the firearm on the basis of dissimilar firing pin marks alone would be misleading and erroneous. It is possible to establish linkage only if other identifying marks are available in addition to dissimilar firing pin marks.

In a murder case, one 12-bore fired cartridge case was recovered from the scene of the crime. The fired cartridge was sent to the laboratory for safekeeping, because the involved gun could not be seized. The accused, after committing the crime, evaded arrest and interrogation for a few days. In the meantime, the accused handed over his licensed gun to an arms dealer for repair. The dealer was directed to replace the firing pin, on the plea that its protrusion was occasionally ineffective, which led to misfires. The accused also obtained a receipt from the arms dealer mentioning the details of the gun deposited, make, serial number, etc., and the nature of the job assigned. Thereafter, the accused surrendered himself to the police and pleaded innocence. He handed over the gun with the changed firing pin. The said gun was sent to the laboratory for linkage with the evidence cartridge that was sent earlier. The firing pin marks on the evidence cartridge, as expected, were distinctly different from those available on the test cartridges fired from the surrendered gun. However, the breech marks present on the evidence and test cartridges were found similar in their individual characteristics. This led to a definite conclusion that it was the gun that fired the evidence cartridge and no other. The defense produced the aforesaid receipt in support of his plea and stressed that the firing pin of the gun could not have fired the evidence cartridge found at the crime scene. The expert, the author himself, during cross examination, produced the photomicrograph showing matching of breech marks, along with dissimilar firing pin marks on the evidence and test cartridges. As imprinting of breech marks on the evidence cartridge was possible only by the development of pressure, evidently it was the gun of the accused that fired the cartridge and none other. The defense plea was

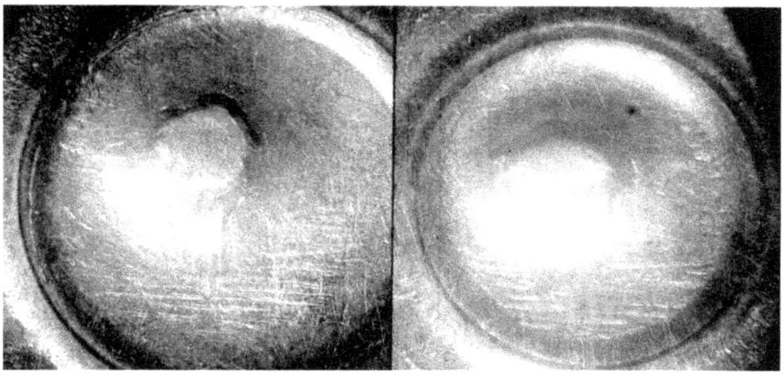

Figure 2.18 Dissimilar firing pin and similar breech marks.

untenable. In addition, the deliberate attempt of the accused to destroy the evidentiary clues was taken seriously in convicting the accused. Similar observation is likely in cases involving crudely manufactured, homemade firearms having detachable firing pin arrangements (Figure 2.18).

Note:

1. It is unsafe to form any opinion on the basis of dissimilar firing pin marks alone. A negative opinion that the questioned cartridge had not been fired from the suspect firearm cannot be inferred unless other marks that are produced by the development of pressure, such as breech, chamber, etc., are available and also are dissimilar.
2. In the absence of other identifying marks, one can safely state only to the extent that the firing pin marks on the questioned cartridge did not tally with the firing pin marks of the suspect firearm.

2.3.2.2 *Firing Pin Periphery Marks*

A deeply indented firing pin hit makes contact with the surrounding area away from the firing pin nose/tip. These marks are called *firing pin periphery marks*. The deeper the indentation, the farther is the periphery contact and its marks. It is independent of usual firing pin marks, though produced by the same firing pin and none other. If marks are sufficient and characteristic, one can safely infer about the linkage of the evidence cartridge with the questioned firearm. Periphery marks may prove helpful when firing pin marks are not identifiable due to tampering or perforated caps.

It has been observed that the tampering of the firing pin is usually carried out by filing, and is often restricted to the nose or tip. The surrounding area often remains intact. Hence, a tampered firing pin generally changes the firing pin nose marks without changing the firing pin periphery marks. The possibility of identifying these periphery marks needs to be probed before forming an opinion on apparently dissimilar firing pin marks. Firing pin periphery marks of poorly finished, substandard firearms are invariably highly characteristic. Periphery firing pin marks also are helpful in perforated caps. The phenomena of perforated caps are due to inappropriate constructional features of the firearm, usually a long firing pin. Illegally made, substandard, improvised, and homemade firearms are more prone to the formation of perforated caps. Cartridges that have perforated caps are devoid of the usual firing pin marks.

2.3.2.3 Firing Pin Marks without Test Firing

In a murder case, four 12 bore cartridges were fired from a 12 bore SBBL gun. After committing the crime, the accused broke his 12 bore licensed gun. The investigating officer recovered all the broken parts of the gun from the possession of the accused. The broken gun parts and the four fired cartridges (recovered from the crime scene) were sent to the laboratory for examination and comparison. On examination it was found that almost all the parts of the SBBL gun were hammered and broken (Figure 2.19).

The action of the gun was badly damaged and even the breech was hammered. Obviously, the gun could not be used for firing test cartridges. On thorough examination of the broken gun parts it appeared that the firing pin remained unprotruded and was not damaged despite hammering on the breech.

On examining the fired cartridges it was observed that the firing pin marks on all the four cartridges were similar. As the gun was broken and unserviceable it was necessary to obtain firing pin marks by adopting a suitable procedure that obviated the necessity of firing. A suitable metal surface softer than metal of the primer was chosen for the purpose. A flattened buckshot was placed on the firing pin and pressed by applying sufficient force. The firing pin marks obtained on test lead specimens tallied with the firing pin marks present on the crime cartridges thereby establishing the linkage of the crime with the licensed broken gun of the accused.

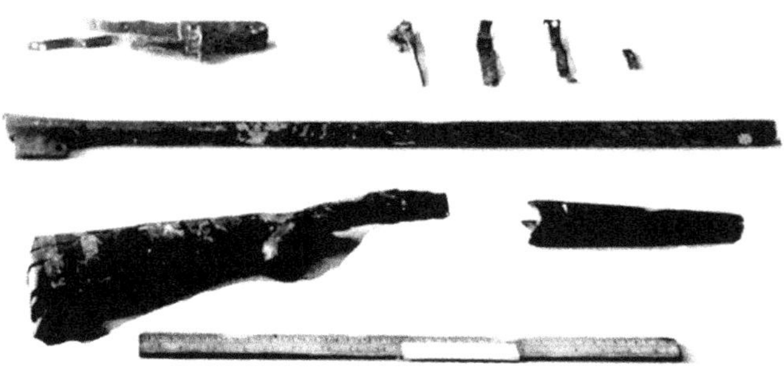

Figure 2.19 Broken gun.

2.4 Extractor and Ejector Marks

There are generally two types of extractors. The first one is the one that imprints its marks on development of pressure. This is made in a recess at the rear end of the barrel. They are common in manual-loading firearms, such as shotguns and revolvers. In revolvers, the recess is at the rear end of the chamber. This type of extractor is usually found in a majority of single-shot homemade firearms irrespective of the type of the ammunition they are designed to fire, whether a high-power rifled cartridge or a usual shotgun cartridge. The extractor is provided in a recess at the rear end of the barrel similar to those of shotguns. The class and individual characteristic extractor marks imprinted by the development of pressure individualize the fired cartridge in respect of the suspect firearm. Identifiable static and sliding extractor marks may be imprinted like those of breech and chamber marks (Figure 2.20).

A high pressure is often required to imprint comparable extractor marks. It serves as an identifying tool for linkage of the fired cartridge in respect to the suspect firearm.

Figure 2.20 Similar static and sliding ejector marks.

The second type of extractor is a claw, commonly found in automatic self-loaders and repeaters. These also are found in a majority of illegally made auto firearms. The extractor claw may imprint its marks without firing, merely by loading and unloading, and, thus, its utility from a forensic point of view is limited.

2.4.1 Extractor Marks by Low-Pressure Round

Imprinting of a comparable extractor mark by low-pressure test rounds is often obligatory in cases involving unusual firearms that have weak constructional material—a common feature seen in homemade and improvised firearms. The procedure for reproduction of extractor marks may need suitable modification depending on allied factors influencing the functioning of the unusual firearm.

In another criminal case, the suspect firearm was a homemade pistol designed to fire 12-bore shotgun cartridges. The evidence cartridge, found at the crime scene, was a 12-bore, 2½-inch fired cartridge case. The primer of the cartridge was perforated and the base was almost separated. However, characteristic marks of the extractor recess were found on the cylindrical portion of the brass head and partly on the paper wall. In the absence of any other identifying marks, a comparable extractor mark had to be obtained that needed development of high pressure. The suspect homemade pistol had inappropriate constructional features and a weak barrel. The lever for closing the breech was loose and the cartridge headspace was excessively high. Two normal load cartridges were fired for test purposes, but they did not produce the required extractor marks. Instead of firing a number of test rounds, preferably heavy load, a new approach was made to imprint the required marks. A thin lead piece was placed on the brass head to make available a softer surface for imprinting clear impressions by the development of a comparatively low pressure. The dimension of the lead piece was such that it could cover more than the width of the brass head and nearly half of the length of cylindrical portion. A flattened buckshot served the purpose. It could conveniently be kept in close contact with the brass head by applying hand pressure. This cartridge was loaded in the chamber, keeping the lead piece just above the extractor. The gap between the extractor and the part of the cartridge that was likely to come in contact on firing was brought down, thereby further reducing the required pressure. Therefore, even a reduced charge was expected to be sufficient for imprinting of extractor marks on the thin lead piece in contact with the base of the cartridge. In the instant case, shot charge was reduced to almost one fourth and the emptied portion was filled in with cardboard pieces. This pressure was found sufficient to imprint class and individual characteristic extractor marks on the lead piece. The extractor marks, so obtained, were examined and compared with the

Figure 2.21 Extractor marks on evidence cartridge.

extractor marks present on the evidence cartridge case. These were found to be similar in their class and individual characteristics. This led to a positive conclusion that the evidence cartridge had been fired through the suspect pistol (Figure 2.21).

This procedure also can be adopted in legally manufactured, branded firearms. This is so if the test live cartridge with the thin lead piece is not a tight fit in the chamber and is loaded easily. It may prove to be of great use if the required extractor marks are not imprinted even after firing a number of test rounds. Depending on the nature of marks and the firearm involved, the shot charge may be reduced accordingly. The reduced charge may be half or less. In some cases, even the entire shot charge may be removed and the emptied portion filled in with additional unfired or fired wads or cardboard pieces. This procedure is very helpful for imprinting of extractor marks in cases involving illegally made, substandard firearms, especially homemade.

2.4.2 Ejector Marks and Tampered Firearms

The ejector is usually a separate unit for ejecting the cartridge in automatic and semiautomatic firearms. The shape and size of the ejector represent the class characteristic parameters and the individual characteristic marks identify the firearm that fired the cartridges. There may be spring-loaded ejectors in hinged-type single- or double-barreled shotguns, which extract and eject the cartridge simultaneously when the breech is opened. The class and individual characteristic ejector marks often prove helpful in establishing linkage especially when other identifying marks, such as breech, chamber, etc., are not available or nonidentifiable.

The tampering of the firing pin and breech by filing is very common. The extractor and ejector are seldom tampered with. The cartridge–firearm linkage may be established if any of the identifying parts of the firearm remain free of tampering. One such part that remains untouched in tampered firearms is the periphery of the recess of the extractor or spring-loaded ejector whose characteristic breaks are imprinted on development of pressure alone. The junction between the spring-loaded ejector and the rest of the chamber provides peripheral or edge marks. These edge marks, if available and characteristic, prove helpful in establishing linkage of the evidence cartridge despite dissimilar firing pin and breech marks.

In another criminal case, the firing pin of the firearm was tampered with. The questioned firearm was a 12-bore SBBL hammered gun. It had a spring-loaded ejector. Three fired cartridges recovered from the crime scene had similar firing pin impressions, but they did not tally with the firing pin of the questioned SBBL gun, This indicated that the evidence cartridges had been fired from the same firing pin, but not from the firing pin of the gun in question. Therefore, the characteristic marks of the tampered firing pin were of no practical utility. The only available marks of forensic significance were ejector edge marks on two of the recovered cartridges. The boundary on the longer side of the ejector had highly characteristic breaks at various places from one end to the other. These marks were evidently reproducible only by the development of pressure being the periphery marks of the spring-loaded ejector of the shotgun. Test cartridges fired from the questioned SBBL gun revealed the presence of similar characteristic peripheral breaks. This led to the conclusion that they were fired from the gun under question, whose firing pin was tampered with. The third evidence cartridge also could be linked with the questioned gun despite absence of the ejector edge marks because all of the three evidence cartridges had similar firing pin impressions (Figure 2.22).

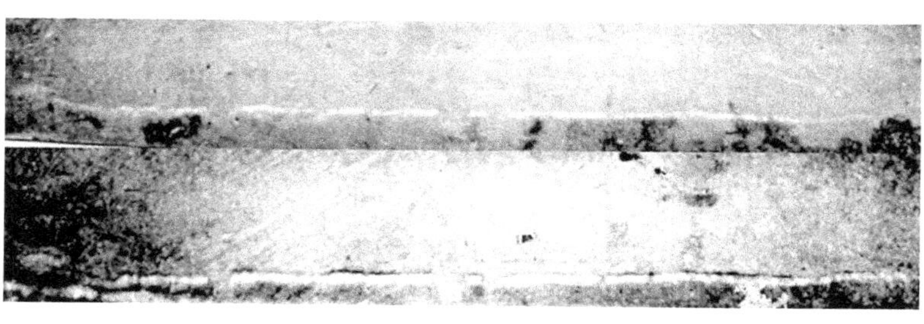

Figure 2.22 Similar ejector periphery breaks.

2.5 Summary of Modified Cartridge Identification Procedures

The identification of fired cartridges by firing pin, breech, chamber, extractor, and ejector marks is known and documented in textbooks on forensic firearm, firearm injuries, and on other allied subjects. There also are popular web sites on the subject. The usual procedure of identification is unavailing in the majority of cases involving illegally made, substandard, and tampered firearms. An alarming increase in the use of these firearms warrants modifications in identification procedures. A detailed study of the criminal cases involving tampered and illegally made, unusual firearms has revealed that it is the reproduction of the marks of the identifying parts of the firearm that is of most concern. The reproduction procedure depends on the constructional features, constructional material, and action mechanism of unusual firearms. The weak barrel restricts the use of high-pressure test rounds. Nonfunctional and unserviceable, tampered, and other unusual firearms call for test marks without firing. Besides, reproduction of marks also depends on the identifying part of the firearm. Modified procedures vis-à-vis identifying parts of the firearm are tabulated for quick reference (Table 2.1 and Table 2.2).

Table 2.1 Reproduction of Marks by Low Pressure Test Cartridges

Identifying marks	Modified procedures for reproducing marks
Breech marks	By reducing shot charge and providing high cartridge headspace
Chamber marks	By developing localized pressure at the bottleneck by firing bottleneck cartridges without bullets
Extractor marks	By placing a thin lead piece on a test cartridge for providing low cartridge headspace

Table 2.2 Reproduction of Marks on Test Specimens without Firing

Identifying marks	Modified procedures for reproducing marks
Breech mark	On flattened buckshot lead surface by light hammering
Chamber marks	By pressing plasticine on glass road in short-barreled firearms
Firing pin marks	On flattened buckshot lead surface by hand pressure

Forensic Investigation of Fired Bullets from Unusual Firearms

3

Projectile identification carries greater evidential values than that of fired cartridges, because it is the projectile that causes the injury. Once the projectile is recovered from the victim's body and is positively linked with the suspect firearm, the criminal is connected with the crime through his/her weapon.

Bullets are cylindro-conoidal projectiles. Their stability in flight is achieved by imparting spin. The desired spin is imparted by rifling the barrel. The rifled firearms that are commonly encountered in crimes are automatic pistols, revolvers, and rifles. A number of parallel spiral grooves are cut longitudinally inside the barrel and have a uniform twist. The twist may be right- or left-handed. The raised portions between the grooves are known as *lands*. The number of lands and grooves are always the same.

When a bullet is fired from a rifled barrel, it expands, sets up, and bottoms the grooves. It is cut by the raised lands creating grooves and moves along the spiral path as it acquires the necessary spin. In doing so, the bullet is engraved with the rifling characteristics signifying the direction/twist of rifling, number of lands or grooves, widths of lands and grooves, and the angle and pitch of rifling. These parameters represent the rifling specification of the manufacturer and are termed as *class characteristic rifling marks.*

The friction between the rifled bore and the moving bullet results in sliding contacts with the imperfections of the barrel, thereby creating striations on the fired bullet. The set of striations represents an integrated effect of imperfections of the barrel and called *individual characteristic rifling marks.* Because bullets follow a preassigned spiral path, the integrated stria pattern is repeated in each firing. The reproducibility of striations makes it possible to ascertain the "thumb print" of the rifled firearm.

The fired bullet, thus, carries class rifling characteristics as well as individual characteristic marks of the rifled barrel. The class characteristic parameters that can visually be identified during field examination are the direction of twist of rifling and the number of lands and grooves. These parameters also can be ascertained visually in rifled firearms as well. A visual comparison often enables the field investigator to eliminate the improbable when the suspect firearm is subsequently apprehended. Whereas, the direction of spiral grooves signifies the twist of rifling in rifled firearms, it is the angular slant of the lands/grooves on the fired bullet that indicates the direction of twist of rifling. If the slant is toward the right, a weapon having left-handed rifling is ruled out and vice versa. The other parameter that eliminates the improbable is the number of lands and grooves. The number can easily be counted on the fired bullet and also on the seized rifled firearm, especially handguns. The seized firearm is eliminated if the number of the lands and grooves is not the same as that on the evidence bullet. Thus, the seized firearm having six lands/grooves is eliminated as improbable if the evidence bullet has five lands and five grooves, and so on. If there are two or more bullets available, then the visual examination of widths of land and grooves is helpful to the extent that they are the same or distinctly different. Because grooves on fired bullet are created by the lands of the rifled bore, the widths of grooves and lands on fired bullets correspond to land and groove widths, respectively, of the firearm. Hence, it must be borne in mind that the land/groove widths on the fired bullet are the negative replica of the rifled barrel. It is usually possible to assess, without making measurements, whether land and groove widths on the fired bullet are same or distinctly different. In some cases, a comparison also can be made by viewing inside the rifled barrel, especially in handguns.

The search is minimized when the laboratory findings are known. A regularly updated data bank of rifling specifications enables the laboratory personnel to ascertain the probable make and model of the firearm from the class rifling characteristics on the evidence bullet. Once the field investigators know the laboratory findings, ascertaining the caliber, make, and model of the seized firearm is a simple task. This information is available on the firearm itself and, thus, no expertise is needed. This investigative aspect is well recognized in "no gun" cases and, therefore, supersedes priority over other cases for expert examination and opinion in forensic laboratories worldwide.

Once the suspected firearms are available, the individual characteristic striations on the fired bullet identify the particular rifled firearm that fired the projectile. To establish the identity, test bullets are fired from the suspect rifled firearm. The class and individual characteristic rifling marks on the test-fired bullets are examined and compared inter se (between themselves) and thereafter compared with those present on the evidence bullet. Whereas similar rifling marks establish linkage, dissimilar marks eliminate the suspect firearm. Identification of the bullet fired from rifled firearms thus poses no problem in establishing linkage or otherwise. Bullet fragments also can be identified if rifling marks are sufficient and identifiable.

It poses a problem if usual, orderly rifling marks are not imprinted on the evidence bullet. This is usually found when the assigned path of spiral grooves is inappropriate due to imprecise bore dimension or irregular rifling. These improper constructional features are commonly seen in illegally made, substandard rifled firearms. The legally manufactured, branded rifled firearms also can have improper constructional features if mismatched ammunition is fired from them. Evidently, the rifling data bank may not prove helpful in either case. Even the resultant striations due to an inappropriate path may at times be misleading and may result in noncommittal inferences.

It is more problematic if the bullet is fired from illegally made, smoothbore firearms that are not rifled, but are designed to fire pistol, revolver, and rifle cartridges. Apparently, the bullet fired from a nonrifled (smoothbore) barrel does not carry rifling marks and, thus, assessing the probable firearm from the fired bullet becomes a difficult task. The prevailing misconception that nonrifled, smoothbore firearms do not imprint identifiable/repetitive marks on fired bullets is the biggest hurdle for making sincere attempts to establish linkage. It usually remains unexplored for seemingly unattainable results and often leads to noncommittal inferences.

The increase in use of illegal firearms in crimes is alarming. It calls for evolving procedures for identifying bullets fired from illegally made, substandard firearms whether rifled or smoothbore. This is a big chunk of firearm evidence over the decade, and, hence, needs detailed discussion.

3.1 Inappropriate Rifled Bore Barrel Marks

The bore dimensions of illegally made rifled firearms are invariably inappropriate. The relative bullet–bore diameter may be under- or oversized. The preassigned spiral path is influenced accordingly and, therefore, the rifling marks on the fired bullets.

3.1.1 Under-Bore Sized Rifled Barrels

Bullets fired from undersized rifled barrels carry deeply engraved land and groove marks. The engravings are markedly influenced by the construction material of the bullet.

3.1.1.1 Lead Bullets

Lead bullets, being soft and malleable, tend to elongate in abnormally undersized rifled bores. During the process, the bullet also is shaved to bring it to the size of the bore. The high velocity forward motion of the bullet, during the process of elongation, tends to slide the bullet from the path and direction of the rifling and, consequently, the bullet may not engage the rifling properly. This results in the imprinting of mixed land and groove marks without clear demarcation. It may be difficult to ascertain even the number of lands and grooves on the fired bullet. The usual procedure of field investigation for eliminating the improbable by visual examination of the rifled barrel may be misleading and erroneous. The available rifling data bank for assessing the probable also becomes redundant. Thus, class characteristic marks cannot be

Figure 3.1 Nonstriated land and groove marks matching on .32 lead bullets fired through abnormally undersized rifled barrel.

compared without firing test bullets in cases involving an abnormally undersized rifled barrel.

Comparison of individual characteristic marks is comparatively easier and more reliable. When the bullet does not travel along the preassigned path of spiral grooves in an undersized rifled barrel, characteristic breaks in the rifling marks are usually observed on fired bullets. Surface irregularities or notches on lands and grooves, if any, also are prominently imprinted on fired bullets. The characteristic break, shape, size, relative position of rifling marks, and nature of shaving can be utilized to identify a fired bullet from the suspect firearm.

In a criminal case, the illegal firearm was a poor copy of a .32 Webley and Scott revolver made by locals of Darra, Afghanistan. The bore was rifled, but its diameter was abnormally smaller. It was .29 inches. As expected, orderly rifling marks were not imprinted on .32 fired lead bullets, but the characteristic breaks in rifling marks were very prominent. The nonstriated rifling pattern was so characteristic and unique that positive identification was possible even by naked eye examination and comparison. However, it is always desirable to examine and compare the test and evidence bullets at a low magnification before arriving at any conclusion (Figure 3.1).

3.1.1.2 *Jacketed Bullets*

Jacketed bullets, being comparatively harder, do not elongate even in unusually smaller diameter rifled barrels. The bullets, after engaging initial rifling, continue to move in the direction and path of rifling until arrested due to oversizing and their inability to elongate. This results in imprinting of identifiable class characteristic rifling marks. Jacketed bullets invariably get lodged inside abnormally undersized rifled bore. The striations present on the jacketed bullets, whether lodged or not, cannot be compared with the nonstriated rifling marks on the elongated lead bullets, though produced by the same barrel. The path traversed by elongated lead bullets is evidently different from the path a nonelongated jacketed bullet travels. Therefore, in the absence of a firearm, comparison of elongated lead bullets with metal jacketed bullets may be misleading both for class and individual characteristic rifling marks.

Note: Jacketed and unjacketed (lead) bullets of the same diameter and caliber fired from abnormally undersized rifled bore may carry distinctly different rifling marks despite being fired from the same rifled firearm.

It is risky to fire jacketed bullets through abnormally undersized rifled barrels as impaction of the bullet may cause the barrel to burst.

3.1.2 Over-Bore Sized Rifled Barrels

The nature of striations depends on the extent of the over-bore size. If it is slightly more, the bullet may manage to bite the lands and move along the spiral path. If it is unusually more, the bullet neither engages rifling nor does it move on the preassigned path of spiral grooves. The bullet, thus, remains unstable during its entire flight, though fired through a rifled barrel. Both aim and range suffer. The very purpose of rifling is defeated. This aspect is taken care of during illegal production of substandard rifled firearms as well. Therefore, oversized rifled bore diameters are uncommon even in illegally made, cheap pistols, revolvers, and rifles.

One often comes across oversized bores in rifled firearms when the chamber is modified or when mismatched ammunition is used. The necessity of modifying the chamber usually arises when the firearm is obsolete and its ammunition is not in production; likewise, if the ammunition of the firearm in hand is not easily available or fairly expensive. Attempts are made to modify the chamber to accommodate cartridges whose bullet diameter is almost identical to the rifled bore diameter of the firearm. However, this may not always be possible. In some cases, the commercially available, nearest caliber may have significantly smaller bullet diameter. Consequently, the bore diameter may be excessively oversized for the smaller bullet that is loaded in the chosen cartridges.

3.1.2.1 Slightly Oversized Rifled Barrels

Bullets fired from slightly oversized, bored rifled firearms engage the rifling, partly or wholly. The rifling marks are usually reproducible on test bullets.

The linkage of the fired bullet with the suspected improvised firearm, therefore, is possible.

In a criminal case, the seized double-barrel firearm was an obsolete firearm, a combination of shotgun and a sporting rifle. The left barrel was an obsolete sporting .32-40 rifled barrel. The evidence bullet recovered in the case was a .303 fired bullet instead of a .32 bore of a sporting rifle. The chamber of the rifled barrel was found to be modified. It was modified to accommodate and fire easily available .303 rifle cartridges. Test .303 cartridges were fired from the modified chamber to obtain rifling marks of the .32 sporting rifle. The rifling marks of the .32-40 rifled barrel were imprinted on .303 test bullets. The rifling marks were properly engraved. Obviously, it was due to insignificant dimensional difference, on firing, between the expanded .303 jacketed bullet and the .32-40 soft nose bullet. The class and individual characteristic rifling marks on the test and evidence bullets established linkage (Figure 3.2).

It is desirable to obtain tests by firing appropriate ammunition, unless the firearm is improvised to fire only mismatched ammunition. In this

Figure 3.2 .32 class rifling characteristics on .303 fired bullets.

case, it was possible to fire a .32-40 sporting rifle cartridge from the modified chamber.

3.1.2.2 Excessively Oversized Rifled Bore

Bullets fired from rifled barrels having appreciably larger diameter do not engage rifling and, hence, do not move on the preassigned path of spiral grooves. Consequently, they make random contacts inside the rifled barrel. The striations are discontinuous and may be overlapping due to random contacts with the raised lands and, thus, are not repetitive. Therefore, the usual procedure of firing test bullets for comparison and opinion cannot be adopted in such cases. It is usually not possible to identify fired bullets in respect of excessively oversized rifled firearms.

3.1.3 Inappropriate Modified Chamber

The chambers are usually modified without using precision instruments. They are crudely made and often inappropriate, though capable of accommodating and firing the chosen mismatched cartridge. The nature of barrel marks is markedly influenced by the varying position of the loaded cartridge in an inappropriate chamber, which is specifically oversized. The fired bullet may not pick up striations if the axis of the loaded bullet coincides with the axis of the rifled bore.

The fired bullet may imprint patch(es) of striations if the axis of the loaded bullet is positioned angularly with the axis of the rifled bore.

3.1.4 Inappropriate/Irregular Rifling

The making of rifled barrels is a precision manufacturing process. It requires sophisticated equipment that can make specified dimensional grooves with minimal permissible tolerance of a few thou for achieving desired ballistics. To make the cost low, the provision of rifling in illegal substandard firearms is made without using precision equipment and, hence, they are often inappropriate. The irregular rifling may be very prominent in crudely made rifled barrels. The width and angle of slant may vary from one land to the other. The groove depth also may vary from one to the other. The varying angle of rifling, land widths, groove widths, etc., in the same rifled barrel, are not found in the rifling data bank of rifled firearms that are legally manufactured. The rifling data bank for assessing the probable make and model is of no practical use in "no gun" cases. Establishing linkage is comparatively easy if the firearm is available. Depending on relative bullet–bore diameter, it may be possible by adopting the procedure detailed above (Figure 3.3).

(a) (b)

Figure 3.3 Varying land widths and angle of slant on bullet fired by irregular rifling.

3.1.5 Mismatch Rifled Firearms

Use of mismatched ammunition is not uncommon. There are pistols, revolvers, and rifles that can conveniently accommodate and fire other caliber cartridges without making illegal improvisations. Mathews has listed a variety of mismatched firearm–cartridge combinations. Adapters also are commercially available for the purpose.

Mismatched bullets have either a loose or tight fit inside a rifled barrel. The rifled firearm, therefore, is undersized or oversized for the bullet, depending upon the type of mismatch ammunition used. Rifling marks vary with the type of the bore. The identification procedure varies accordingly.

If the mismatched rifled bore is slightly more than the bullet diameter, then it is likely that the bullet may not bottom the grooves of the rifled barrel, which results in improper engravings. Partially engaged rifling is often similar to those fired from worn-out rifled firearms. One such example is the .315″/8 mm sporting rifles that can conveniently accommodate and fire 7.62 mm self-loading, service rifle cartridges. The 7.62 mm-fired bullet carries improper rifling marks of a .315 sporting rifle and appears to be fired from a worn-out rifled firearm. There are many more regular branded firearms that can fire mismatched ammunition. The list remains incomplete due to rapidly increasing new makes and models of a variety of branded firearms that are flooding the gun market worldwide.

3.2 Smoothbore Firearms Using Rifled Ammunition

One often comes across unusual firearms that are designed to fire pistol, revolver, and rifle cartridges, but their barrels are not rifled. The unrifled barrels are known as smoothbore barrels, and the firearms as smoothbore firearms. The term "smoothbore" firearm is a misnomer because the interior of a smoothbore barrel is never perfectly smooth. The finely finished interior of a smoothbore barrel that shines like a mirror has innumerable, randomly distributed irregularities in the form of elevations and depressions, if viewed under a microscope. Thus, smoothbore firearms simply signify that their barrels are not rifled. Evidently, the bullets fired through smoothbore barrels would not carry orderly barrel marks like those of rifled barrels. In such a case, the question arises whether bullets fired from smoothbore barrels also provide valuable evidentiary clues like those fired from rifled barrels. The issues that need to be addressed are:

- Whether smoothbore barrel marks can positively be identified as having been caused by a smoothbore firearm. This calls for a detailed study of the nature of barrel marks that are likely to be imprinted by varying constructional features of smoothbore firearms using rifled ammunition.
- Whether smoothbore barrel marks provide necessary data for assessment of probable constructional features that differentiates one smoothbore firearm from the other firing the same caliber ammunition. This necessitates the introduction of new class characteristic parameters for identifying the type of smoothbore firearms from fired bullets.
- Whether fired bullets can positively be linked with the smoothbore firearm that has no preassigned path like spiral grooves of rifled barrels.

The author has made an exhaustive study of barrel marks on bullets fired from a variety of unrifled (smoothbore) firearms. A large volume of experimental work involving about 1,000 firearms has revealed that, not only the fired bullet can invariably be linked with the smoothbore firearm, but a probable assessment of inappropriate constructional features also can be made by introducing new class characteristic parameters. The details are discussed separately below:

- Nature of smoothbore barrel marks
- Caliber and type of firearm from fired bullet when smoothbore firearm is not available and introduction of new class characteristic parameters
- Linkage of fired bullet with the available smoothbore firearm

3.2.1 Smoothbore Barrel Marks Using Rifled Ammunition

Smoothbore firearms are not meant to fire rifled ammunition, hence, there is no specified path of travel, such as spiral grooves. In contrast to rifled firearms, their bore diameters are nonspecific as well. They may be under- or oversized for the bullet and sometimes even both, under *and* over. The movement of the bullet, thus, depends upon the relative bullet-bore diameter. It makes contact with the sides of the smoothbore barrel accordingly and is scratched, creating striations. In addition to relative bullet-bore diameter, the nature of barrel marks is influenced by the chamber–bore alignment. Unlike regular branded, rifled firearms, the chamber may not always be aligned. The axis of the loaded bullet may or may not coincide with the axis of the bore and, accordingly, the chamber may be coaxial or noncoaxial, aligned or misaligned. The inclination of the loaded bullet determines the direction of its entry inside the smoothbore and possible barrel contact points. The other important constructional feature that influences the barrel marks is the characteristic protrusion(s) inside the bore, if any, especially those having sufficient height and width. Thus, the three important variables that influence the nature of barrel marks are bore size, chamber alignment, and characteristic protrusions inside the bore.

3.2.1.1 Undersized Smoothbore Barrel Marks

A bullet passing through an undersized bore is a tight fit. It imprints continuous striations from base to the ogival portion or even beyond. The nature of continuous striations varies with the bullet–bore alignment whether coaxial or noncoaxial.

3.2.1.1.1 Coaxial Bullet–Bore A coaxial bullet enters into the bore with its axis almost coinciding with the axis of the bore. The coaxial bullet makes continuous contact inside the undersized smoothbore resulting in continuous straight striations. The unidirectional forward motion of the bullet creates parallel striations. The resultant striations on fired bullets, thus, are continuous, straight, and parallel completely around the periphery (Figure 3.4).

3.2.1.1.2 Noncoaxial Bullet–Bore A noncoaxial bullet enters into the bore at an angle. It creates inclined striations. A misaligned or loose chamber makes the bullet noncoaxial with the axis of the bore. Hence, a loose or misaligned chamber causes the bullet to enter angularly down the undersize

Figure 3.4 Continuous straight and parallel striations from undersized smoothbore .38 pistol.

Figure 3.5 Inclined parallel striations from undersized smoothbore pistol.

Figure 3.6 Straight parallel striations having grooves.

bore. If the angularity continues throughout its travel in the undersized bore, then the striations are inclined, continuous, and parallel (Figure 3.5).

3.2.1.1.3 Unusual Surface Joints Undersized, smoothbore firearms, having characteristic surface protrusions and longitudinal joints, create groove(s) on fired bullets in addition to parallel straight or inclined striations (Figure 3.6).

3.2.1.2 Oversized Smoothbore Barrel Marks

Bullets passing through oversized bore barrels are loose. The loose bullet tumbles during its travel inside the barrel. It makes random contacts with

Figure 3.7 Straight and partly inclined discontinuous striations.

the sides of the barrel at different places and at different angles imprinting discontinuous straight or inclined striations. The discontinuous striations are invariably in patches, located at various places including at the tip. Angular contacts imprint inclined striations. Multiple discontinuous contacts, partly or wholly, on the same portion, imprint overlapping striations. Consequently, the patches of discontinuous striations are wholly straight or wholly inclined or both straight and inclined in separate as well as overlapping patches (Figure 3.7).

Thus, discontinuous striations are either wholly straight or wholly inclined or partly straight and partly inclined. There may be insignificant striations if the loose bullet leaves the oversized barrel without making appreciable contacts. The nature of resultant striations varies with the bullet–bore alignment whether coaxial or noncoaxial.

3.2.1.2.1 Coaxial Bullet If the bullet enters into a very loose bore coaxially, then it may not touch the sides of the barrel during its entire passage through the bore and may not carry striations. This usually occurs in short-barreled firearms.

3.2.1.2.2 Noncoaxial Bullet Firearms having misaligned chambers invariably imprint single-patch striations. The misaligned chambers tend to propel the bullet in a particular direction at a particular angle. Thus, the initial impact creates straight or inclined striations (Figure 3.8). The striations overlap if the portion of initial impact on the bullet also touches the barrel more than once.

The striations on the fired bullet are often unique if the oversized firearms, having misaligned chambers, also have characteristic protrusions inside the bore.

The bullet makes angular contacts due to misalignment in an almost similar manner, imprinting inclined striations on one side and creating irregular grooves on the other side due to protrusion in each firing (Figure 3.9(a)(b)).

Figure 3.8 Inclined initial contact marks from misaligned oversized .315 pistol.

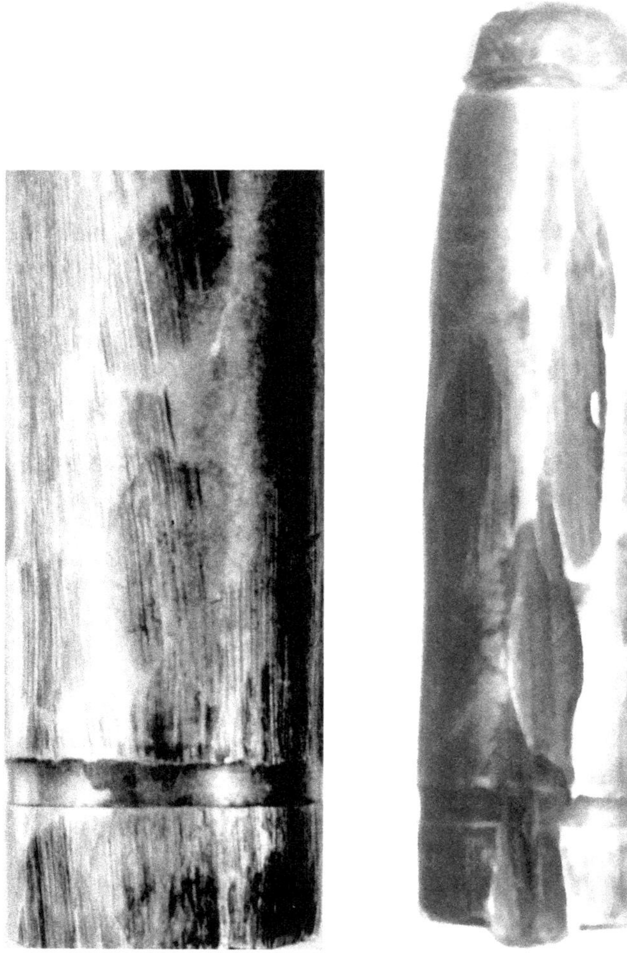

(a) (b)

Figure 3.9 (a) Inclined striations on the outer side; (b) irregular grooves on the other side; and (c) similar irregular grooves on fired bullets. *(continued)*

3.2.1.3 *Variable Smoothbore Barrel Marks*

The bullet–barrel contact is influenced both by under- and oversized portions of the mixed-sized bore firearms. The fired bullet creates striations all around the periphery from the undersized part of the barrel and random discontinuous striations from the oversized part of the barrel. The resultant striation depends upon the relative position of the under- and oversized portions inside the barrel.

3.2.1.3.1 Tapered Barrels In tapered barrels, the undersized portion is invariably only near the muzzle end. The over-bore sized portion is at the

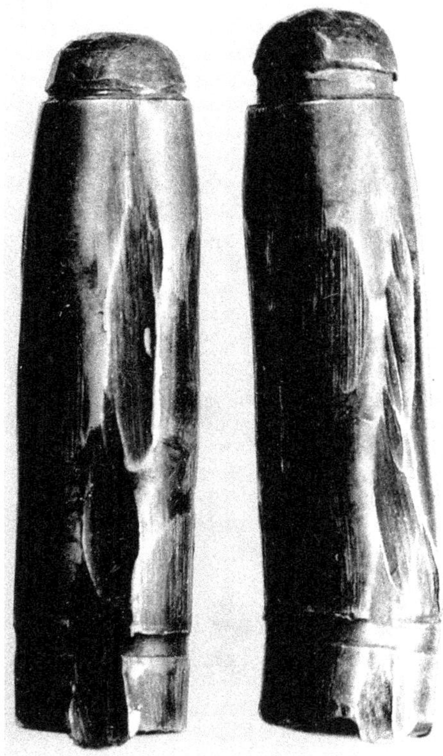

(c)

Figure 3.9 *(continued)* (a) Inclined striations on the outer side; (b) irregular grooves on the other side; and (c) similar irregular grooves on fired bullets.

rear end. The bullet makes continuous contact with the undersized portion of the barrel near the muzzle without touching the initial oversized portion of the bore.

Thus, striations, besides being continuous all around the periphery, also are parallel, straight, or inclined depending on the angle at which the bullet enters into the undersized portion of the bore. Firearms having tapered barrels behave like undersized bore firearms (Figure 3.10).

3.2.1.3.2 Nontapered Variable Bore Firearms In contrast to tapered barrels, the undersized bore portion may be near the breech. Alternatively, the under-bore portion may be between two or more oversized portions.

As under-bore creates continuous striations and over-bore discontinuous striations, the resultant striations are continuous patch or patches of overlapping striations. Continuous striations are created before or after the imprinting of random striations depending on the sequence of under and over

Figure 3.10 Continuous parallel striations from mixed-size bore.

portions of the bore inside the barrel. Therefore, it is apparent that mixed-size smoothbore barrels create:

- parallel, straight, or inclined continuous striations or;
- overlapping straight and/or inclined continuous striations in patches.

3.2.2 Class Characteristic Parameters of Unusual Firearms: New Parameters

The rifling marks on a fired bullet vary with the constructional features of the rifled bore. The marks signify the rifling specifications of the firearm that fired the bullet. Likewise, smoothbore barrel marks also vary with the constructional features of the smoothbore firearm. However, there are no specific specifications because smoothbore firearms are not meant to fire rifled ammunition. There is an exhaustive rifling specification data bank maintained by manufacturers and laboratory personnel and, hence, ascertaining the probable make and model by comparing it with the available rifling specifications data bank is routine work in "no gun" cases. However, there obviously is no data bank for smoothbore firearms because of dimensional diversity from one firearm to the other, manufactured/made at different sources, without conforming to any specification. In fact, no specification exists that can be considered as class characteristic data to differentiate one from the other, using the same caliber ammunition. So, also, there is no relevance of make or model. This calls for introduction of new class characteristic parameters that can assess the probable smoothbore firearm. It is only the nature of smoothbore barrel marks that can be utilized to assess the probable constructional features of the firearm in "no gun" cases. Therefore, the plausible class characteristic parameters that can be ascertained from the nature of stria pattern include:

- Bore size
- Chamber alignment
- Characteristic longitudinal joints or raised portions inside the bore

3.2.2.1 Assessment of Bore Size from Barrel Marks

3.2.2.1.1 Bore Size from Continuous Striations Bullet carrying continuous striations indicate its passage through a barrel having a partly or wholly undersized bore. An assessment of probable firearms, whether rifled or smoothbore, can be made by evaluating the nature of continuous striations.

- Continuous straight striations all around the periphery indicate absence of spiral grooves. It also indicates that spin has not been imparted to the fired bullet. The involved firearm is obviously a non-rifled firearm.
- Continuous straight striations having one or two straight grooves indicate that the probable firearm, besides being smoothbore and undersized, also has longitudinal joint or characteristic protrusions inside the bore.
- Continuous straight striations having additional patches indicate that the bullet has made random contacts as well. The bullet, after or before making continuous contact with the undersized portion of the bore, has made contacts with the oversized portion of the barrel. Thus, the probable firearm is a mixed smoothbore firearm having both under- and over-bore size. The possibility of an undersized smoothbore firearm is ruled out.
- Continuous inclined striations without lands/grooves also indicate that spin was not imparted to the bullet and, hence, the probable firearm is not a rifled firearm.

3.2.2.1.2 Bore Size from Discontinuous Striations Bullet carrying discontinuous striations in patches on its cylindrical portion or beyond indicates that it has made random contacts with the sides of an oversized bore barrel irrespective of the nature of striations in the same or different directions, located at one or different places, and overlapping or nonoverlapping striations. The oversized bore firearm may be smoothbore or a rifled firearm. A worn-out rifle and mismatched ammunition also provides an oversized bore for the fired bullet. The loose bullet makes random contacts with the raised lands. In some cases, it may engage rifling (grooves), though loosely. If grooves are engaged even partly, the fact that the bullet has been fired from a rifled barrel is almost certain. If the bullet does not engage rifling, it becomes difficult to ascertain whether the oversized bore barrel is smoothbore or rifled. Usually, additional evidence available in support of the smoothbore firearm is a very wide patch, far more than the usual land width of a rifled firearm. If a patch of continuous striations covers almost half of the cylindrical portion or more, then an oversized rifled firearm becomes improbable.

3.2.2.1.3 Bore Size from a Single Striation Patch A single patch of striations that covers only a part of the fired bullet indicates that the bullet is loose throughout its entire travel including at the point of contact. It indicates that the involved firearm is an oversized smoothbore or an oversized rifled firearm.

3.2.2.1.4 Bore Size from Insignificant/Faint Striations Patches A small patch or patches of insignificant or faint striations indicates that the bullet is very loose even at the point of contact and it has made random contacts with the barrel. The plausible inferences that can be drawn in such a case are that the bullet has passed through an oversized rifled firearm including a worn-out rifled firearm, or an oversized smoothbore firearm. The possibility of an undersized or a mixed-sized bore firearm is ruled out.

3.2.2.1.5 Bore Size from Bullets without Striations A fired bullet without striations is possible only if it does not make contact with the sides of the barrel throughout its passage down the bore. This is expected when fired from an excessively oversized bore firearm whether rifled or smoothbore. The shorter the barrel, lesser are the chances of bullet contacts. A .38 revolver bullet fired from an oversized .45 short-barreled revolver may not make barrel contacts, but a .303 bullet fired from a .410 long-barreled, smoothbore musket is usually scratched at one or two places.

Therefore, a fired bullet without striations indicates an excessively oversized smooth or rifled bore firearm. The possibility of a under-bore or mixed-bore firearm is ruled out. Bullets without striations or carrying faint striations pose additional identification problems. They often appear like unfired bullets. If such a bullet is recovered from the crime scene and the suspect firearm is not seized, then it becomes necessary to ascertain whether the evidence bullet has ever been fired from a firearm or not.

3.2.2.1.6 Bullet Appearing as Unfired, Whether Fired or Not A fired bullet appears as unfired if it does not carry barrel marks. Presence of firearm discharge deposits on a bullet are helpful in ascertaining whether the bullet appearing as unfired is a fired one.

- Physical Examination—The hot gases, developed by rapid conversion of propellant into gases, constantly come in contact with the base of a bullet during its travel inside the bore. The outer surface of the bullet also comes in contact with the escaping hot gases from the sides. The bullet is partly or wholly enveloped by the discharge gases if it travels without barrel contact. Significant blackening is often present on bullet cannelures. It is usually unnoticeable on the grayish black surface of metallic lead.
- Chemical Examination of Propellant Combustion Products—The combustion products of propellant contain compounds of nitrite ion. The presence of nitrite ion on a fired bullet can readily be detected by diazotization and coupling reaction. The then commonly used gries reagents, α-napthylamine and sulphanilic acid in acetic acid, prove helpful. The reagents are prepared as follows:
  1. 0.03 gm of α-napthylamine is boiled for a few minutes in 100 ml of water and mixed with 30 cc of glacial acetic acid.
  2. 1 gm of sulphanilic acid is dissolved by warming in 100 ml of 30% acetic acid.

  Chemical tests are carried out on the base cavity, and cylindrical and ogival portions of the bullet.

  The base cavity of the unjacketed bullet and exposed base cavity of a jacketed bullet are treated with a few drops of the mixed reagent solution (1) and (2). Development of a pink color indicates the presence of a firearm discharge deposit on the questioned bullet.

  To detect the discharge deposit on the cylindrical and ogival portion of the bullet, a strip of filter paper treated with a mixed solution of reagent (1) and (2) is pressed on the surface. Development of a pink color on blackened surfaces, cannelures, engraved/scratched portions, or on exposed soft nose indicates the presence of nitrite ion. Presence of nitrite ion on the metal jacketed portion, including the flat jacketed base of a soft-nose bullet, can usually be detected only for a short period after firing, probably a couple of weeks or so. However, nitrite can usually be detected, even after years from firing, on exposed lead-based cavities, on soft-nose, or on cylindrical and ogival portions of lead bullets. The adsorption of propellant gases is more on a lead surface compared to other jacketed metal surfaces. Bullets, even after five years from their firing, revealed the presence of nitrite on lead-based cavities. Since jacketed and unjacketed bullets have lead-based cavities and soft-nose bullets have a nose of lead, the presence of nitrite on exposed lead on these three basic types of bullets, usually encountered in criminal cases involving illegal firearms, is usually expected.

- Examination of Gun Shot Residue (GSR) Particles and Elemental Analysis—The development of high temperature also results in vaporization of primer, bullet, and cartridge case material. The extent of vaporization depends upon the time interval during which the temperature remains effective. The resultant molten or vaporized material on rapid condensation results in the formation of micrometer-sized particles, referred to as gun shot residue (GSR) particles. The GSR particles, having characteristic morphology, are deposited on the fired bullet.

  In the case of oversized firearms, the developed temperature is often far less compared to that developed by regular branded firearms using appropriate ammunition. The formation of GSR particles is significantly influenced both qualitatively and quantitatively. A bullet without barrel contact is expected to contain GSR particles in addition to combustion products of the propellant. Sometimes, partially burnt or unburned powder particles are present on the base cavity of fired bullets. If the bullet makes barrel contact (significant or insignificant), then an additional deposit of barrel fouling also is transferred onto the bullets at the point of contact.

  The base, cylindrical, and ogival portions of the bullet are examined under scanning electron microscopes for locating GSR particles having characteristic size and morphology. On locating the GSR particles, their chemical composition is determined by an energy dispersive x-ray analyzer. Identification of GSR particles by their morphology and chemical composition establishes that the bullet is one that has been fired.

- Examination by Elemental Analysis—The portion of the bullet carrying faint scratches is examined for presence of transferred metal of barrel fouling. Besides chemical tests for detection of iron, elemental analysis is carried out by energy-dispersive x-ray analysis (EDXA), coupled with the scanning electron microscope (SEM). The relevant portion is examined under the SEM and is subjected to elemental analysis by EDXA. The spectra invariably reveals presence of iron on fired bullets, especially those fired from rusted barrels of crudely homemade firearms. The x-ray spectrum of the jacketed portion of a .315 soft-nose bullet fired from a smoothbore country-made, oversized bore pistol is shown in Figure 3.11. Presence of iron on a

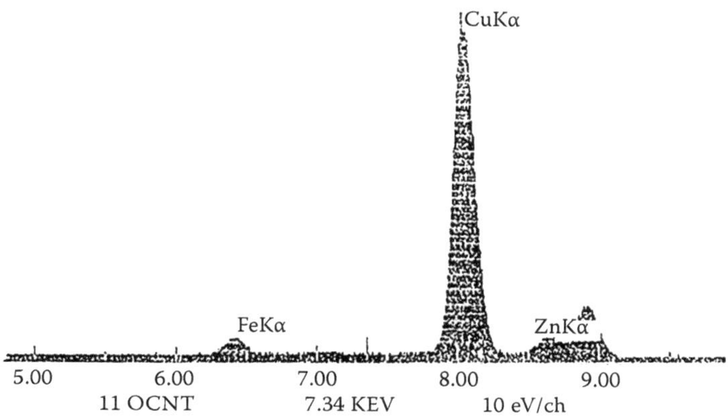

Figure 3.11 EDAX of bullet appearing as unfired.

portion carrying scratches and its absence on other portions acts as a corroborative evidence of firing.

3.2.2.2 Assessment of Chamber Alignment From Barrel Marks

It is usually possible to evaluate chamber alignment from the nature of striations on fired bullets.

1. Chamber alignment from continuous striations:
   a. Continuous parallel straight striations indicate that the bullet has entered into the undersized bore portion of the barrel in coaxial position and the chamber is properly aligned.
   b. Continuous inclined parallel striations indicate that the bullet has entered into the undersized bore portion in an inclined position and the chamber of the firearm is either misaligned or loose.
2. Chamber alignment from discontinuous striations:
   Discontinuous striations whether inclined or straight, parallel or nonparallel essentially indicates that the bullet has passed through an oversized bore firearm. It is not possible to ascertain whether the direction, position, and overlapping of striations are due to random movement of the bullet inside the over bore-sized barrel or due to alignment of the chamber or positioning of the bullet inside the loose chamber. Therefore, it is usually not possible to predict the chamber alignment from discontinuous striations.
3. Chamber alignment from single striation patch:
   A single striation patch indicates that the bullet has touched only once during its travel inside an oversized bore. There are two possibilities. Either it is due to a misaligned chamber or due to a random contact.

Figure 3.12 Similar initial barrel contact marks.

a. If it is due to a misaligned chamber, then the same portion of the barrel comes in contact with the bullet in each firing due to similar inclined positioning of the bullet in the chamber. The repetitive character of single patch stria on two or more bullets indicates that the involved firearm has a misaligned chamber. In a criminal case, similar single patch striations on three .315 crime bullets led to the conclusion that the chamber of the involved oversized bore firearm was misaligned (Figure 3.12).
b. If it were due to random contact, then the bullet would not touch at the same place. The point of contact may vary depending upon its inclination in loaded position that may vary from round to round. Therefore, it is apparent that alignment of the chamber can be ascertained only if two or more bullets are available. The chamber is misaligned only if the single striation patch is repetitive on each. If only one bullet carrying a single patch striation is available, then it can only be inferred that the probable firearm is an oversized bore firearm and no opinion on the alignment of the chamber can be formed.

4. Chamber alignment from multiple striation patches:
   Two or more (multiple) patches of striations are always possible by random multiple barrel contacts in oversized firearms, irrespective of the chamber alignment. Therefore, it is usually not possible to ascertain whether the chamber is misaligned, loose, or appropriate if the bullet has multiple patches.
5. Chamber alignment from absence of striations:
   A bullet without striations indicates that it has not made contacts with the sides of the barrel during its entire travel inside the bore. Since there is no bullet–barrel contact, the only plausible inference is that it is an oversized firearm whose chamber is not significantly misaligned.

3.2.2.3 Assessment of Longitudinal Joints or Protrusions from Barrel Marks

Bullet-carrying grooves or unevenly spaced grooves extending from base to ogival portion or beyond indicate that the bullet has passed through a bore having longitudinal joints or characteristic protrusions between the chamber and the muzzle. In short barreled smoothbore firearms, the presence of longitudinal joints/raised portions can be corroborated by visually examining the bore when the firearm is recovered.

3.2.3 Identification of Bullets Fired from Smoothbore Firearm

The underlying principle of identifying bullets fired from a smoothbore firearm is also based on the same universally accepted fact that no two barrels are microscopically identical and every barrel has its own characteristic surface profile. The striations produced by the surface profile imperfections of smoothbore barrels are individualistic and, hence, utilized to link the firearm.

However, the integrated stria pattern may not be repetitive because there is no preassigned path in smoothbore barrels like those of spiral grooves. There exists diversity in stria pattern from one round to the other. As such, reproducibility of stria pattern on test bullets becomes uncertain. However, linkage can be established only if barrel scratch marks on the evidence bullet are reproduced on the test-fired bullets. In view of these, linkage of the fired bullet with the suspect smoothbore firearm is often considered as an insoluble problem. Apparently, the only problem in the identification of fired bullets is to reproduce barrel scratch marks from the requisite portion of the barrel. Imprinting of barrel marks depends on the movement of the bullet inside the unrifled bore. The relative bullet–bore diameter and the relative chamber–bore alignment markedly influence the movement of the bullet inside the bore. Thus, the procedure of reproducing barrel marks varies with the constructional features of the smoothbore firearm. Once the required barrel marks are reproduced, the identity of the evidence bullet is established by comparing marks under a comparison microscope. Various methods of reproduction of stria patterns and identification procedures for all possible variables of constructional feature that influence the movement of the bullet are discussed below.

3.2.3.1 Undersized Smoothbore Firearms

The bullet is a tight fit in an undersized smoothbore barrel. It comes in close contact with the surface irregularities of the barrel throughout its periphery in a similar manner in each firing. This results in the formation of repetitive integrated stria on fired bullets. Therefore, the usual procedure of obtaining test bullets can be adopted in such cases, though the firearm is a smoothbore and not rifled. Test bullets are fired from the suspect undersized smoothbore firearm. The characteristic integrated barrel marks are examined and compared with the marks on the evidence bullet to establish linkage or otherwise (Figure 3.13(a)(b)).

3.2.3.1.1 Under-Bore Sized Firearms Having Longitudinal Joints The usual procedure of test firing also can be adopted in undersized smoothbore barrels having longitudinal joint(s) or significant protrusions. The undersized bore imprints corresponding groove(s) on fired bullets, in addition to continuous striations, on each firing. The groove serves as a reference point for comparison (Figure 3.14).

3.2.3.1.2 Undersized Bore Having Non-aligned Chamber The nature of striations varies with the alignment of the chamber and so also the procedure of reproducing barrel marks on the fired test bullets.

3.2.3.1.3 Misaligned Chamber The misalignment of the chamber poses no problem in reproducing barrel marks because it forces the bullet to enter into the undersized bore at the same angle and at the same position in each firing. The integrated striations are inclined parallel and continuous, and they are repetitive. Therefore, the usual procedure of firing test bullets from the suspect firearm is adopted in such cases. Barrel marks on fired test bullets are compared with the evidence bullet to establish linkage (Figure 3.15).

3.2.3.1.4 Loose Chamber This poses a practical problem in obtaining proper tests. The loaded cartridge in a loose chamber may occupy uncontrollable varying positions from round to round. The direction of bullet in the loaded position may vary accordingly. It may be almost coaxial or noncoaxial. The striations are straight or angular depending upon the position of the loading of the bullet/cartridge inside the loose chamber. Test bullets carrying striations in the direction similar to the evidence bullet can be obtained only by a trial and error method. To obtain proper test bullets, a number of rounds

(a)

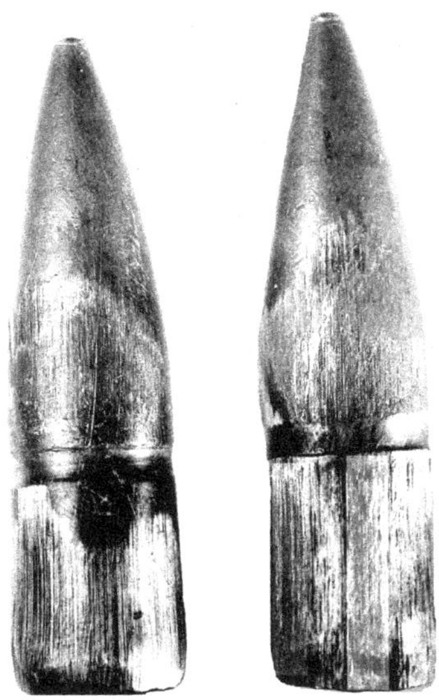

(b)

Figure 3.13 (a) Straight striations. (b) Similar striation from tapered barrel; (c) straight striation matching on evidence and fired test bullet from undersized barrel. *(continued)*

(c)

Figure 3.13 *(continued)* (a) Straight striations. (b) Similar striation from tapered barrel; (c) straight striation matching on evidence and fired test bullet from undersized barrel.

Figure 3.14 Matching of grooves created due to longitudinal joints in undersized smooth bore firearm.

Figure 3.15 Repetitive inclined striations.

may have to be fired by manually varying the position of the cartridge inside the loose chamber. It is a difficult task and it may not always be possible to do so. Those having dissimilar directions are unsuitable for comparison.

3.2.3.2 *Oversized Smoothbore Firearms*

Bullet passing through an oversized bore makes random contacts with the sides of the barrel. The location and direction of striations due to random contacts vary from one round to the other. The integrated stria are not repetitive and, hence, usual bullet identification procedure, by firing test bullets, cannot be adopted. The identification technique has to be modified.

The striations due to random contacts can be identified if the striations from the relevant portion in the same direction are duplicated. The reproducibility of marks becomes a difficult task. The same can be ensured only if the entire barrel marks from breech to the muzzle end are obtained. This is possible if oversized bullets (slightly more than the bore diameter) are fired as test bullets instead of firing similar loose bullets. This would ensure striations from all portions of the barrel. On firing, the test bullet probably would move almost in the direction of the axis of the bore. It would make contact all around the periphery imprinting straight striations. Lead bullets, being soft, can easily pass through slightly oversized bore barrels and, thus, are best suited for firing oversized test bullets. However, limitation of chamber shape/size and bore dimension coupled with the danger of bursting of the barrel restricts the choice of commercially available, desired unjacketed ammunition. Appropriate oversized lead bullets may not always be found loaded in regular branded ammunition. In such cases, firing of factory-made ammunition having unsuitable oversized lead bullets is risky. It is desirable to obtain required marks without firing. Thus, instead of test firing oversized lead bullets, cylindrical lead slugs of slightly more than the bore diameter are pushed straight from chamber to muzzle end by means of an iron rod or the like. Lead bullets or slugs can easily be pushed through a short-barreled, smooth bore firearm, but it is very difficult to do so in long barrels. These pushed-through oversized test bullets/slugs carry integrated barrel marks due to continuous bullet–barrel contacts in the direction more or less parallel to the axis of bore. Striations from the relevant portion are located and compared with the evidence bullet for establishing linkage.

This procedure of identification can be adopted only if the evidence bullet carries identifiable coaxial straight striations wholly or partly in combination with inclined or mixed striations at one or different portions (Figure 3.16).

This procedure of reproducing relevant patch(es) of straight striations is inapplicable, if striations are interfered with or masked by additional contacts on the same portion, whether angular or straight. In such a case, the striations (inclined, straight, or mixed) on the questioned bullet would invariably exhibit distinct dissimilarities with the resultant striations on the test bullets that are continuous, straight, and parallel. Hence, forming a negative opinion based on dissimilar marks may be misleading and erroneous. The extent of chamber alignment and over-bore size significantly influence the nature of striations on fired bullets and, thus, the procedure for reproduction of marks is varied.

3.2.3.2.1 Excessively oversized bore firearms Bullets fired from excessively oversized firearms are very loose. They often do not carry significant barrel marks if the chamber is aligned. The linkage is usually not possible in such cases. If striations are significant and almost straight, then the bullet can be identified by firing/pushing oversized lead bullets/slugs. If striations are inclined due to random angular contacts then identification, ordinarily, is not possible.

Marks on fired bullets are usually reproducible if the chamber of the firearm is considerably misaligned because the axis of the bullet in loaded position is always tilted in a particular direction. The tilted bullet always touches the same portion of the barrel at the same angle. The striations due to initial angular impact are reproducible in each firing. The usual procedure of obtaining tests by firing using the questioned firearm is adopted for establishing linkage (Figure 3.17).

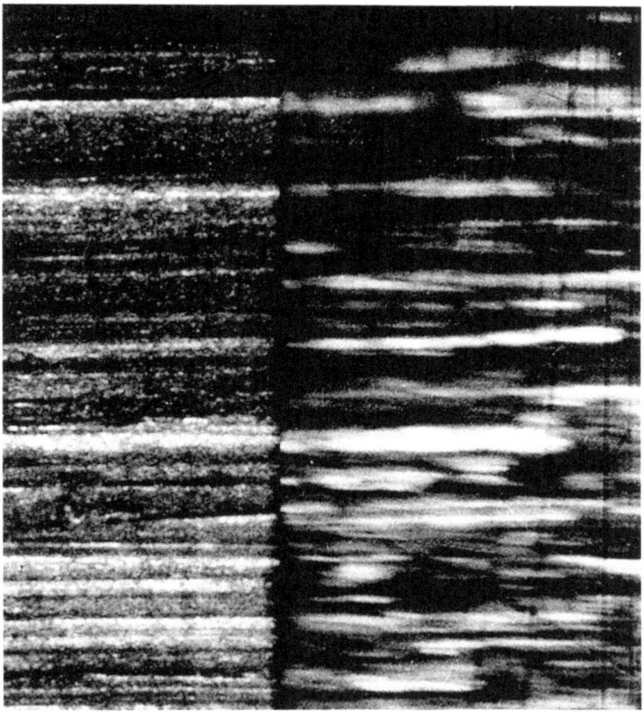

Figure 3.16 Matching of barrel marks on .303 fired bullet with .38 pushed lead slugs (.34″).

3.2.3.2.2 Very slightly oversized bore firearms If the chamber is considerably misaligned, then the bullet, after making its first angular impact, makes repeated contact (without appreciable sideways shift) with the sides of the very slightly oversized barrel. This results in almost straight or slightly tangential multiple contacts producing zigzag overlapping and jumbled marks. Patches of identifiable zigzag marks are sometimes reproducible by firing test bullets thereby establishing linkage. If the relevant patch is not produced in a similar manner on test bullets, then linkage cannot be established (Figure 3.18).

3.2.3.2.3 Summary: Bullet Identification Procedures Bullet identification procedures differ with the type of oversized bore and chamber alignment. It is not possible to determine the extent of the varying of these. To ascertain proper identification procedures in oversized firearm cases, three to five test bullets of the same caliber as that of the evidence bullets are fired from the firearm. Test bullets are compared amongst themselves under a comparison microscope. Similar/dissimilar patches of striations on test bullets determine proper identification procedure.

Figure 3.17 Striations matching of barrel marks of misaligned chamber.

Figure 3.18 Matching of zigzag marks from very slightly oversized .303 pistol.

- If at least one patch of striations (straight or inclined) is repetitive and similar on all test bullets, then, obviously, the questioned oversized firearm is the one which has a misaligned chamber. The repetitive patch is compared with the marks on evidence bullets and linkage is established if there is a positive match.
- If there is no repetitive patch on test bullets, then they cannot be utilized for comparison. For obtaining proper tests, slightly oversized lead bullets/slugs are pushed through the barrel almost straight from chamber to muzzle end. A positive match of one or more patches of straight striations on test and evidence cartridges indicates linkage, whether any other distinct dissimilar patch of striations from other portions of the same barrel is present or not. If there is no positive match, then identification is not possible. Because distinct dissimilar striations on bullets fired from the same barrel are possible in case of oversized firearms, a careful evaluation is necessary while forming an opinion on dissimilar marks, whether a bullet is positively linked or not. In general, an opinion on dissimilar marks should not be given.
- If test bullets carry insignificant/faint striations or no striations, then it becomes evident that the firearm is excessively oversized and the chamber is not excessively misaligned. Bullet–firearm linkage, in such cases, cannot be established. In the absence of striations, only physical and chemical examinations of the evidence bullet are carried out to ascertain whether it is one that has been fired.

3.2.3.3 *Mixed-Sized, Smoothbore Firearms*

Striations by a mixed-sized bore firearm is influenced both by under- and oversized portions of the barrel. Undersized bore creates continuous and repetitive striations and oversized bore imprints patch or patches of striations in the same or in different directions. The location of under- and over-bore portion of the mixed-bore barrel influences the nature of resultant striations. The identifying marks, thus, depend upon the constructional features of the mixed-bore barrel and so also the identifying procedure.

- Tapered barrels, having undersized portions near the muzzle, imprint repetitive, straight, or inclined continuous striations. They behave like undersized bore firearms. Hence, usual procedure of obtaining tests by firing bullets from the suspect firearm is adopted. Fired test bullets are compared with the evidence bullets and linkage is established (Figure 3.19).

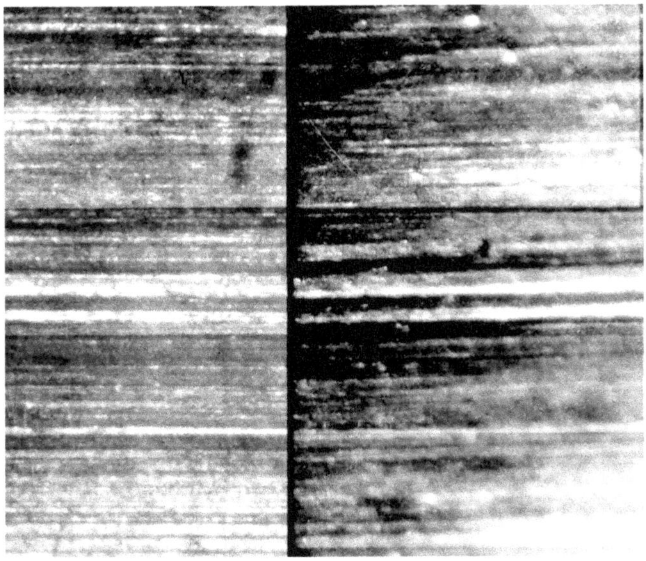

Figure 3.19 Repetitive barrel marks from tapered barrel.

- The undersized portion between the chamber and the muzzle usually creates overlap striations. Additional striations are created by oversized portion(s) before and/or after formation of striations by undersized portions of the barrel overlap. They often are unsuitable for identification. Striations that are due to undersized portions, if not interfered with and identifiable, can be utilized for identification. In practice, an identifiable patch is rarely found unless the chamber is somewhat misaligned, and that, too, if the marks due to misalignment remain without interference. It is desirable to fire test bullets for identifiable patches, if any. The usual procedure of identification by firing test bullets is adopted in either case.

Forensic Investigation of Fired Shot Charge of Unusual Firearms

4

The projectiles, other than cylindroconical, that are of forensic interest are spherical shot/pellets used in shotgun cartridges. Shotguns are smooth bores and their cartridges are usually loaded with a large number of spherical shot/pellets of a lead alloy of varying sizes. Shot sizes are designated by their diameter and weight. Their designation differs from one country to another. Bigger and smaller shot also are designated differently. The bigger shot, which are used for big game hunting, such as deer, bear, etc., are popularly known as buckshot in the United States (American standards). Their sizes vary with the type of game. They are designated as buckshot (000), buckshot (00), BB, etc. Likewise, the bigger shot, for large game, are known as LG shot in British/Indian specifications. They are SG for small games, SSG, and so on. The shot that is used for bird hunting and the like are designated by shot numbers depending on the size of the shot/pellet, such as no. 1 shot, no. 4 shot, etc. The size of spherical shot may be as low as .050 inch for no. 12 and as high as .38 inch for buckshot (0000). The total number of shot/pellets varies with the load. The load is usually 1⅟₁₆ ounce in a 2½ inch/65 mm 12-bore cartridge. The nomenclatures for size and number of shot/pellets as per American standards and British specifications are known (Table 4.1 and Table 4.2).

Shotguns are popular guns among big and small game hunters. The licensing policy for possession of shotguns is comparatively liberal even in countries that enforce strict gun licensing policies. Therefore, shotguns are the most sought after firearms by civilians, especially in developing and underdeveloped countries. Consequently, there is a great demand for shotgun ammunition as well. Numerous ammunition factories are engaged in the manufacture of shotgun cartridges worldwide. Besides branded factory-made ammunition, home loading of shotgun cartridges also is very common among the game hunters. Lead alloy shot, steel shot, wads, etc., are commercially available for those making shotgun cartridges at home. Shotgun ammunition is, thus, comparatively cheap and easily available. The easy availability of shotgun ammunition has resulted in the illegal making of homemade/improvised/converted firearms that are especially designed to fire shotgun ammunition. Homemade 12-bore pistols are encountered frequently in criminal cases in India.

One often comes across pellets and wads recovered from the victim's body or from the crime scene in cases involving shotguns and illegally made firearms using shotgun cartridges. According to Hatcher, "Little or nothing

Table 4.1 Pellet Sizes

No.	American Specification (diameter in inches)	British/Indian Specification (diameter in inches)
1	0.16	.143
2	0.15	.135
3	0.14	.125
4	0.13	.120
5	0.12	.110
6	0.11	.102
7	0.10	.095
8	0.09	.087
9	0.08	.080
10	0.07000	.070

Table 4.2 Buckshot Sizes

American Specification (diameter in inches)		British/Indian Specification (diameter in inches)	
Buck 000	.36	LG	.360
Buck 00	.34	SG	.332
Buck 0	.32	Special SG	.298
1 Buck	.30	SSG	.269
2 Buck	.27	AAA	.214
3 Buck	.25	AA	.194
4 Buck	.24	A	.180
Air rifle	.175	BBB	.170
BB	.18	BB	.161
B	.17	B	.154

can be proved by pellet evidence found at the crime scene or from the victim's body. The experts are, therefore, called upon to examine shotgun projectiles to identify the shot size or shot number or to estimate the range." In fact, even range estimation is a difficult task in "no gun" cases. The usual criteria of range estimation by spread of pellets that apply to regular factory-made shotguns is apparently inapplicable to illegally made, substandard firearms because of their inappropriate constructional features. There are varied problems associated with pellets and wads as projectiles. One comes across a variety of unusual, ambiguous, and misleading exhibits while examining cartridges, pellets, and wads fired from illegally made firearms, especially homemade pistols. One often needs an innovative approach to arrive at significant forensic inferences. Some of the case-oriented practical problems of forensic interest that need discussion include:

1. Dispersion of pellets and possible misleading range determination
2. Linkage of fired pellets with suspect firearm
3. Misleading inference on number of fires from fired pellets
4. Pellets without striations appearing like unfired, whether fired or not
5. Determination of reloaded shot size from fired shot shell
6. Dispersion of wads and reconstruction of shooting incidents
7. Unusual barrel marks on fired wads
8. Unusual chamber marks on fired wads

4.1 Dispersion of Pellets and Possible Misleading Range Determination

In shotgun firing, the pellets start dispersing as soon as they come out of the muzzle. The dispersion increases progressively in a roughly conical shape. The increasing degree of dispersion with the increasing distance of firing provides valuable data for the estimation of the range of fire. The dispersion is significantly influenced by two main factors:

1. Type of wad
2. Barrel dimension

4.1.1 Type of Wad

The main purpose of wad is to barricade the escape of propellant gasses into the pellet charge and to cushion for smooth propulsion of rapidly accelerating charge of pellets inside the barrel. The spread of pellets depends on the type of wad or wad column. The type of wad depends on the type of shotgun cartridge, whether cupped or uncupped.

4.1.1.1 Uncupped Shotgun Cartridge and Spread of Pellets

A traditional shotgun cartridge has a wad column generally consisting of an overpowder wad, an aircushion or a felt wad, and an undershot wad. The shot charge is firmly held in position between the undershot wad and a closing disk or crimp at the top. A single plastic wad that serves the purpose both for sealing and for cushioning replaces the wad column. The aircushion, felt, and single plastic wad behave differently in sealing the bore, thereby controlling the spread of pellets.

4.1.1.1.1 Aircushion Wad and Spread of Pellets Cartridges having a wad column containing an aircushion wad have the following drawbacks for an even spread of pellets:

- The pellets that are touching the periphery of the cartridge come in direct contact with the hard surface of the barrel during their passage inside the bore. The pellet–barrel contact from breech to muzzle results in the deformation of the peripheral shots. The distorted pellets become asymmetrical, and are scattered far away from the middle of the shot pattern. They are known as *flyers* or *stray* pellets. The area of the pellet spread increases with the flyers/stray pellets that strike away from the main pellet pattern. The enlarged area depends on the number of flyers and extent of their deformation.
- The hot propellant gases may escape from the sides of the powder wad and air cushion wad. The escaped gasses enter into the shot column. Some of the pellets may partially melt and fuse together. The fused pellets also become asymmetrical as they are formed by joining two or more partly melted pellets. The spread is affected by the asymmetrical fused pellets.
- The scattering of pellets takes place in the air by the wad column travelling at the rear. The wad may enter into the charge of pellets and scatter it considerably depending on the wad column. The column containing the aircushion wad travels with three more cardboard wads at the rear and an overshot wad in front of the charge of the pellets. There is comparatively pronounced scattering thereby affecting the disperse area of pellets.

4.1.1.1.2 Lubricating Felt/Fiber Wad and Spread of Pellets Cartridges loaded with lubricating felt/fiber wad overcome the drawbacks to some extent on two counts. It improves sealing of the propellant gasses and provides better cushioning for smooth propulsion of the rapidly accelerated charge of pellets. The pellet pattern may further be scattered if the felt wad enters into the rear part of the moving charge of pellets after leaving the firearm. There may be a plastic wad in addition to a short fiber/felt wad. The plastic wad seals the bore and the fiber/felt wad cushions the rapidly accelerating charge of pellets.

4.1.1.1.3 Uncupped, Single Plastic Wad An uncupped, single plastic wad replaces air cushion, overpowder, and undershot wad.

It is a cylindrical wad, with its two ends that serve as undershot and overshot wads. In between the two, there are small-width spiral strips with cuts that are equally spaced. The strips and the empty spaces between them provide the necessary cushioning. This wad effectively serves the purpose of sealing the bore as well as cushioning the propulsion of rapidly accelerating charge of pellets inside the barrel. This being a single wad reduces the scattering of pellets compared to those that are caused by three separate wads traveling at the rear of the charge of pellets in air.

Note: In uncupped cartridges, the deformation of pellets due to their sliding contacts with the inner wall of the barrel remains an important factor of an uneven wider pattern. The flyers/stray pellets that fly far away from the center of the pattern have to be excluded for a fair correlation between the range and the spread of pellets. It is usually a difficult task. An approximate assessment is invariably made by ascertaining the percentage of pellets enclosed in a 30-inch circle fired from a distance of 40 yards.

4.1.1.2 Cupped Shotgun Cartridge and Spread of Pellets

Cupped cartridges minimize the aforementioned drawbacks to a large extent. The cartridge has an integral cupped wad. The charge of pellets is contained in a plastic cup, which prevents direct pellet–barrel contacts. This minimizes the formation of asymmetrical flyers/stray pellets, thereby reducing the scattering of pellets in air.

The cup is connected to a laminated plastic wad that acts as a power piston of a shock absorber. The plastic wad seals the bore and provides necessary cushioning for a smooth movement of a rapidly accelerating charge of pellets. The plastic cup has generally three to four splits. The split opens like wings after the cup emerges out of the barrel and the shot column is projected.

4.1.2 Barrel Dimension

4.1.2.1 Choke

The spread of pellets is significantly influenced by the bore dimension of the firearm. The spread can be controlled by constricting the bore at the muzzle end known as a *choke*. The tapering for the constriction starts from a point usually about 1 to 1¼ inches from the muzzle end. The constriction varies between 3 to 40,000th of an inch. Depending on the extent of constriction, the choke is designated as full choke, half choke, modified choke, etc. (Table 4.3).

Table 4.3 Extent of Muzzle Constriction and Choke Designation

Designation	Muzzle Constrictions in Thousandths of an Inch
Full choke	40
Three-quarter choke	30
Half choke	20
Quarter choke	10
Improved cylinder	3 to 5
True cylinder	None

Table 4.4 Varying Dispersion of Pellets at 40 Yards

Choke	Percentage of Dispersed Pellets in a 30-in. Circle at 40 Yards
Full choke	70
Three-quarter choke	65
Half choke	60
Quarter choke	55
Improved cylinder	50
True cylinder	40

The constriction compresses the shot charge all around the circumference during its travel at the muzzle end. The shot column is longitudinally extended depending on the extent of constriction. The radial spreading of pellets is considerably reduced restricting the area of spread. The spreading of pellets is more when it is a true cylindrical bore without a choke. The variation in percentage of pellets in a 30-inch circle with the degree of choke from a distance of 40 yards provides a comparative assessment of the pellet spread pattern. The documented data are reproduced in Table 4.4.

Usually, one of the barrels of a double-barrel shotgun is a choked barrel. There are interchangeable choke adapters that can be fitted in the barrel. The end of the barrel is threaded for that purpose. Adapters are screwed into the threaded barrel to provide desired choke. Interchangeable choke adapters are commercially available and are used for the intended game that requires varied pellet spread. Even a wider pellet spread is sometimes required for certain games, such as skeet. The deformation of pellets causing flyers has also a considerable influence on the density of pellets at a particular distance.

4.1.2.2 Barrel Length

The pellet distribution is greatly influenced by the barrel length. The shotgun, being a shoulder firearm, has a barrel length of about 26 to 30 inches. When a shotgun is fired, the shot charge moves en masse up to a distance of about 3 to 5 feet making a single, large hole in the target, popularly known as a rat hole. The hole is usually 1 to 1½ inches in diameter. Individual pellets start surrounding the rat hole after a distance of 2 to 3 yards of firing. Thereafter, the dispersion of pellets increases with the increase in firing distance in a roughly conical shape. A very rough assessment about the range, without experiments, can be made from the area of the distribution of pellets. The spread of pellets in inches roughly corresponds to firing distance in yards for a true cylindrical barrel. As for example, 5-inch dispersion is expected roughly from a firing distance of 5 yards; likewise, 10-inch dispersion from 10 yards, and so on. Almost all pellets make individual holes from a range of about 10 yards and beyond. In cases of buckshot, the individual shot makes separate holes from a firing range of only about 5 yards.

For estimating range of fire, experimental firings are conducted with the suspect firearm in each case, preferably with the same type of ammunition as used in the crime. A similar pellet spread pattern is obtained by firing at various ranges and an opinion on probable range of fire is formed. However, it is usually difficult to form an opinion beyond a range of 10 yards by comparing the spread experimentally. Usually, the center of pattern and the total area of spread of pellets, including flyers, may not be available on a small-sized human target from such a distance.

4.1.2.2.1 Unusual Firearms and Misleading Range Determination The aforementioned criteria are evidently not applicable in cases involving improvised/illegally made, substandard firearms because of their inappropriate constructional features as outlined in Chapter 1. In the majority of cases, especially with homemade firearms, the *barrel length* is usually less than 6 inches in order to make it handy and concealable. This affects the burning of the propellant, development of temperature, and required sustained pressure inside the barrel. This reduces the propelled velocity of the emerging shot charge, thereby influencing the dispersion of pellets. The en masse shot charge coming out of the muzzle disperses quickly, resulting in a wider spread compared to a usual long-barrel shotgun firing. The shorter the barrel, the lesser is the range of the rat hole formation. The individual pellets start surrounding the rat hole at comparatively shorter distance of fire. The pellet spread at any particular distance is also wider compared to a long-barreled shotgun firing (Figure 4.1(a)(b)).

In addition to barrel length, the spread is affected by inappropriate *chamber and bore dimensions*. A variable bore diameter disperses the pellets before expelling out of the muzzle. The dispersion takes place inside the barrel itself. Oversized chamber dimension also gives rise to pellet spread inside the barrel. The spread is much wider at any particular distance compared to a long-barrel, regular shotgun fire. An exhaustive study of pellet spread pattern of 12-bore, homemade, short-barreled pistols revealed that the spread also increases in a roughly conical shape with the increase in firing distance. Usually the spread is two to four times that expected from the firing of a regular long-barreled shotgun. A spread of 6 inches usually corresponds to an approximate firing distance of only 6 feet or so, compared to 6 yards of a long-barreled, regular shotgun firing. This approximation may be helpful in eliminating or corroborating the probable reconstruction of the crime scene at the investigation stage, in "no gun" cases.

Caution: While forming an opinion on the spread of pellets, it is essential to mention the type of firearm to which it pertains. The range for the same

(a)

(b)

Figure 4.1 (a) 12-bore, homemade pistol barrel length of 3.6 inches; (b) pellets surrounding rat hole from a 6-inch firing distance.

spread differs significantly depending on the involved firearm whether it is a small-barrel, improvised/homemade pistol or a regular long-barrel shotgun. In the absence of specific mention, it may be misleading at times, because the possibility of firing of an improvised/homemade, short-barrel pistol using shotgun cartridges cannot be ruled out, especially in areas of great demand of illegally made, cheap firearms.

4.2 Linkage of Fired Pellets with Suspect Firearm

The most important evidence that a fired projectile can provide is its linkage with the suspect firearm. The underlying principle involves presence of identifiable barrel marks on the evidence projectile and its reproducibility on test projectile/specimens. Usual and modified procedures for reproducing barrel marks on cylindro-conical bullets, including those fired from illegally made, substandard rifled and smoothbore firearms, were discussed in Chapter 3. It remains to be seen whether identifiable marks also are produced on pellets fired from smoothbore, unrifled firearms, and, if so, can it be reproduced by adopting similar procedures especially when unusual firearms are used?

4.2.1 Barrel Marks on Fired Shot/Pellets

In a shotgun cartridge, pellets occupy different rows and columns depending on their size and number. Pellets on the sides come in contact with the walls of the cup/cartridge. The larger the size, the higher is the percentage of pellets in contact with the walls of the cup/cartridge. On firing, they come in contact with the walls of the barrel while passing through the bore. Whereas pellets loaded in uncupped cartridges come in direct contact with the inner wall of the barrel, it is the cup in cupped cartridges that comes in contact with the inner surface of the barrel. The sliding contacts of pellets from breech to muzzle register barrel marks. As expected, the indirect sliding contacts of pellets of the cup often do not create significant striations. Barrel marks are comparatively prominent on pellets that are in direct barrel contact. As expected, the striations are imprinted on only one side of the pellet. Smaller pellets are scratched only by a small portion of the barrel. Bigger shot, such as buckshot/LG/SG, etc., are scratched by a comparatively larger portion of the barrel. Therefore, identifiable striations are likely to be imprinted on bigger pellets, though only one segment of the barrel comes in contact. These barrel marks on the pellets can be identified if they are unique and reproducible.

It is known and was discussed in Chapter 3 that the internal surface of a smoothbore barrel, being microscopically uneven, also bears randomly distributed, innumerable rough spots of elevations and depressions. Therefore, sliding striations that are caused by the surface irregularities of the smoothbore barrels also are characteristic and unique and, thus, can safely be utilized to individualize the firearm.

4.2.2 Reproducibility and Identification of Barrel Marks

Knowing that barrel marks on a segment of the barrel are identifiable, the same can be utilized to link the suspect firearm provided those marks are reproducible. As fired pellets carry marks from one segment of the barrel, it becomes obligatory to obtain barrel marks from the same segment/portion on test-fired pellets. However, the statistical probability of pellets touching exactly identical portions of the barrel on subsequent firing is very small. It is obviously because of the uncontrollable variation in positioning of the cylindrical cartridge inside the chamber. Even a slight variation changes the points of pellet–barrel contact considerably. It is also virtually impossible for a cylindrical cartridge to manually manipulate in a manner such that pellets occupy exactly the similar positions in subsequent test firings. Under the circumstances, it is almost impossible to reproduce the markings from the same set of surface irregularities by firing test cartridges. Therefore, the usual procedure of reproducing barrel marks by firing test cartridges loaded with similar-sized pellets cannot be adopted. In view of the inability to reproduce similar barrel marks on test-fired pellets, the identification of pellets fired from smoothbore shotguns is considered an insoluble problem.

Sinha et al. suggested a procedure for reproduction of marks from the requisite points/area of the barrel, which was modified by the author by a foolproof procedure. The underlying principle is that the. The marks from any particular area of the barrel are ensured if marks from the entire surface are obtained. Therefore, instead of barrel markings from a particular area, marks from the entire surface from breech to muzzle are obtained. To achieve the objective, instead of test firing, a cylindrical lead slug, slightly larger than bore diameter, is chosen as a test specimen. It can easily be made by casting in the laboratory. A flexible steel strip of about ½-inch width is chosen for preparing the cast. The steel strip is turned to form a cylinder of the required, slightly bigger diameter. A lead cast is made by pouring molten lead shot. A slightly bigger lead slug, thus prepared, is pushed through the bore from breach to muzzle to carry marks from the entire surface of the bore. In doing so, it carries the marks from the required portion as well. The relevant marks are located on test slugs. A comparison of marks on the test lead slugs with the marks on the evidence pellet, if similar, establishes linkage (Figure 4.2).

However, it is a problem in choosing an appropriate larger diameter slug, especially if the firearm has appreciable variation in bore size from chamber to muzzle end. If it is a choke barrel, the test slug, which is slightly bigger at the breech, is fairly larger at the constricted portion near the muzzle. It is also evident in tapered homemade pistols having a markedly over-bore size near the breech and excessively undersized bore near the muzzle. Thus, it is not only a hard task to choose correct slug diameter, but it is also cumbersome to push them from breech to muzzle.

In addition to difficulty in pushing, one also may find it difficult to push it straight. The diameter of such a slug, being more than shotgun bore

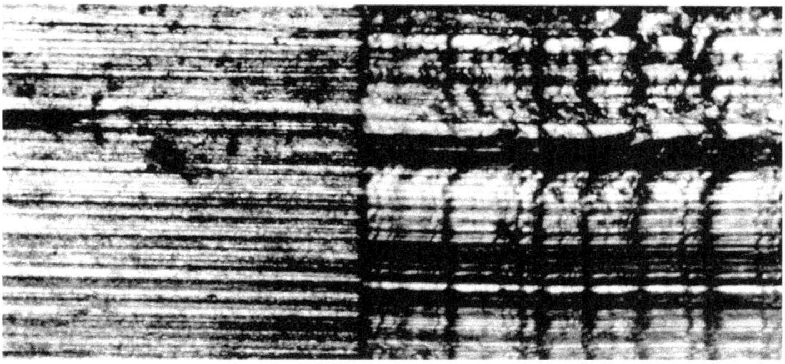

Figure 4.2 Matching of barrel marks on pellets and lead slugs.

diameter, is always unwieldy. Not only does it require a considerable force, but also, at times, it may be stuck in between. Therefore, pushing of oversized lead slugs is not a practical solution for obtaining barrel marks in the majority of cases.

The modified procedure suggested by the author that obviates the necessity of pushing oversized lead slugs from breech to muzzle. The difficulty in pushing the cylindrical lead slug has been overcome by exerting a greater force. The expanding gas, on firing of a cartridge, is the only recourse to exert required forward force to propel a slightly oversized projectile. Thus, a shotgun cartridge loaded with a single projectile of a larger bore diameter can only serve the purpose. However, shotgun cartridges are not loaded with a single projectile whose diameter is more than the bore diameter of the shotgun. This is because of the possibility of bursting the barrel while passing through a choke barrel. In addition, the projectile being a spherical ball has the disadvantage of inadequate surface contact and possible rotational motion inside the barrel. Above all, it is not commercially available in different sizes and, thus, cannot meet even the basic requirement of a larger diameter projectile. Thus, cartridges that are loaded with the usual factory-made, single spherical ball are unsuitable for test firing. A wider surface can be made available if the projectile has a cylindrical surface instead of spherical, but shotgun cartridges are not loaded with cylindrical shot. To achieve this objective, a traditional 12-bore, live paper cartridge is chosen for test firing. The loaded shot is removed after taking out the overshot wad or by opening the crimp. Cotton soaked in water is wrapped on the outer wall of the emptied portion. Lead or lead shot is melted in a small crucible. Molten lead is poured uniformly into the cartridge to fill about ¼ to ½ inch of the empty cylindrical portion. The molten lead solidifies soon. The diameter of the lead cast inside the cartridge becomes almost equal to that of the sealing air-cushioned wad. The remaining empty portion at the top is filled with cardboard/wad pieces.

(a)

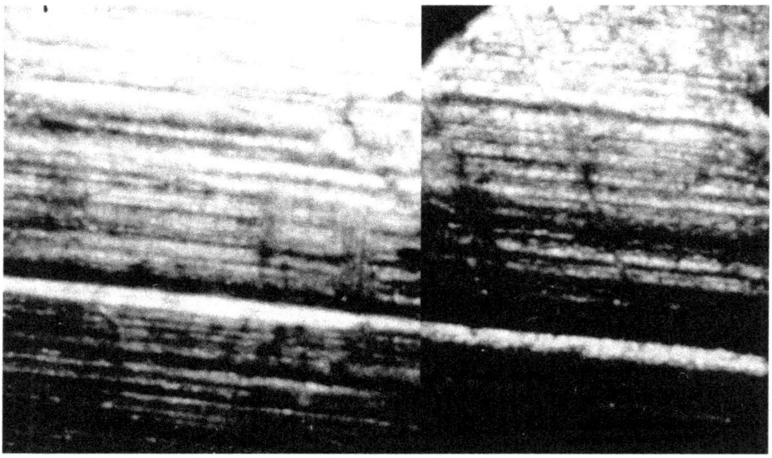

(b)

Figure 4.3 (a) Barrel marks on fired lead slug, (b) Matching of barrel marks on fired lead slugs.

On firing, the lead slug fills the bore tightly and registers barrel marks. Test cartridges having lead cast, so prepared, are fired in a bullet recovery box to obtain test-fired slugs. The fired lead slugs carry barrel contact marks around the entire cylindrical periphery, if the bore diameter is less than the wad's diameter, such as less than .73 inch for 12 bore (Figure 4.3).

The test slugs are examined inter se (between themselves) under a comparison microscope for repetitive barrel marks and thereafter lead slugs are compared with the barrel marks on the fired shot. Striations matching all around the periphery establish linkage (Figure 4.4).

Fired pellets recovered from the crime scene or from the victim's body carrying sufficient striations from different segments of the same barrel are separately compared with test slugs. Positive match of striations are usually obtained in each case, if fired from the same firearm (Figure 4.5(a)(b)).

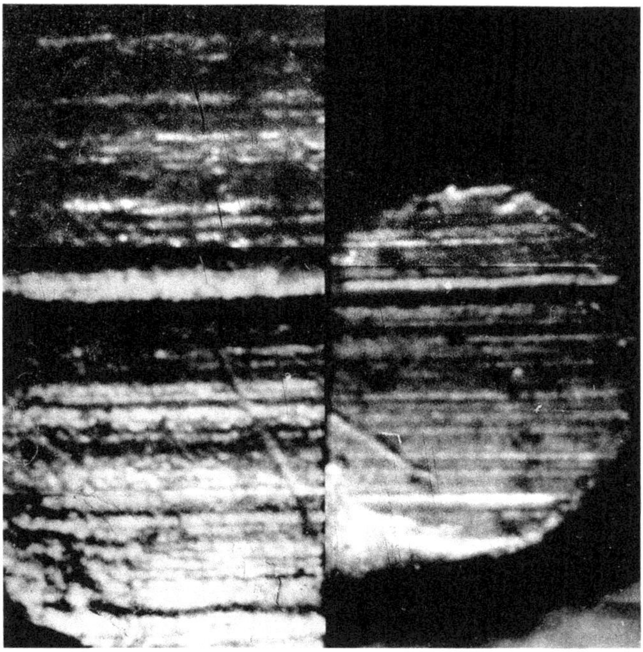

Figure 4.4 Matching of barrel marks on fired lead slug and fired lead shot.

Note: This procedure of obtaining barrel marks is suitable for undersized, illegally made/homemade pistols having a bore diameter less than the sealing wad, e.g., .73 inch for 12 bore.

4.3 Misleading Conclusion on Number of Fires from Fired Pellets

In cases of bullet fire, the number of fired bullets carrying identifying barrel marks signifies the number of fires. If two bullets carry matching barrel marks, it signifies two fires. Likewise, there are three fires if three bullets carry identifiable barrel marks, and so on.

The number of pellets that carry barrel marks depends on their distribution inside the cartridge or the cup that houses the pellets. The pellets on the sides are the ones that come in contact with the barrel during their travel inside the bore. They carry sliding barrel marks. The likely number of pellets carrying barrel contact marks may be ascertained by examining the lead impressions on the inner walls of the cartridge or the cup. The impressions

(a)

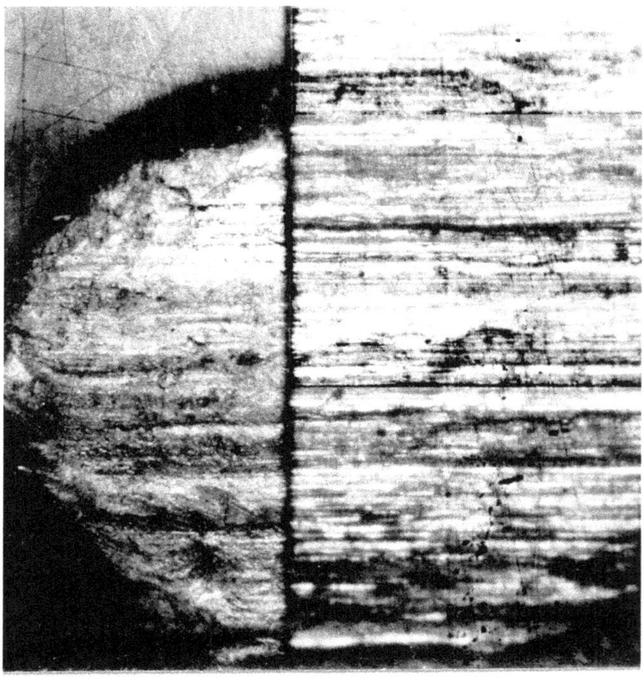

(b)

Figure 4.5 Matching of different barrel segment marks on fired pellets and fired slugs.

are comparatively clearer and noticeable on the inner walls of the traditional paper or plastic uncupped cartridges and, therefore, suitable for ascertaining the possible number of pellet–barrel contacts.

Shotgun cartridges loaded with bigger lead shot, such as buckshot, LG, SG, etc., bear distinct lead impressions on the inner walls of uncupped cartridges. There are six impressions at six different places corresponding to six LG shot loaded in the cartridge. On firing, each LG pellet makes sliding contacts with a separate segment of the inside barrel from chamber to muzzle. As each pellet touches separate segments, no two pellets carry the same marks despite being fired from the same firearm. Those carrying characteristic striations can be identified in respect to the suspect firearm by adopting the procedure mentioned above. Linkage is usually possible, if the involved firearm is an underbore, homemade pistol having a muzzle diameter less than the sealing wad, which is about .73 inch for 12-bore.

Similarly, there are nine impressions in an SG cartridge corresponding to nine pellets. These impressions represent column-wise distribution of pellets inside the uncupped SG cartridge. There are three rows and six columns. Three columns bear two impressions in each. The other three have only one impression. Each column of the cartridge, when loaded in the chamber, faces a separate segment of the barrel. On firing, the shot in each column move along the directed segment of the barrel. The pellets contained in the column touch the same segment of the barrel and are scratched. Each of the pellets of the same column is likely to carry similar barrel marks. Thus, there are three sets of two pellets each having similar barrel marks. Of course, each set carries distinctly separate barrel marks that differentiate from one set to the other (Figure 4.6).

Likewise, the number of columns and rows of pellets varies with the type of the load, such as buckshot (00), (o), BB, SSG, SSSG, etc. The number of pellets contained in each column varies accordingly. This determines the number of pellets pointing to the specific segment of the barrel they travel on firing. They carry similar barrel marks in each set. The number of sets carrying similar marks from different segments of a barrel varies accordingly.

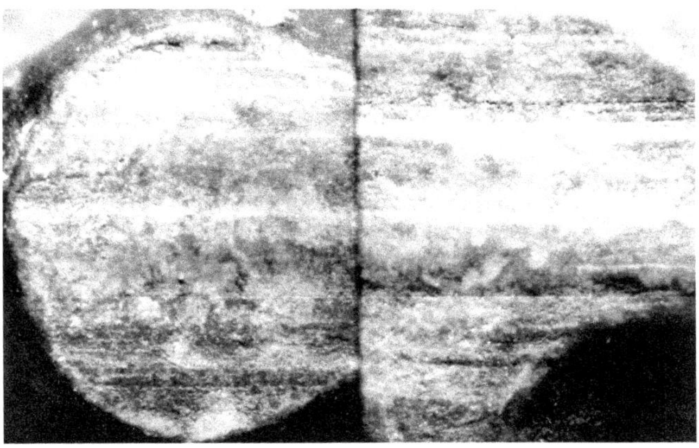

Figure 4.6 Barrel marks matching on a set of two SG pellets.

Table 4.5 Pellet Impressions on Inner Walls of 12-Bore, 2½-inch K.F. IOF Cartridges

Cartridge	Total Number of Pellets	Pellet Impressions	
		Number of Columns	Number of Rows
No. 1	109	20	4
No. 2	128	28	4
No. 4	180	34	5
No. 6	292	39	6

In contrast to bigger pellets, the number of columns and rows is many more in cartridges loaded with smaller pellets (1 to 10).

The set of smaller pellets likely to come in contact with the same segment of the barrel also may be ascertained by the number of columns and rows of nonoverlapping impressions. An Indian ordnance, factory-made, 12-bore, 2½-inch K.F. no. 1 cartridge has as many as 20 columns and 4 rows to accommodate about 110 pellets. The number of probable pellets carrying striations from the same segment of the barrel, therefore, can be ascertained.

The number of columns and rows of pellets contained in 12-bore, 2½-inch, Indian ordnance factory, K.F. cartridges, loaded with no. 1, 2, 4, and 6 pellets, usually encountered in criminal cases in India is listed in Table 4.5.

It can be seen from the table that there are as many as five pellets in a column in cartridges loaded with no. 4 and no. 6 pellets. All five such pellets are expected to come in contact with the same segment of the barrel imprinting similar striations. Smaller pellets also may carry similar identifiable characteristic striations (Figure 4.7).

4.4 Pellets without Striations Appear as Unfired, Whether Fired or Not

It can be seen from Table 4.5 that not all pellets loaded in a cartridge come in contact with the sides of the wall of the cartridge/cup. The smaller the size, the more pellets that do not touch the sides of the wall of the cartridge or the cup. A sizeable number of small pellet remains away from the sides of the barrel and are recovered in almost spherical or slightly deformed condition. They look like unfired pellets. Cases are on record where a small-sized, unfired pellet was planted inside a self-made skin-deep hole to support the plea of self-defense. In the absence of barrel marks, the nature and extent of mutilation may not prove helpful in arriving at the right conclusion, whether fired or not. In such cases, detection of adsorbed discharge residues on the

Figure 4.7 Matching of barrel marks on no. 4 pellets.

pellet may prove helpful. The gaseous product of combustion envelops the entire shot charge shortly after leaving the barrel. The propellant gases may also escape through the sides of the moving shot charge inside the barrel. Fired pellets coming in contact with the escaping gases reveal the presence of nitrite ion of propellant gases. The adsorption of nitrite ion on the fired pellet can be detected by a diazotization and coupling reaction. The reagents used are α-naphthylamine and sulfanilic acid in acetic acid. Pellets are placed on filter paper, keeping them fairly apart. A drop of the mixed reagent solution is added to the pellets. Appearance of a pinkish color at the point of contact on the filter paper indicates the presence of nitrite. A detectable amount of nitrite is usually present on fired pellets even after a considerable lapse of time, even after a year or so. Some of the pellets, especially badly mutilated, may not reveal the presence of nitrite, even in traces. It is usually due to partial removal or dilution of a small quantity of deposited residues by excessive flow of blood over them. Discharge residues also may be masked heavily by the upper thick layers of dried blood. When pellets that do not hit the human target and are recovered from the crime scene do not show the presence of nitrite, even in traces, in some cases, it may be due to deformation or deposition of negligible amount of discharge residues. However, the fact remains that, whereas the presence of discharge residues confirms the pellets have been fired, its nondetection does not lead to conclude otherwise.

4.5 Reloaded Shot Size from a Fired Shell

The wounding capability of a spherical shot depends on its weight and diameter. The more the diameter, the greater is the wounding capability. Therefore, bigger shot is preferred to achieve greater wounding effect on a human target beyond close range. However, bigger shot cartridges are comparatively less common. Smaller pellets are commonly used for small game and target practice. Indian ordnance-manufactured, 12-bore shotgun cartridges that are commonly available are loaded with no. 1, 2, 4, 6, and BB shot. There had been criminal cases in which smaller pellets were replaced by bigger shot to achieve greater wounding effect. In such a case, it is often argued that the evidence cartridge was not loaded with buckshot that has been recovered from the victim's body or from the crime scene, which convincingly suggests that neither the evidence cartridge nor the suspect firearm are involved in the crime. The type of the load, i.e., the shot size, imprinted on the fired cartridge or on the fired overshot wad found at the crime scene, in such cases, does not correspond to the shot recovered from the crime scene or from the victim's body. It becomes necessary, in such cases, to ascertain whether the evidence cartridge was indeed loaded with bigger buckshot contrary to the mentioned load of smaller shot on its outer wall, or on the closing disk/top wad found at the crime scene. It is desirable to ascertain the original as well as replaced shots from the fired cartridge in question.

It has been discussed in section 4.3 that lead impressions of the pellets at their points of contact are usually available on the inner walls of the uncupped cartridge. These impressions reveal the number and size of pellets loaded in the cartridge. On firing, the impression at the point of contact spreads with the forward movement of the pellet inside the cartridge and is retained after firing. The number of spread impressions can easily be determined if they are few in number and are distributed symmetrically. A fired LG cartridge has six spread impressions occupying distinctly different positions (Figure 4.8).

The probable size can be ascertained from the distribution of loaded shot impressions on the walls of the fired cartridge. Two or more shots in the same column follow the same path one after the other inside the cartridge. The number of lead spread after firing depends only on the number of columns irrespective of the number of pellets in each column. Therefore, the number of impressions may not be similar to those available on an unfired cartridge. These impressions can be seen clearly by cutting the mouth of the fired cartridge and can be located and identified by chemical tests. Filter paper impregnated with 50% acetic acid is placed inside the fired cartridge without overlapping at the end. The filter paper is pressed in place by a clean glass rod or by a tube preferably of the diameter almost equal to

Figure 4.8 Six LG shot spread impressions on 12-bore fired cartridge.

that of the mouth of the fired cartridge. The filter paper is taken out and unfolded on a clean glass plate. Another filter paper treated with a .02% sodium rhodizonate solution in distilled water is placed on it. Red spots of lead rhodizonate appear corresponding to each lead spread. Smaller pellets that follow the same path of travel produce overlapping and smudged lead impressions. The number of pellet impressions that merged in the smudged lead impressions cannot be assessed.

Therefore, it is apparent that it is only the streak of lead impressions that determines the shot that moved inside the cartridge irrespective of the fact whether they are a reloaded or original load. Examination of a fired cartridge case reveals the impressions left behind by the original loaded shot as well as by the movement of the reloaded shot. The original shot impressions remain undisturbed to a great extent after the shot is replaced. On firing, the reloaded shot is pushed out by the forward movement of the gases, producing streaks corresponding to their movement inside the cartridge. A part of the original shot impressions is also masked by the spreading impressions of reloaded shot. Because original shot impressions remain unaffected after firing, the original as well as reloaded shot can be ascertained. The original impressions of the replaced shot are between the reloaded shot impressions (Figure 4.9).

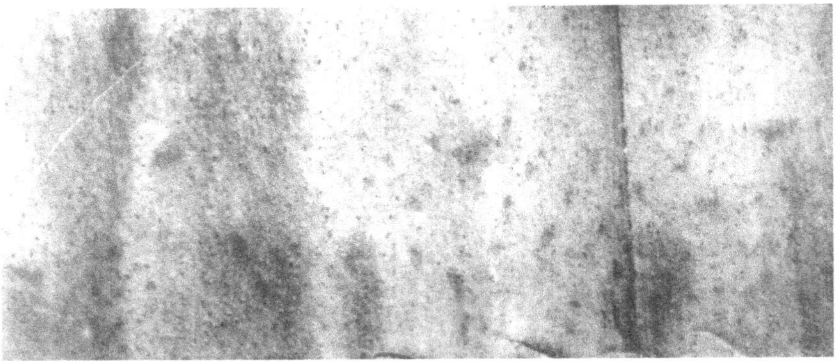

Figure 4.9 Original smaller and replaced bigger shots impressions on a fired cartridge.

If buckshot is replaced by smaller shot, as is often found in crimes in India, the number of streak impressions and their symmetric distribution determines the size and number of reloaded shot. Because original smaller shot impressions are partly masked, it is usually not possible to ascertain their size and shot number. However, it can positively be inferred to the extent that the cartridge was originally loaded with smaller shot. The original and reloaded shot impressions can be examined conveniently by cutting the tubular portion of the cartridge or by chemical tests by adopting the procedure mentioned above. If the buckshot is replaced by smaller shot, then determination of reloaded shot from a fired shell is usually not possible.

4.6 Dispersion of Wads and Reconstruction of Shooting Incidents

Wads are essential components of a shotgun cartridge. They vary widely in shape and size. Wads are ejected with shot as a single column of projectile from the muzzle. They are projected with the same velocity as that of shot charge and are carried to a considerable distance from the shooter. They move initially along with the pellet charge for about 6 feet. Thereafter, they begin to separate. Their separation takes place in accordance with their location and weight. The wad, moving in front of the whole shot and wad column, if any, separates first. The wads moving behind the shot column separate variedly depending on their makeup and the type of cartridge used. Their trajectories depend on their velocity at the time of separation, ballistic coefficient, angle of projection, angle of separation, etc. The distance of projection of various wads and their wounding capabilities provide significant forensic inferences in cases involving shotgun firing. Their presence or absence at the crime scene or inside the human body provides valuable clues in reconstructing the shooting incident.

4.6.1 Wads at the Crime Scene

The types of wads that are usually loaded in uncupped and cupped cartridges and their influence on the spread of pellets have been discussed above in section 4.1.1. There is a wide variety of wads that are commercially available for home loading of shotgun cartridges. The presence of wad at the shooting incident is helpful in assessing the probable location of the firer. Therefore, the distance up to which the evidence wad is likely to travel when fired from the questioned firearm needs to be known. A rough assessment of the distance of travel of usually loaded wads in branded ammunition is generally available in text books and related literature. In view of ever-changing propellant, and shape, size, and construction material of wads, to form an opinion, it is desirable to effect an experimental firing.

In a criminal case, the victim was hit by pellet spread of shotgun fire. The firearm was a 12-bore SBBL gun and the ammunition used was a 12–bore, 2½-inch Indian ordnance, factory-make cartridge. The victim was sitting on the boundary wall of his house. The assailant fired at him while passing in front of the victim's house. The assailant alleged that it was a mistaken, unintentional firing when under the impression that it was a ferocious barking dog. It was a fairly considerable distance (about 100 feet or so). The visibility at that time was low in the village due to setting darkness in late hours of the evening.

On examining the site, an air cushion wad was found lying near the boundary wall, 100 feet away from the shooter. However, the documented expected distance of travel of the air cushion wad is only about 40 feet. Thus, the disputed distance was the main deciding issue in the case. The evidence cartridge was a commonly used, traditional, uncupped Indian ordnance, factory-make shotgun ammunition. The wadding consisted of an overshot wad, an undershot wad, an air cushion wad, and an overpowder wad. Air cushion wad, being heaviest, travelled more than other wads. Experimental firings from the gun in question with the ammunition of the same make revealed that the air cushion wads travelled far more than a distance of 40 feet. It travelled nearly four times the reported distance, which had been documented decades ago. It travelled up to about 150 feet, a distance that needed due consideration while deciding the case on the disputed issue of range of fire.

The experiments also revealed that the distance of travel of a wad, besides weight, is influenced by the shape and size, velocity at the time of separation from the shot charge, direction and speed of wind, elevation of gun, and, finally, the nature of surface of impact, whether plain, smooth, or muddy.

Sinha et al. conducted exhaustive experiments with 120 rounds of the then commonly used, traditional 12-bore cartridges of Indian ordnance factory manufacture, consisting of an overshot wad closing disk, an undershot wad, an air cushion wad, and an overpowder wad. The overpowder, overshot, and undershot are thin card board disks. The gun was kept horizontally at a height of 4 feet above the ground and fired in and against the direction of wind (10–15 knots [11.5–17 mph]). The firings were performed on dry, plain, and wet muddy ground. After firing, the distance of the projection of various wads was recorded. The distance of travel of various intact and split wads on dry plain and wet muddy ground, when fired horizontally at a height of 4 feet from the ground, is tabulated in Table 4.6.

It can be seen from the table that the distance of projection of intact wads is 10–40 feet for overshot wad, 35–60 feet for undershot wad, 70–80 feet for overpowder wad, and 110–150 feet for the air cushion wad. Some of the wads split after emerging from the barrel. They are overshot, overpowder, and undershot lightweight cardboard disks.

4.6.1.1 Flight of Closing Disks

In addition to traditional uncupped cartridges, closing disks also are used in cartridges having plastic piston wads loaded in uncupped or cupped cartridges. The disk travels ahead of the shot charge. At close range, it enters into the rat hole due to heavy impact of the shot charge from behind. It travels in front of the shot charge partly or wholly until it forces its entry into the central rat hole by the backward impact or makes a sideways separation to move away from the shot charge. The sideways separation increases as the distance increases from the muzzle until it strikes the target or drops on the ground. The fired closing disk often gets sliced or fragmented. They vary in shape, size, and thickness, and, therefore, do not show consistency in their flight. The location of an intact or fragmented closing disk, found at the place of shooting, determines the position of the firer. It aids in the investigative aspect of reconstruction of the shooting incidents. Therefore, it is always desirable to ascertain the likely distance of travel by experimental firings using similar ammunition.

An unusual phenomenon of *backward projection of a sliced/fragmented closing disk* has been observed while firing against the wind. Its distance of travel at the rear depends on the speed of blowing wind against the shooter. It has been observed that the wind of even 10 to 15 knots (11.5–17 mph) blowing against it has resulted in a rearward thrust of the sliced parts to a distance of 8 feet behind the shooter. As expected, the lighter sliced parts are blown farther at the rear. Thus, assessing the probable position of the firer from the sliced/fragmented closing disk is usually a difficult proposition and, at times, may be misleading.

Table 4.6 Flight of Traditional Shotgun Wads in Favor of and Against Wind

Pellet Size Number	Overshot Wad		Undershot Wad		Overpowder Wad		Air Cushion Wad	
	Favor	Against	Favor	Against	Favor	Against	Favor	Against
No. 2	32 ft intact 5–20 ft split	30 ft intact (-) 8– +15 ft split	40–60 ft intact	40 ft intact	70 ft intact	70 ft intact 60 ft split	125 ft intact 120–150 ft (both sides open)	130 ft (one side open) 120 ft (both sides open)
No. 4	40 ft intact 15–30 ft split	(-) 4– +20 ft split	35–50 ft intact	45–55 ft intact	45–65 ft split	12–35 ft split	130–150 ft intact 120–150 ft (one side open)	148 ft intact 110 ft (both sides open)
No. 6	10–20 ft intact	5–15 ft split	30 ft split	30–35 ft split	16–60 ft split	70–80 ft intact 18–25 ft split	110–150 ft intact 35 ft completely open	150 ft intact 135 ft (both sides open)

Caution: A caution is needed when forming an opinion on the probable position of the firer from a split closing disk found at the place of shooting incident.

4.6.1.2 Flight of Cushion/Sealing Wads

4.6.1.2.1 Air Cushion Wads The flight of intact fired air cushion wads is generally consistent. Like other cardboard wads, some of the air cushion wads may not retain their shape and size. They may be sliced or fragmented. The fired cushion wads are found in four different forms. They are intact, one side open, both sides open, and in ribbon form (Figure 4.10).

The flight of air cushion intact wads is generally consistent to a great extent, except when opened in ribbon form after separating the cardboard disk. The flight of intact cushion wads is forensically significant because the usual plastic cushion wads loaded even in cupped cartridges also remain intact. Reasonable assessment of flight of various wads of desired gun–ammunition combination can be made by firing a number of rounds in favor of and against the direction of wind at any normal speed. The mean of the distances travelled in both directions denotes the probable distance of intact fired wads.

4.6.1.2.2 Mathematical Formulism A mathematical formulism has been proposed by Jauhari et al. for evaluating trajectory of shotgun wadding by using the McShane solution of normal equation of motion detailed in Chapter 5, for trajectory of projectiles fired horizontally at subsonic velocity. To compute the trajectory, ballistic coefficient of wads is calculated. Since wads are unstable projectiles, they tumble and their frontal area continues to change during the motion. This results in a varying ballistic coefficient during their flight in air. Therefore, an average ballistic coefficient is calculated by using the Cummings approximation. The trajectory parameters of wadding components of a typical 12-bore shotgun cartridge of Indian ordnance,

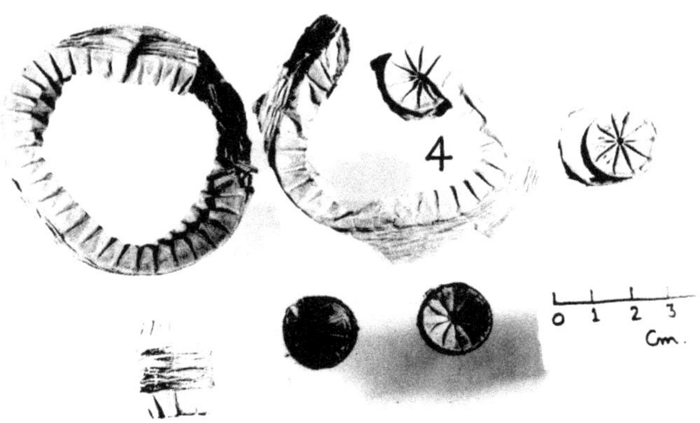

Figure 4.10 Different forms of fired air cushion wads.

Table 4.7 Summary of Calculated Theoretical Values of Flight of Traditional Shotgun Wads

Distance of Travel in Feet	Overshot Wad Drop in Feet	Undershot Wad Drop in Feet	Air Cushion Wad Drop in Feet	Overpowder Wad Drop in Feet
60	−3.1340	−0.6601	−0.2153	−0.2205
80	> 4 ft	−3.8243	−0.7182	−0.7441
100		> .4 ft	−2.2504	−2.3621
110			−3.9412	−4.1000
120			> 4 ft (-)−6.8763	> 4 ft (-)−7.3180

factory manufacture has been computed by Jauhari et al. for a drop of 4 to 5 feet (Table 4.7).

It can be seen from the table that the horizontal distance of travel is about 60 feet for the overshot wad, about 80 feet for the undershot wad, and 110 feet (approximately) for the overpowder and air cushion wads. A comparison of maximum range values calculated theoretically with the experimental values reveals that there is some measure of agreement between the two except for air cushion wads. The observed distance of travel of air cushion wads is comparatively more than the calculated values. This signifies that the ballistic coefficient of the fired air cushion wad is more than that of the theoretically calculated values of wad, which was an unfired air cushion wad. Air cushion wads, being made of cardboard, are compressed longitudinally by the expanding propellant gases. This makes for lateral expansion, thereby reducing the thickness of the air cushion wads. The reduction in thickness changes the ballistic coefficient of the emerging fired air cushion wad. A comparison of the experimental values of maximum range of 110 to 150 feet with the theoretical calculated maximum range of 110 feet suggests an acceptable assessment of probable distance of travel. The probable distance of projection of these wads is well within their calculated distances of projection.

4.6.1.2.3 Plastic Wads The plastic wads that are loaded in cupped or uncupped cartridges often retain their shape and size during their travel in air. The ballistic coefficient of unfired plastic wads can be determined by using the Cummings approximation. Because their shape and size usually do not change during firing, the probable distance of travel can be assessed by applying the McShane solution of equation for trajectory parameters. In "no gun" cases, the assessment of theoretical calculated probable distance may be helpful at the investigative stage. The calculated distance is expected to be in close agreement with the observed firing distances. The same may be verified experimentally.

Note: The probable distance of travel of wads loaded in cupped and uncupped cartridges can be computed by using the Cummings approximation and the McShane solution of trajectory parameters. For moderate accuracy of forensic work, it can be assumed that the probable distance of projection of fired wads is nearly similar to their theoretically calculated distances of projection.

4.6.2 Unusual Firearms and Flight of Wads

The velocity of an emergent shot charge varies with the constructional features of illegally made/improvised, substandard unusual firearms. The escape of expanding gases affects the development of requisite pressure thereby affecting the discharged velocity of the ejecta (including those of wads). Because constructional features of unusual firearms do not conform to standard specifications, their influence on the emergent velocity is very significant. The firearm-related factors affecting the velocity of the discharge ejecta are the shape and size of the chamber, bore diameter from breech to muzzle, and the barrel length.

The larger the chamber diameter, the greater is the expansion of the cartridge case. The elastic limit is exceeded if the chamber diameter is comparatively very high. This may lead to longitudinal or circumferential fractures. The gases may start escaping through these fractures even before the shot charge leaves the cartridge. The conversion of propellant into gases is affected even inside the cartridge. This results in a considerable decrease in the velocity of the emergent shot charge, including wads. The velocity is expected to be considerably less compared to even those firearms whose chamber is not excessively oversized.

Like an oversized chamber, the gaseous escape also increases with the increase in overbore diameter. The more the gaseous escape, the lesser is the development of pressure. This lowers the velocity of the emergent wads.

Illegally made, unusual firearms are short barreled. They are usually 4 to 7 inches, compared to about 26 to 30 inches in length of regular factory-made branded shotguns. The extent of conversion of propellant into gases is decreased in short barrels. This affects the sustained pressure on the moving shot charge and wads inside the barrel. This lowers the emerging velocity. A usual variation of a few inches of barrel lengths is not expected to markedly influence the ballistics if the chamber and bore size are similar, provided it exceeds all burnt points.

In view of the above theoretical considerations, it is apparent that the velocity of the emergent wads is affected by all the three factors: chamber shape and size, bore diameter, and barrel length. One can often infer from a plausible reasoning of the three variables that among the three factors, the diameter of the chamber influences the most and the length of the barrel, the least. Thus, an excessively larger chamber diameter coupled with an excessively oversized bore diameter is likely to markedly decrease the velocity. Likewise, a very short barrel length is expected to markedly decrease the emergent velocity, especially if it is less than all burnt point lengths.

4.7 Unusual Barrel Marks on Wads

The constructional material of wads is usually cardboard, fiber, felt, and plastic. They are unsuitable for picking striations from the barrel. Therefore, identifiable barrel marks are neither expected nor found on fired wads. Even the sealing and cushion wads that remain in continuous contact with the sides of the barrel do not carry identifiable sliding striations. The crudely finished barrels that carry comparatively prominent surface irregularities are likely to imprint identifiable barrel marks on fired wads. The muzzle of a sawed-off shotgun may carry marked surface irregularities at the cut end. The wad passes through the crude cut and picks up identifiable surface irregularities. This may be helpful in linking the fired wad with the sawed-off shotgun. Warlow has reported such a case. A characteristic pattern of striations was obtained on a12-gauge plastic cartridge wadding fired from a sawed-off shotgun with a rough muzzle end. The matching pattern of marks on the evidence and tests was helpful in establishing linkage of fired wads with the questioned sawed-off shotguns.

While conducting a series of experiments to study the flight and identification of wads fired from homemade firearms, the author also has come across the matching pattern of barrel marks on fired wads. Characteristic barrel marks have been observed even on cardboard air cushion wads. It is usually possible in the case of a tapered barrel having an undersized portion almost at the muzzle tip. The air cushion wad remains intact while travelling inside the overbore diameter of the tapered barrel. The intact wad passing through the underbore diameter at the muzzle tip may not squeeze if the diameter is very slightly less than the air cushion wad. Besides the squeezing effect, the reduction in the thickness of the air cushion wad is also insignificant. The cylindrical surface is blackened at places by the escaped gases. The partly blackened, unsqueezed air cushion wad makes barrel contact during its passage through the undersized portion near the muzzle end. Sliding barrel marks are imprinted on the fired cushion wad. Sometimes, repetitive and identifiable barrel marks are imprinted on the unfolded cylindrical surface of the fired air cushion wads (Figure 4.11).

Figure 4.11 Characteristic indentations on fired wads.

If the undersized portion of the tapered barrel is considerably long, squeezing and folding of layers takes place and barrel contact marks are not decipherable. Clearly demarcated and identifiable repetitive barrel marks on fired air cushion wads are not expected from unusual firearms having under- or oversized bore and nontapered, mixed-sized bore barrels.

4.8 Cartridge Splits and Unusual Chamber Marks on Fired Wads

The phenomenon of cartridge split is often found in cases involving unusual firearms having an excessive overchamber diameter. The larger the overchamber diameter, the greater is the expansion of the cartridge, on firing. Excessive expansion may exceed the elastic limit of the cartridge. This tends to split the cartridge. The split may be either longitudinal or circumferential or both. It is more pronounced on paper shotgun cartridges compared to metallic cartridges of rifled firearms. The split may result in marked fractures leading to partial or complete separation (Figure 4.12).

Associated with the expansion of cartridge, oversized chamber allows the escape of gases inside the chamber itself. The expanding gases start escaping through the split/fractures even before the shot charge leaves the cartridge. If

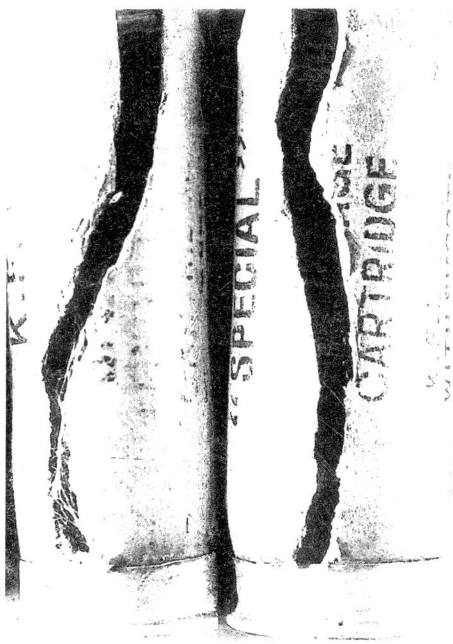

Figure 4.12 Paper cartridge splits from a 12-bore shotgun.

the split (due to fracture or partial separation) provides considerable space, the wad beneath may come in direct contact with the walls of the chamber. The movement of the wadding is arrested until it moves ahead along with the shot charge. The shortly arrested wad is pressed against the wall of the chamber through the fracture until the expansion continues. In doing so, it imprints the characteristic static shape and size of the chamber at the point of contact. The presence of static chamber marks can be utilized to identify the fired wad in respect of the firearm. The impressions are likely to be identifiable if the marks are sufficient and repetitive. With a larger surface area of wad contact, the impressions are likely to be characteristic, especially if it is a crudely finished barrel. It is sufficient and identifiable if the static marks on the wad are retained during its forward travel inside the barrel. This may be achieved if the marks on the wad are not interfered during its onward journey inside the barrel. This is possible if the bore diameter is also significantly more than the wad's diameter. While experimenting with 12-bore homemade pistols having marked oversized chambers and bore diameters, besides almost similar fractures on paper shotgun cartridges, identifiable static chamber marks on wads have been found as well in some cases. Air cushion wads having larger surface area have been found to carry identifiable chamber marks. However, repetitive indentations on wads may not always be obtainable in most firearms, even though they have oversized chamber diameter. A number of test rounds have to be fired for test purposes so that the wad touches the relevant portion of the chamber partly or wholly. On obtaining proper tests, static marks are compared under low magnification. A positive match establishes linkage (Figure 4.13).

Caution: Whereas, a positive match establishes linkage, dissimilar marks do not lead to conclude otherwise. Identification of wads by static marks is possible only in rare cases.

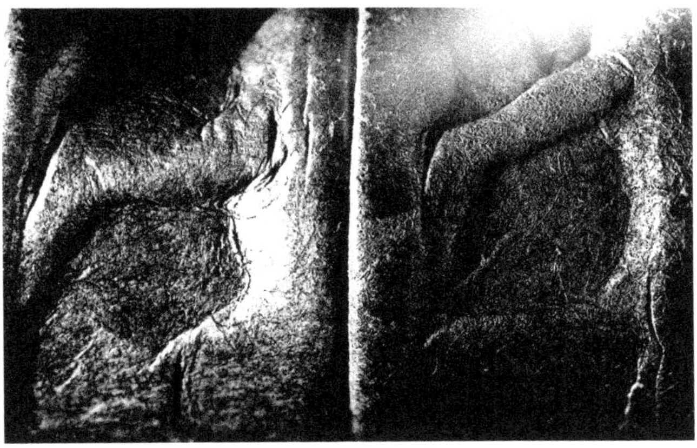

Figure 4.13 Characteristic static chamber marks on fired wads.

Note: In "no gun" cases, it is essential to assess the type of firearm for evaluating range from spread of pellets and presence or absence of wads. The documented data of regular branded firearms is inapplicable for unusual firearms. It may be wrong to comment on the range of fire unless the probable type of firearm is rightly assessed; however, it may not always be possible. It may be possible, though, if the evidentiary clues found at the crime scene or inside the wound are apparently suggestive of probable and improbable, such as:

- Characteristic splits/fractures on the evidence empties signify that the involved firearm is an unusual firearm having an oversized chamber.
- Characteristic static chamber marks on wads signify that the involved firearm is an unusual firearm having an oversized chamber as well as oversized bore diameter.

Unusual Firearms and Medico-Legal Evidence

5

Medico-legal examination of firearm injuries is an important aspect of a criminal investigation. It yields a wealth of information. It assumes great forensic significance in evaluating investigative, scientific, and legal aspects of crimes involving firearms. The role of a forensic pathologist/autopsy surgeon, who examines the injuries and records the wound profile, is highly significant. All possible details of the gunshot wound are required to be recorded with due care and caution. They can include the following:

1. Shape and size of the bullet hole
2. Presence or absence of close-range phenomena
3. Presence or absence of abraded and dirt collar
4. Probable caliber of bullet and type of firearm from bullet hole
5. Entry hole and direction of fire
6. Projectile–tissue interactions and the track
7. Exit wound

For a meaningful interpretation of the wound profile in the court of law, the medical officer is expected to have the basic understanding of the firearm discharge, the trajectory of the projectile through the air, and the potentiality of the projectile at impact. However, for an easy understanding of the text in hand, the relevant details of wound ballistics, though known and documented, have been briefly summarized, wherever necessary.

5.1 Shape and Size of Bullet Hole

The shape and size of the bullet hole is influenced by the stability and velocity of the projectile at impact. The stability depends on the constructional features of the projectile. The lower part of a cylindro-conical bullet is heavier than its upper part. The center of gravity of such a bullet is behind the center of pressure. Consequently, there is an overturning tendency of the bullet during its flight. The overturning is overcome by imparting the spin, which keeps the bullet stable in flight, though some tail wobbling (up to a couple of feet) takes place before it is stabilized. The bullet also tumbles during the last phase of its trajectory before it finally hits the ground. The spin-stabilized bullet traverses in a nose-on position. It strikes the target nose on and creates a circular or an oval hole depending on the angle of fire. A circular hole indicates a right-angle fire and an oval (elliptical) hole, an angular fire. The major axis of the oval shape varies with the angle of fire. The smaller the angle of fire, the greater is the major axis of the elliptical hole. Thus, bullets fired from rifled firearms create varying shapes depending on the angle of fire. The wobbling/tumbling bullet creates an irregular hole and sometimes a keyhole. The criteria of formation of circular, oval, irregular, or keyholes hold well if the involved firearm is a legally manufactured, standard, rifled firearm and the ammunition used is appropriate.

This may not necessarily be true if the firearm is an illegally manufactured/made, substandard rifled or unrifled firearm either using appropriate or mismatched ammunition. In such cases, the direction of the emergent bullet does not depend alone on the angle of fire. It also depends on the makeup of the functional parts of the substandard firearm, generally inappropriate, especially the barrel. The inappropriate constructional features of the firearm affects the direction of the emergent bullet considerably, thereby influencing the shape and size of the bullet hole, irrespective of the direction of fire.

The significant inappropriate constructional features include:

- Unrifled bore using rifled ammunition
- Irregular rifling/bore dimension of the rifled bore barrel

5.1.1 Unrifled Bore Using Rifled Ammunition

When a spin-stabilized rifled bullet is fired from an unrifled barrel, the emergent bullet tends to tumble during its entire trajectory. In the absence of rifling, the movement of the bullet depends on bullet–barrel contacts inside the barrel. This is influenced by the relative bullet–bore diameter from breech to muzzle, whether under-, over-, or mixed-sized bore. The axis alignment of the bullet with the bore, in loaded position, is another important factor. These factors contribute to the formation of shape and size of the bullet hole. Most of the homemade and low-cost, illegally made, unrifled firearms designed to fire rifled ammunition vary widely in their relative bullet–bore diameter and relative bullet–bore axis. Therefore, the shape and size of the bullet hole varies from one round to the other by the same firearm–ammunition combination; so, also, one firearm to the other, using similar ammunition. These result in the formation of varying shapes and sizes of bullet holes that are unlike those formed by regular factory-made rifled firearms. The formation of various shapes and sizes of bullet holes by a variety of illegally made, unrifled firearms are discussed below.

5.1.1.1 *Undersized, Unrifled Bore*

Bullets passing through an undersized, smoothbore barrel get elongated to fit the undersized bore. The elongation alters the shape, size, and symmetry of the bullet. The symmetrical bullet becomes asymmetrical inside the barrel. Its length is increased and diameter is reduced (Figure 5.1(a)(b)).

The center of gravity of the asymmetrical bullet is shifted away from the central axis of the bullet. This results in yaw. It makes the bullet strike the target at an angle depending on the extent of yaw. It may hit the target in an inclined or straight-on position even at fairly close ranges forming oval

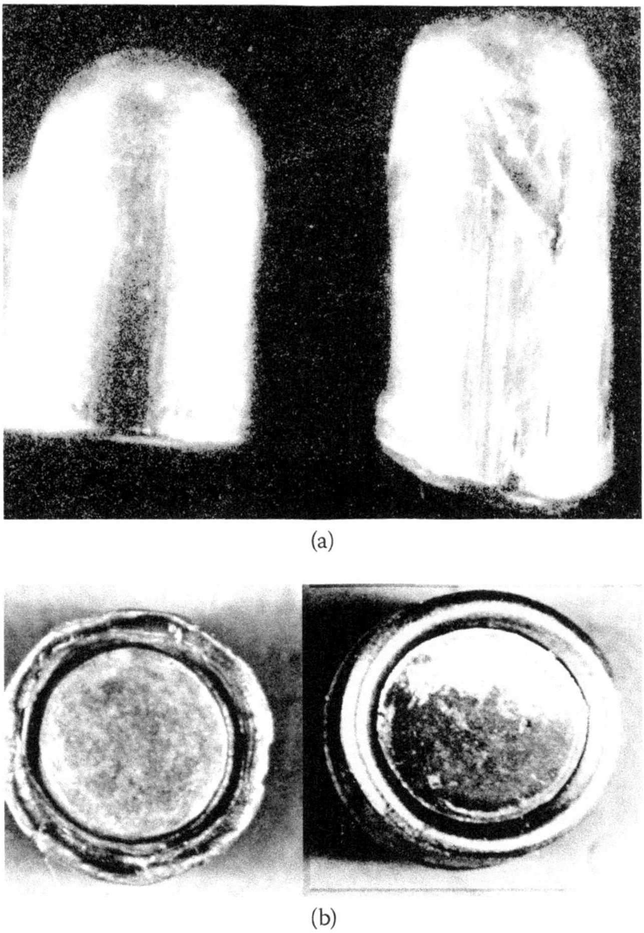

Figure 5.1 (a) Elongated bullet length: Original L = .44 inch and elongated L = .54 inch; (b) Reduced bullet diameter: Reduced dia = .26 inch and original dia = .31 inch.

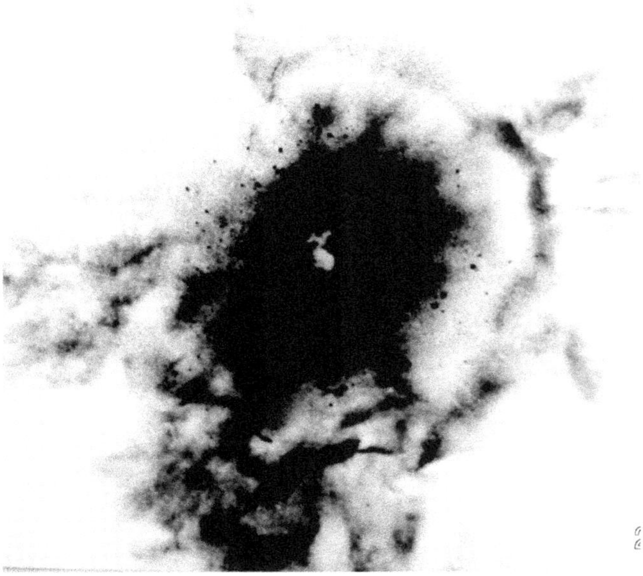

(a)

(b)

Figure 5.2 (a) Oval hole from 6 inches fired from .32 homemade pistol (m.d. 3 inches); (b) keyhole from 4 feet fired from .32 homemade pistol (m.d. 3 inches).

holes and keyholes. The possibility of keyhole formation increases with the increase in firing distance (Figure 5.2(a)(b)).

Sometimes, undersized, nonrifled bores also form almost circular bullet holes. This is possible if the emergent bullet moves with its nose pointing onward until it starts wobbling/tumbling. This is usually observed from a

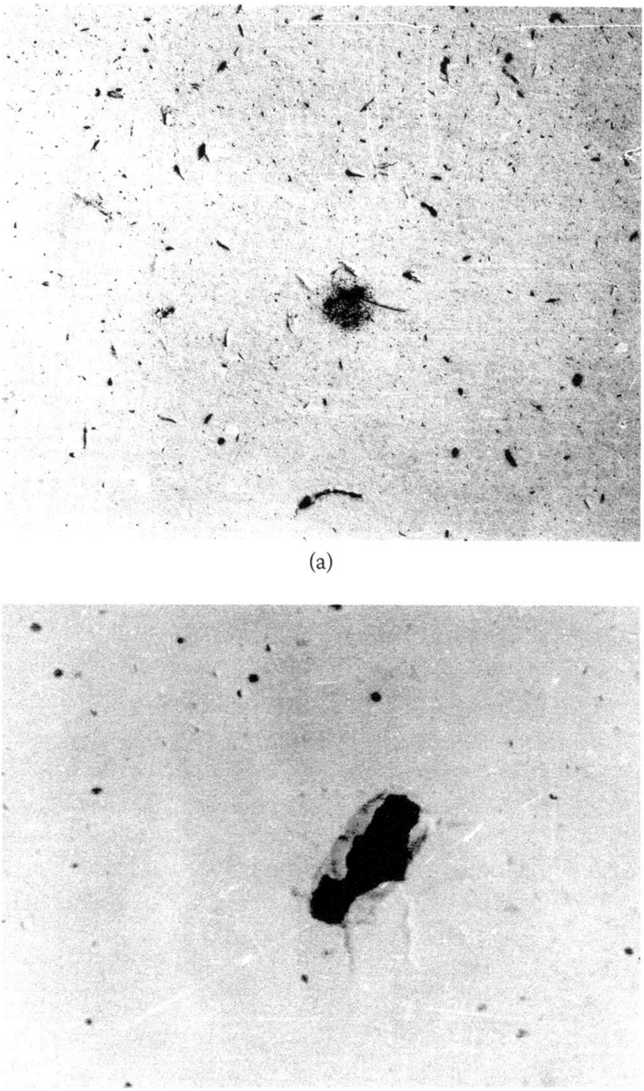

(a)

(b)

Figure 5.3 (a) Circular hole from 4 inches and (b) elongated keyhole from 12 inches (.38 homemade, nonrifled pistol muzzle diameter .35 inch).

very close range. With the increasing distance, the tumbling effect dominates the onward journey forming an elongated hole or a keyhole (Figure 5.3(a)(b)).

The shape of the bullet hole is not solely dependent on the angle of fire. Therefore, an opinion on the direction of fire from the shape of the hole, at times, may be misleading.

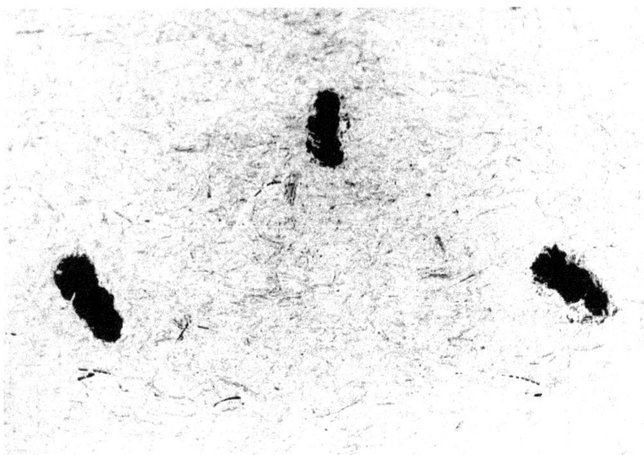

Figure 5.4 Keyholes from oversized .38 homemade pistols (m.d. 4 inches) at varying positions on fixed target at 12 inches.

5.1.1.2 Oversized, Unrifled Bore

Oversized, nonrifled firearms usually create keyholes. This is due to random contacts of the bullet with the sides of the barrel during its movement inside an oversized, nonrifled bore. It makes the direction of the emergent bullet unpredictable. Such a bullet is unlikely to hit the target in nose-on position and, hence, keyholes are usually formed, and are often clearly demarcated. Sometimes, oval holes also are formed from very close ranges. Variation in the direction of the emergent bullet changes the direction and position of the keyholes. Hence, the locations of the keyholes vary significantly from one round to another. The orientation and position of keyholes may change from round to round as well. The figure of merit also changes in each firing (Figure 5.4).

5.1.1.3 Unusual Bent Bullets

The phenomenon of bending of bullets was discussed in Chapter 3. The phenomenon, though rare, has been observed while firing from oversized bore firearms having significant misaligned chambers. The misaligned chamber makes the loose bullet strike at an angle inside the bore. This changes the original direction of the motion. If the forward motion is momentarily restricted, then the bullet may bend at the point of initial impact. The bent bullet creates curved keyholes on the target (Figure 5.5(a)(b)).

5.1.1.4 Variable Unrifled Bore and Bullet Holes

Mixed-size, unrifled (smooth) bore firearms usually create oval or keyholes. They may also create a circular hole if the undersized portion is near the

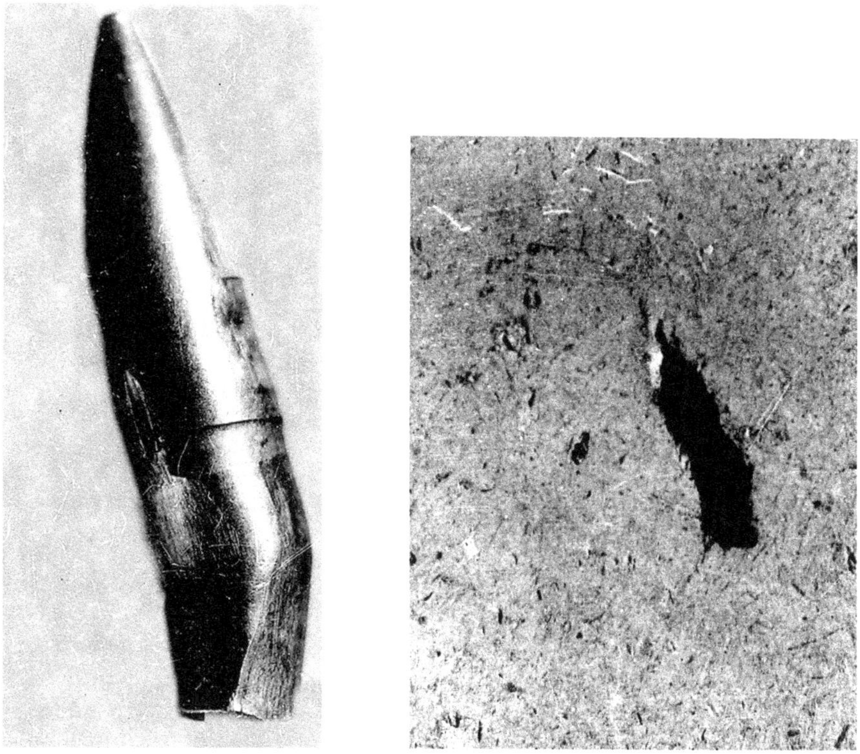

(a) (b)

Figure 5.5 (a) Bent bullet and (b) curved keyhole.

muzzle. This is usually found in homemade firearms having tapered barrels. The bullet passing through the undersized portion of the tapered barrel behaves as one fired from an undersized bore barrel. In such a case, the bullet continues to pass through an undersized bore while coming out of the muzzle. The emergent bullet may move in a nose-on position for a short distance. During its short nose-on travel, the bullet usually creates a circular hole. It is accompanied with wide and densely distributed unburned powder particles.

Variable (mixed) bore, unrifled firearms may create oval holes as well as keyholes even from close ranges (Figure 5.6).

5.1.2 Unusual Rifled Firearms

The shape of the emergent bullet is markedly influenced by the inappropriate bore dimension of illegally made, substandard rifled firearms. The shape of the bullet hole varies accordingly. The emergent bullet is usually elongated if the chamber of the substandard rifled firearm is designed to accommodate

Figure 5.6 Oval hole and keyhole from .315 mixed-bore, homemade pistol from 6 inches.

and fire cartridges that load bullets greater in diameter than the rifled bore. The bullet fired from such a barrel elongates to bring it to the smaller size of the bore. The elongation is conspicuous in the case of abnormally undersized rifled bore barrels. It makes a significant change in the shape, size, and symmetry of the two halves of the fired bullet. The center of gravity of the bullet is shifted and its central axis is tilted to its heavier half. The emergent bullet, thus, strikes the target angularly toward right or left from the line of fire, depending on the under-bore size of the unusual rifled firearm and the alignment of the chamber; the elongation and asymmetry of the bullet would vary, which, in turn, would result in the variation of the eccentricity of the oval hole on the target.

Note: It is likely that substandard, under-bore sized, rifled firearms may create oval holes even at close range on the target placed at right angles. This may be misleading to an unwary examiner.

5.2 Presence or Absence of the Close-Range Phenomena

It is often necessary to distinguish between a close and a distant firing. Investigation of cases involving close-range firing, such as suicide, struggle, murder, and alleged self-defense, may often be aided by ascertaining the firing distance. An approximate estimate can be made by studying the close-range phenomena on the body or the clothes of the victim.

It is the firing process that needs to be reviewed for the basic understanding of close-range phenomena. The propellant inside the cartridge, on firing, converts rapidly into gases. The gases develop very high temperature and pressure. The rapid development of the pressure results in the unseating of the projectile, pushing it through the barrel, and finally propelling it out of the muzzle with a high velocity. The high temperature, hot gases that follow the projectile carry firearm discharge residues. They are propelled out of the muzzle with a high velocity. The discharge residues travel in almost a conical shape. The emerging hot gases cool quickly and, hence, the effect of hot gases is limited to a very small distance. The discharge particles also do not travel far. The effect of the expelled hot gases and the firearm discharge provides the necessary data for approximate estimate of close firing distance.

The following effects of the firearm discharge that signify close-range phenomena are worth mentioning;

- Burning
- Scorching
- Blackening
- Powder tattooing
- Metal vapor smudging
- Projectile scrapings/Bullet chips
- GSR particles
- Unusual firearms and contact shots

5.2.1 Burning

The propellant gases emerge out of the muzzle at a very high temperature. It produces flame when it encounters the atmospheric oxygen. The thermal effect of the flame has a burning effect on the bare skin and singeing of hair. The flame is limited to a few inches. According to Hatcher, "Burning is a phenomenon that does not occur under any circumstances at all when the distance from muzzle is greater than about 7 inches. Even the 7-inch distance is for a service rifle. Few pistols will burn at a distance beyond about 2 inches, regardless of the loading, assuming, of course, that black powder is not being used."

5.2.2 Scorching

The hot powder gas travelling beyond the flame has a similar scorching effect on the bare body and on hairs. The scorching effect persists so long, the tem-

Figure 5.7 Cloudy appearance of blackening around the bullet hole.

perature is very high. Because the propellant gas cools quickly, the scorching effect is limited to a few more inches beyond flame.

Note: The hairs surrounding the bullet hole are singed, often clubbed, and swollen by burns due to flames or by scorching heat.

5.2.3 Blackening

The cooled, discharged powdery, gaseous deposit appears as dirty black soot. It is known as *blackening*. The black soot travels beyond scorching range. Due to blackening, the area around the bullet hole often presents a cloudy appearance (Figure 5.7).

The blackening, being a dirty gaseous deposit, can be removed by wiping, but scorching or burning cannot. This differentiates between blackening and scorching. The soot/smoke (blackening effect) is more pronounced in the case of black powder compared to smokeless powder and it travels farther.

5.2.4 Powder Tattooing

The burning of the propellant is never complete inside the barrel. Therefore, the firearm discharge usually contains unburned or partially burnt propellant grains/particles. They also are projected out of the muzzle with a high velocity. These particles move farther than smoke, being heavier than the propellant gases. The fast moving, partially burnt and unburned propellant particles embed into the pores of the skin at close range and appear similar to a tattoo, thus, powder tattooing. They travel farther than blackening. Their distance of projection also is limited because they are lightweight particles. The characteristic pattern of powder grains/particles is exhibited on the intervening target like clothes, if any. The nature and spread of powder pattern depends on the factors contributed by the firearm and ammunition besides distance of fire.

5.2.4.1 Unusual Firearms and Powder Tattooing

The burning of the propellant is invariably incomplete in unusual firearms. This is mainly due to inappropriate constructional features. Their barrel lengths are usually shorter and bore dimensions are irregular compared to their branded regular firearms counterpart. The moving projectile is unable to seal the bore. This invariably causes incomplete combustion of the propellant. Hence, the density of unburned and partially burnt powder grains/particles is comparatively far more. This phenomenon is usually observed from the variable bore of an illegally made, unusual firearm. Because the bullet is loose at one or more places in variable bore firearms, partially burnt/unburned powder particles are densely distributed around the wound/bullet hole (Figure 5.8(a)(b)).

5.2.5 Metal Vapor Smudging

The high temperature inside the barrel results in vaporization of metallic constituents. Those having vaporization temperatures lower than hot powder gases are expelled out of the muzzle as metal vapors. The metal vapors, being heavier, travel farther than the propellant gases and also beyond blackening. The metal vapors form part of the discharge ejecta and are projected as a compact smudged vapor around the bullet hole. Their distance of projection is usually more than the blackening, but less than unburned/partially burnt propellant grains/particles that cause powder tattooing.

5.2.6 Projectile Scrapings (Bullet Chips)

The friction between the moving projectile and the bore scrape the metallic projectile. The scrapings of the bullet that are cut by the lands of the rifled barrel are small bullet chips/pieces. The bullet chips that do not melt or vaporize are projected from the muzzle as solid metal particles. The bullet chips, especially from lead bullets, are much heavier than propellant grains. Therefore, their distance of projection is far more than lightweight propellant particles that cause powder tattooing. These scrapings also deposit like powder tattooing on the bare body and provide characteristic patterns on the clothing. Their distance of travel is dependent on their shape, size, and velocity.

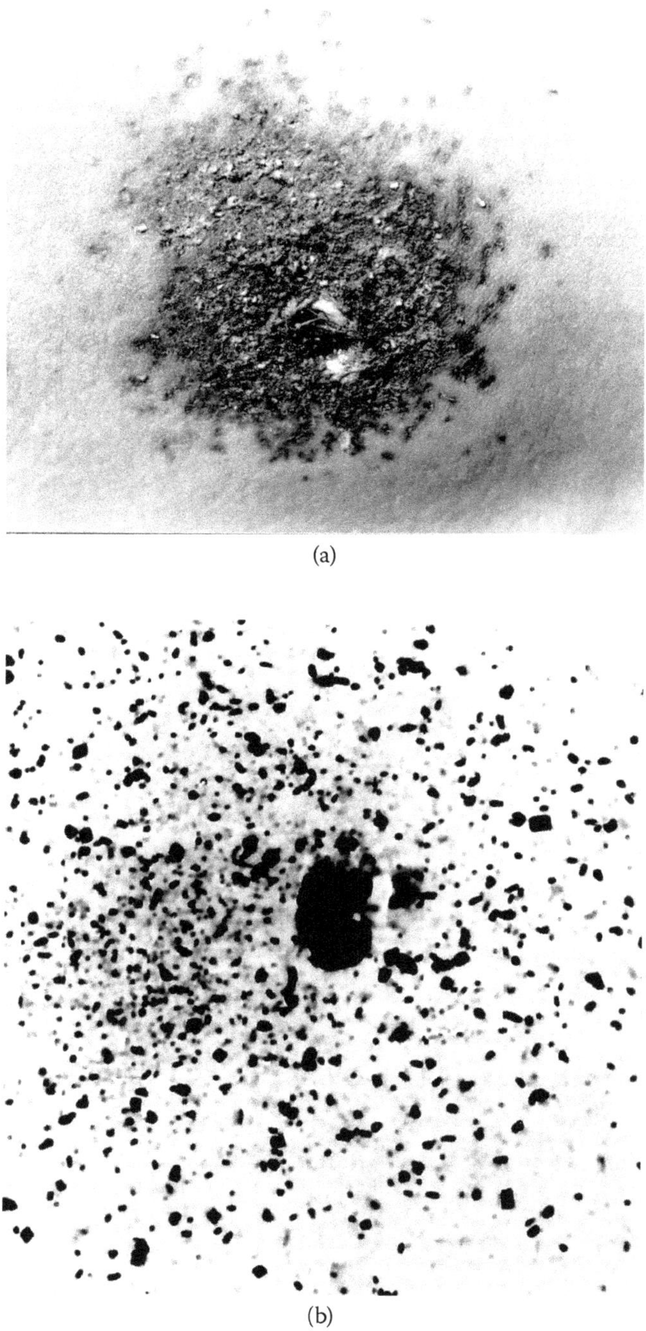

(a)

(b)

Figure 5.8 Wide and dense powder tattooing from homemade firearms around (a) bullet wound and (b) bullet hole.

The distribution of small bullet chips on the bare body is akin to powder tattooing. It may not be possible to differentiate between the two on visual examination of firearm injuries.

5.2.7 Gunshot Residue (GSR) Particles

GSR particles are caused by the condensation of the vapors of metallic constituents of the primer, cartridge case, and the projectile. These particles have characteristic size, morphology, and elemental composition. They are generally spherical in shape, having a fused appearance. They are varying micron-sized particulates composed primarily of lead with minor amounts of antimony, barium, etc. The particulates may contain copper as well, in cases of copper-coated or metal-jacketed bullets. The details are, however, out of the preview of the present discussion. The GSR particulates are projected along with other firearm discharge. The GSR particles varying in size and elemental composition travel at varying distances.

5.2.7.1 Absence of Close-Range Phenomena

It is needless to mention that the aforesaid close-range phenomena are absent at distant firings. In addition to distant firing, any of the cited close-range phenomena also is absent if the muzzle is in close contact with the body. In such a case, the discharge from the muzzle is driven into the bullet track inside the body. Consequently, the effect of burning/scorching, blackening, powder tattooing, etc. is not seen around the bullet hole; instead, they are observable in the bullet track inside the body. However, traces of these effects also may be present at the periphery of the wound/bullet hole. A firm and hard muzzle contact invariably leads to muzzle imprint surrounding the wound/bullet hole (Figure 5.9(a)(b)).

5.2.8 Unusual Firearms and Contact Shots

It was discussed in Chapter 1 that the muzzle thickness of illegally made, substandard firearms may not be uniform all around the circumference and the wall thickness may be abnormally less. In cases of contact shots, the surface of the muzzle that comes in contact with the body may be uneven and very sharp. These variations affect the firm grip and, consequently, the muzzle imprint (Figure 5.10).

5.3 Abraded and Dirt Collar

The phenomenon of abraded and dirt collar around the wound/bullet hole assumes forensic importance in evaluating firearm injuries. Its presence is observed from close as well as distant firing range.

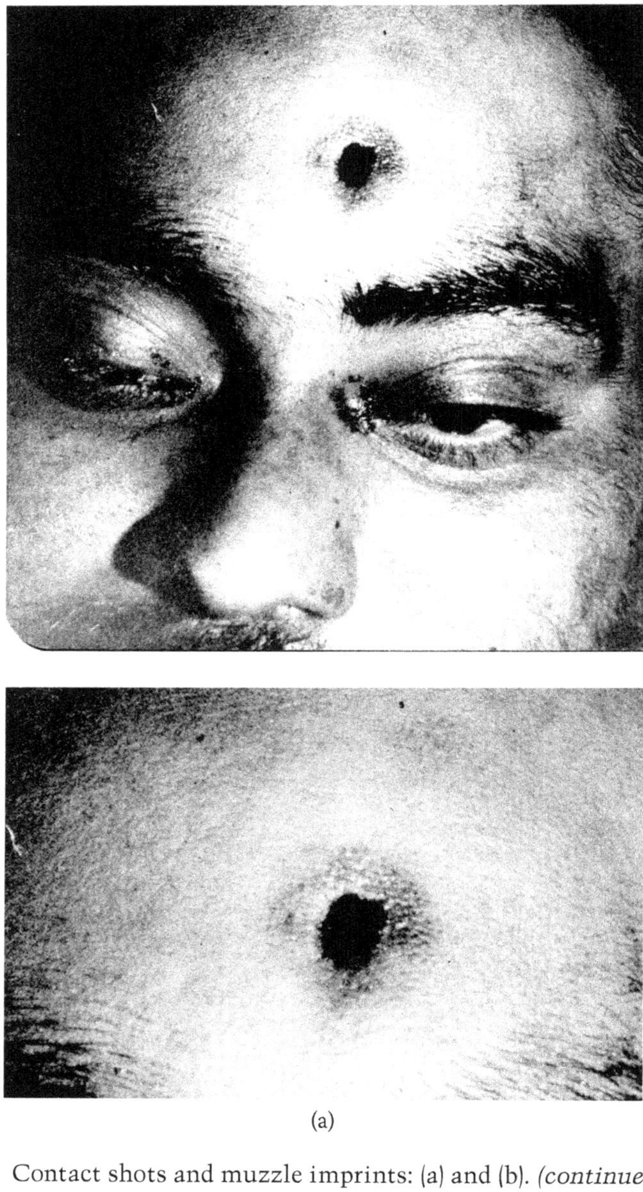

(a)

Figure 5.9 Contact shots and muzzle imprints: (a) and (b). *(continued)*

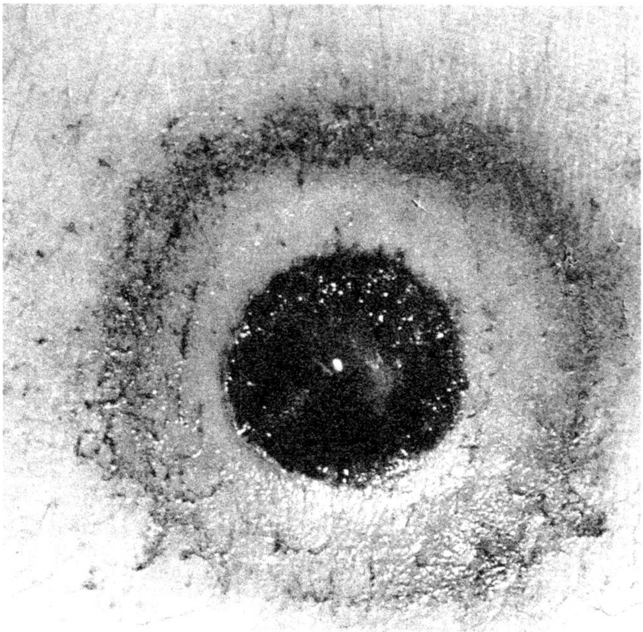

(b)

Figure 5.9 *(continued)* Contact shots and muzzle imprints: (a) and (b).

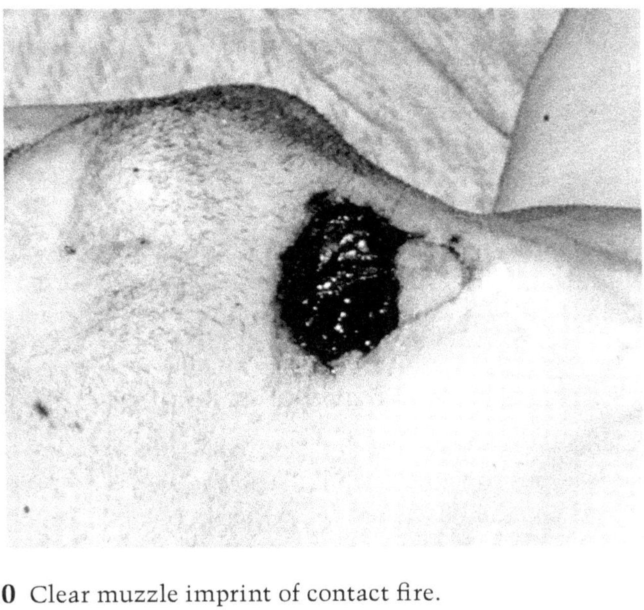

Figure 5.10 Clear muzzle imprint of contact fire.

5.3.1 Abraded Collar

When a bullet strikes the skin, it stretches and splits the skin to allow its entry. In doing so, the edge surrounding the bullet hole is abraded due to rubbing or scraping of the skin against the inverted epidermis. The zone of epidermal abrasion immediately surrounding the edges of the wound is termed *abraded collar.* It darkens on drying.

5.3.2 Dirt Collar/Ring

The bullet picks up dirt, soot, and other soiled material of the barrel during its travel inside the bore. They are transferred to the skin around the edges of the wound/bullet hole, which gives rise to a dirt ring. In addition, the wiping of lubricated or unjacketed lead bullets also contributes to the dirt deposit around the wound/bullet hole edge. The dirt ring, in some cases, may cover the abraded collar.

5.3.3 Visual Examination of Firearm Injuries and Caution Needed

The medico-legal examination of firearm injuries is primarily a domain of a forensic medicine specialist. The medical officer, who examines the firearm injuries and performs postmortem, records the presence of close-range phenomena upon visual examination. The visual examination may sometimes be misleading, especially if the autopsy surgeon is not from the field of forensic medicine. One often comes across reporting of misleading observations by unwary medical examiners, especially nonspecialists attending medico-legal cases in remote rural areas. This is quite common in India. The observations that usually confuse the unwary medical examiners include:

- Dark rings around the bullet hole due to abrasion and dirt may be confused with charring and blackening.
- Bullet scrapping may be confused with powder tattooing. Insect bites appearing like powder tattooing has been reported as well. Intermediate target scrapings also may look like powder tattooing.

5.3.4 Blackening and Blackened Bullet Periphery

The difference between blackening and blackened edges around the wound/bullet hole clearly must be understood. Blackening is due to propellant gaseous deposit and not the blackened bullet periphery. For an illustration, a .45 revolver was used for the firing of lead bullet and white filter paper targets were used for a bullet wipe (Figure 5.11 and Figure 5.12).

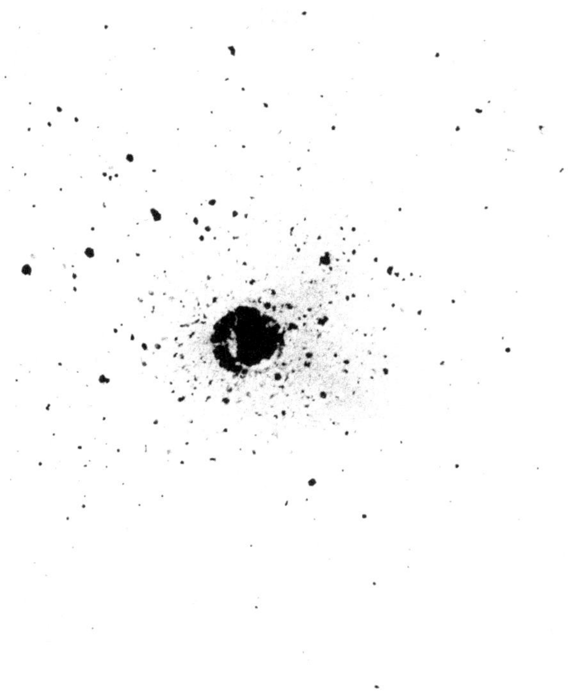

Figure 5.11 Blackened bullet wipe on periphery.

It can be seen in Figure 5.11 that there is a blackened periphery on the filter paper target, blackening surrounding the bullet hole, and powder tattooing. The blackened periphery is obviously not due to abraded color. It is the lead bullet wipe. On the other hand, in Figure 5.12(a), there is neither blackening nor powder tattooing surrounding the bullet wound, but a blackened bullet hole periphery. Therefore, it is evident that, associated with blackening, the phenomenon of powder tattooing also is observed around the bullet hole. If blackening is present, powder tattooing must be present. Thus, presence of powder tattooing is a necessary condition for the deposit of blackening due to powder gases. Therefore, to make the observations unambiguous, the medico-legal examiner must record the presence of powder tattooing along with blackening. The blackened edges due to abraded collar, bullet wipe, or dried blood appearing as blackening may also be evaluated similarly. Absence of powder tattooing signifies blackening from sources other than powder gaseous deposit.

In addition to powder tattooing, dispersion of pellets is another distinguishing factor in cases involving shotgun firing. It has been discussed in Chapter 4 that dispersal takes place beyond close range. The area of dispersion of pellets depends on distance of firing. Hence, dispersion of pellets

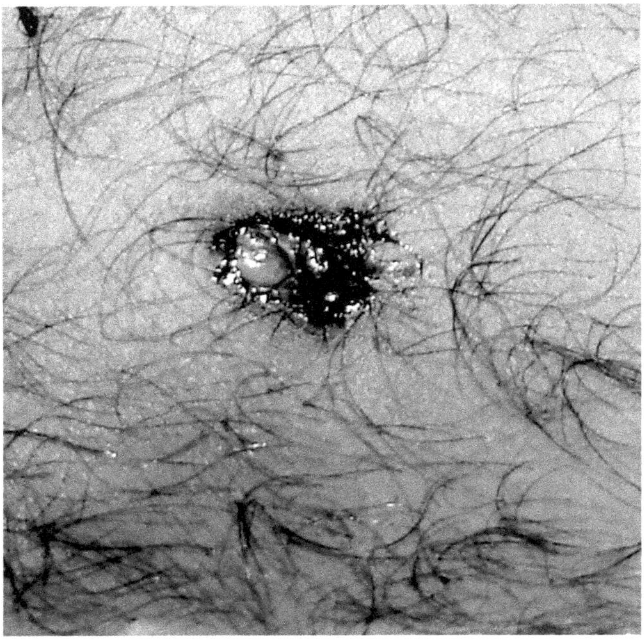

(a)

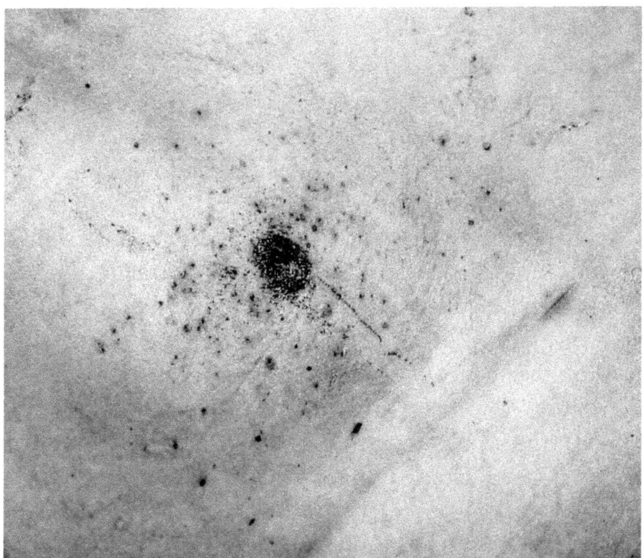

(b)

Figure 5.12 (a) Absence of blackening and powder tattooing around the bullet wound but blackened periphery; (b) powder tattooing from 7.65 mm country-made auto pistol and blackened periphery.

conveniently can be taken as an additional important factor for assessing the presence or absence of blackening in shotgun firing.

In a murder case, the empty cartridge found at the crime scene was positively linked with the licensed shotgun of the accused. The eyewitnesses had stated that the assailant had fired his licensed shotgun from a distance of about 8 to 10 meters. The autopsy surgeon reported that there were six separate holes in the victim's body in an area of about 10 inches. The recovered projectiles were LG shot. The dimension of the six holes also revealed that they could have been caused by firing a shotgun using LG shot. In addition to wound dimensions, the autopsy report also indicated the presence of a blackening around all of the wound holes. On the basis of blackening, the autopsy surgeon stated that it was a close-range fire of about a couple of feet or so. In view of the evidence of the medical examiner on the probable distance of firing, the defense pleaded outright rejection of eyewitness accounts. The opinion of the ballistics expert was sought on the issue. The author, on studying the postmortem report, suggested a distant firing on the basis of a very wide dispersion of clearly separated individual shots in an area of about 10 inches. The author stated plausible reasons in support of his opinion, which was contrary to the opinion of the autopsy surgeon. It was explained that pellet dispersion and close-range blackening are distance-related physical phenomena of shotgun firing. A wider pellet distribution of separated shots cannot occur along with blackening simultaneously. One is a close-range phenomenon and the other a distant range. Hence, only one of the observations is correctly recorded. It cannot be imagined that there can be any confusion on the part of the attending autopsy surgeon about the number of wound holes, their varying locations, and specific dimensions. Therefore, the observation of widely distributed, six separate wound holes is evidently correctly recorded. The observation of blackening on all the wounds, as it appears, was apparently due to dirt, abraded color, or dried blood. Thus, it was possible to corroborate a distant firing solely on the basis of dispersion of pellets despite reporting of blackening on all the wound holes.

In cases of rifled firearms, it is only the powder tattooing that confirms the presence of blackening around the bullet hole due to gaseous deposit and not due to bullet wipe or abraded collar. Therefore, it is essential that presence or absence of powder tattooing must be recorded along with blackening. This would obviate the ambiguity in differentiating close and distant firing. Ideally, the relevant portion should be cut and forwarded to a forensic laboratory for examination.

5.3.5 Detection of Powder Particles on the Bare Body

Sinha et al. suggested a simple method to detect powder particles around the wound/bullet hole. The procedure utilizes formation of dye by the then commonly used reagents for diazotization and coupling reaction. Previously prepared, chemically treated filter papers are used to detect powder particles around the wound/hole. The procedure for the preparation of reagent solutions and test papers is simple; so also is the detection of a powder pattern.

Preparation of reagent solutions:
0.1 g of a-napthylamine is dissolved in 100 ml of boiling distilled water
0.5 g of sulphanilic acid is dissolved in 100 ml of distilled water
10 g of citric acid is dissolved in 100 ml of distilled water

Equal volume of each of the three reagent solutions is mixed.

Preparation of test papers:
Whatman filter papers of 4-inch diameter are used for the preparation of test papers. Filter papers are dipped in the mixed reagent solution for two to three minutes. Thereafter, the soaked filter papers are dried in a vacuum desiccator. The dried test papers can be used for about two to three months if protected from light and air like those of photographic papers.

Procedure for detection of powder pattern:
The chemically treated test paper is placed over the area surrounding the wound. A wet filter paper is placed over the test paper and pressed tightly against the skin surrounding the area suspected to carry powder particles. Pink spots are developed corresponding to the burnt propellant indicating the presence of nitrite ion. Unburned propellant grains that do not develop pink spots are lifted. A transparent cellophane tape is pressed against the skin to pick up visually identified, unburned propellant particles. Ideally, the tape should be handed over to the investigating agency for laboratory examination. Alternatively, a simple and convenient procedure may be adopted, in continuation, to identify unburned propellant by a diazo color reaction. A fresh test paper is placed over the lifted particles of the tape. The reagent paper is placed on a glass plate keeping the tape downward. A wet filter paper is placed over the reagent paper and pressed with a warm press for a few minutes. The propellant burns and diazo-coupling reaction takes place. Pink specks are developed showing presence of nitrite ion. The color fades with the passage of time. It can be retained by pasting cellophane tape on both sides of the specks and photographed for record.

The reagents and test papers are prepared in the forensic laboratory and properly stored. The test paper should form part of the crime scene kit of the investigating agency attending the crime scene and supplied to the medical officer, if needed, during medical examination.

Note: The possibility of omission and error attending visual examination by an unwary examiner is minimized.

5.4 Probable Caliber of Bullet and Type of Firearm from Bullet Hole

Having studied the likely shape and size of bullet holes caused by a variety of illegally made, unusual firearms, it has to be seen whether an assessment of the type of the bullet, caliber of the bullet, and the type of the firearm can be made from bullet hole.

5.4.1 Caliber from Bullet Hole

It is usually not possible to determine the caliber and bullet diameter from a circular, oval, or an irregular, atypical, elongated hole. An approximate estimate of diameter of the bullet from a circular hole is sometimes possible if the target is fairly nonelastic, like wood.

An assessment of the caliber of the bullet is possible only from a clearly demarcated keyhole. It is often created by a high CRH pointed bullet fired from unusual firearms having inappropriate constructional features. Its diameter and cross-sectional dimension can conveniently be determined especially on the victim's clothing (Figure 5.13).

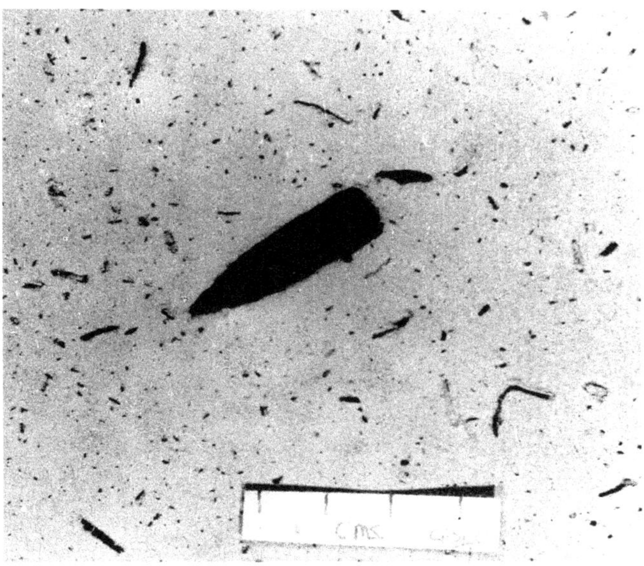

Figure 5.13 Clearly demarcated keyhole of a .303 bullet having high CRH 7.

If the keyhole is not clearly demarcated, then it may not be possible to determine the dimensions of the hole. This is usually observed in low CRH handgun (revolver/pistol) projectiles. However, a rough assessment of the type of the handgun bullet is often possible.

5.4.2 Determining the Type of Firearm from a Bullet Hole

Determination of the type of firearm from a bullet hole is usually a difficult task. In some cases, it may be possible to assess the probable as well as improbable. The shape and size of the bullet hole is helpful in determining the probable/improbable by incorporating presence or absence of powder tattooing and casualty criteria.

5.4.2.1 Type of Firearm from Shape and Size of Bullet Hole and Keyhole

Significantly dense, unburned/partially burnt, widely distributed propellants around a clearly demarcated keyhole suggest that the probable firearm is an oversized bore firearm. It may be either an oversized smoothbore firearm or a mismatched oversized rifled firearm.

It is often possible to eliminate the improbable if an assessment of the caliber of the bullet is made from the bullet hole.

1. Rifled firearms that are not capable of accommodating cartridges loaded with such a bullet can safely be eliminated as improbable. So, illegally made, smoothbore unusual firearms that cannot load and fire such a cartridge also can be eliminated as improbable.
2. In the absence of burnt/unburned propellant particles, it is not possible to eliminate regular rifled firearms using appropriate ammunition because a keyhole formation is also possible by a rifled firearm. A keyhole is possible from a ricocheted bullet. Also, a bullet in its last phase of its trajectory may create keyholes. Since a bullet fired from a regular rifled firearm usually traverses more than 1,000 meters or so, such an unusually far distance can easily be eliminated in the majority of criminal cases as improbable on the basis of circumstantial and eyewitness evidence. The distinguishing close-range phenomenon of widely distributed, unburned/partially burnt propellant particles, coupled with insufficient wounding effect suggests involvement of a nonstandard, oversized, smoothbore firearm as highly probable (Figure 5.14).

5.4.2.2 Type of Firearm from Curved Keyhole

Curved keyholes are formed by bent bullets. The caliber of the bullet can be determined from clearly demarcated curved keyholes. The phenomenon of

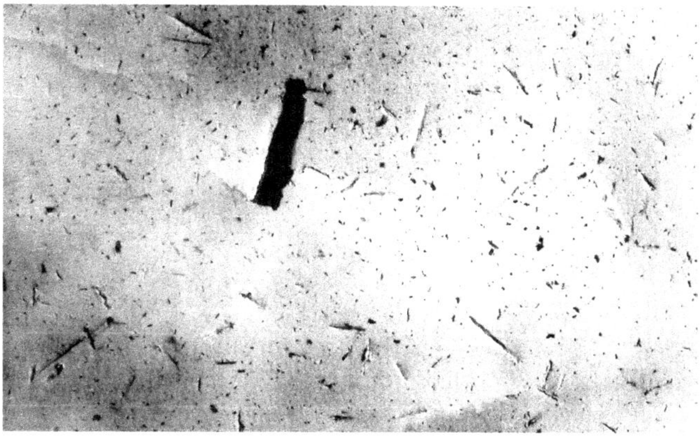

Figure 5.14 Keyhole from a .315 bullet. Caliber of smoothbore, unusual firearm is obviously the caliber of the bullet.

bending of the bullet has been dealt with in Chapter 3. It has been seen that it is usually expected from a slightly oversized barrel having an excessively misaligned chamber or by a ricocheting bullet.

- The possibility of involvement of a slightly oversized, rifled firearm is highly improbable because angular impact of the bullet, if any, is more likely to engage rifling, though loosely, rather than bending of the bullet.
- A curved keyhole surrounded by powder particles eliminates the possibility of having it caused by a ricocheted bullet. Slightly oversized, smoothbore firearms having excessive misaligned chambers can only be considered as highly probable firearms in such cases.

5.4.2.3 *Type of Firearm from Circular and Oval Holes*

It is usually not possible to ascertain the type of firearm from circular or oval holes. However, it is possible to eliminate the improbable in some cases. One of the determining factors is distribution of unburned/partially burnt powder particles around the bullet hole at close range.

- The burning of propellant is significantly incomplete in tapered barrels having an undersized bore near the muzzle. This results in widely distributed, unburned/slightly burnt, propellant particles (especially tubular and solid chord propellants) around the bullet hole. Smoothbore, tapered barrels, having an undersized bore near the muzzle end, sometimes create circular or oval holes like usual branded rifled firearms. Thus, widely distributed, unburned/partially burnt, powder particles around circular or oval holes do not rule out the possibility of a smoothbore or a mismatch rifled firearm.

- Absence of close-range phenomena around the circular hole coupled with significant wounding effect is usually expected from a regular rifled firearm. The probability of involvement of an illegally made, smoothbore or a mismatch rifled firearm is remote, though cannot be ruled out.

5.5 Entry Wound and Direction of Fire

An entry wound is an important part of firearm injury. It is the point of entry into the body. A combined reading of the above deliberations characterizes the entry wound. The characteristics of an entry hole are inverted margins, presence of abraded and/or dirt color, presence of close-range phenomena, etc. In fact, the entry wound itself provides a wealth of information that is helpful in evaluating varied problems of medico-legal importance and in reconstructing the shooting incident. In the majority of cases, the attending autopsy surgeon is unaware of the firearm used in the crime, whether recovered by then or not, as well as whether the involved firearm is illegally made or regular branded. Needless to say, the use of unusual firearms cannot be ruled out in any crime. Therefore, possible variations that are expected by the use of illegally made, unusual firearms must be borne in mind or else the observations may lead to an erroneous conclusion. The salient features of entry wounds that need special attention are reviewed and summarized for the benefit of the readers, and for exercising caution wherever necessary.

1. Inverted margins indicate an entry wound. The misconception that the entrance hole is smaller than the penetrating bullet diameter is no longer valid. The entry wound may be small or large, regular or irregular, depending on the composition (elasticity and density) of the underling tissues. Sometimes, the abraded collar is mistakenly included making the entry wound larger. It must be carefully demarcated while measuring the entry hole dimension.
2. One may observe an elongated narrow zone of abraded collar, if the bullet strikes at an angle. The abrasion is wider on the sides from where the sliding bullet strikes the body. The direction of the abrasion, from wider to narrower side, determines the direction of the entry of the bullet. It also signifies the probable direction of the wound track. The abraded and dirt collar is usually present irrespective of the firing distance. The presence of an abraded and dirt collar provides a positive proof of entry wound.
3. Ordinarily, a circular wound of entrance suggests a right angle fire and an elliptical angular fire. On the contrary, illegally made firearms, designed to fire pistol, revolver, and rifle cartridges, usually

create oval holes and keyholes, irrespective of the bore, whether rifled or smoothbore. Therefore, whereas a circular hole indicates a right angle of fire, an oval hole may not necessarily signify it to be an angular firing. A caution is needed while forming an opinion on the direction of the firing distance from an oval entry hole.

4. It is not possible to assess the direction of fire from a keyhole wound of entrance caused by illegally made, substandard rifled or smoothbore firearms, using rifled ammunition. The keyhole formation from the same distance and angle are so varying (see Figure 5.6) that it becomes difficult to assess the probable direction of track from the direction of the bullet tip. The keyhole may be upside down from the same distance and, hence, needs caution while coming to a conclusion on the issue.
5. Ordinarily, the entry hole does not provide adequate data for determining the caliber of the bullet. It is usually possible from a keyhole wound of entry. The majority of illegally made, unusual firearms form keyhole entry wounds irrespective of the firing distance. The cross-sectional dimension of the keyhole is usually possible to measure. This determines the probable caliber. In such cases, it is essential to take a scaled photograph of the keyhole, if it is the only one on the body.
6. Presence of blackening, powder tattooing, hair singeing, etc., is positive proof of an entry wound. It also suggests a firing distance of close range. The presence of the close-range phenomenon is helpful in corroborating or eliminating suicide, struggle, homicide, and in reconstructing the shooting incident. The area and density of unburned and partially burnt powder particles is often helpful in suggesting possible use of illegally made firearms. In such cases, merely mentioning the presence of powder tattooing may not be sufficient. Preferably, they should be photographed. The possible ambiguity must be taken care of while noting blackening. The details of the close-range phenomenon must be noted with due care and caution.
7. The presence of a muzzle imprint is a positive proof of the gunshot wound of entry. It indicates a contact shot firing, very common in suicide. The wound track, in such cases, must be probed for firearm discharge to substantiate a firm muzzle–body contact during firing. Presence of a scorching effect, blackening, powder particles, and other close-range phenomena in the wound track is inevitable in such cases and, thus, must be recorded. Sometimes, the nature of a muzzle imprint may indicate possible use of illegally made firearms. Presence of conspicuous cut marks, due to the sharp edge of the muzzle/slide, indicates a poorly finished, illegally made pistol. It should be photographed and noted (Figure 5.15).

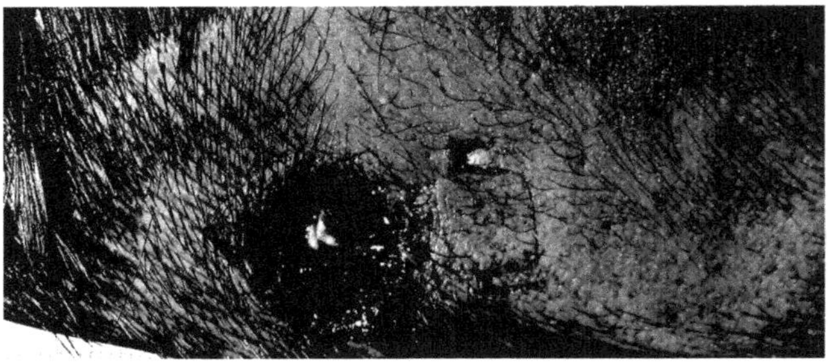

Figure 5.15 Sharp muzzle cut imprints of contact fire by 7.65 mm country-made pistol.

8. If there is more than one gunshot wound hole, it is obligatory to ascertain whether they are entry holes, and, if so, the number of firings. Ordinarily, the number of entry holes corresponds to the number of firings. But, it may not always be true, especially if they are tandem bullets or fragmented bullets. These phenomena must be understood clearly with special reference to unusual firearms.
   a. Tandem bullets: The phenomenon of tandem bullets is observed when a bullet lodged inside the bore is kicked by another bullet fired subsequently. The two together move in tandem inside the bore. They are projected out of the muzzle as a single projectile and move in tandem in the air for a short while. The bullets in tandem, being unstable projectiles, separate after a short distance in the air. The higher the emergent velocity, the farther is the distance at which separation takes place. They make a single hole of entry until they are separated, and make separate entry holes after they are detached. The separated bullets may hit the same or different targets depending on the extent of separation and distance between the two targets. The separated bullets exhibit different direction of fire. In the absence of a firearm, it may appear as the two fired at varying angles. It may be misleading and needs caution while deciding on the angle of fire.

      A lodged bullet is not uncommon in unusual firearms. It is usually due to inappropriate constructional features of the firearm and an improper firearm–cartridge combination. For an easy understanding of the text, the process of propulsion of a projectile is briefly reviewed again.

      The burning of propellant is never complete in unusual firearms due to inappropriate constructional features. This results in the development of low pressure compared to counterpart regular firearms using similar ammunition. If the developed pressure is very low, it may only be sufficient to unseat the bullet, but may not be sufficient to propel the bullet out of the muzzle. Such a bullet is lodged inside the barrel. Incomplete burning is usually expected from firing of a homemade or an old cartridge.

A bullet also may get stuck when fired from illegally made, cheap pistols using inappropriate ammunition. This usually happens if it passes through an abnormally undersized rifled firearm. The bullet elongates while passing through the undersized rifled bore. If it is a lead bullet, being soft and malleable, elongation may not be difficult despite rifling. The elongated lead bullet is usually propelled out of the barrel. On the other hand, if it is a metal jacketed bullet, it may not elongate to the extent to fit into the undersized rifled bore and may get stuck. The bullet is lodged inside the bore, and may be forced to propel out of the muzzle by subsequent firing of a cartridge loaded with an unjacketed lead bullet. In such a case, the two different types of bullets move in tandem. They are likely to be separated quickly due to low emergent velocity. Both the bullets may strike the victim's body if fired from a short distance, making single or two-parted bullet holes. A caution is needed while observing the injuries or deposing on the issue. The possible use of an illegally made, unusual firearm cannot be ruled out.

b. Fragmentation of bullet and multiple holes: A bullet may make multiple holes if it fragments before hitting the target. One may encounter such a phenomenon if the bullet passes through a crudely finished barrel of unusual firearms. The fragments often occur near the cannellure. The fragmented piece may make separate holes (Figure 5.16(a)(b).

9. Contact gunshot wounds are larger than the bullet's diameter. Presence of blackening, powder tattooing, and other close-range phenomena around the wound are invariably absent. A tight barrel–body contact may not always be possible in the case of unusual firearms. The muzzle end may not be uniformly finished in crudely manufactured, unusual firearms. This results in partial gaseous escape from the loose end. The presence of close range effect on a part of skin surrounding the contact wound is expected in such cases.
10. Presence of wad inside the wound or its impact on the body indicates an entry wound. Dispersion of pellets from unusual firearms is wider compared to standard shotguns. Only a part of the dispersed pellets may be available on the body. In such cases, ascertaining the range may be difficult (Figure 5.17).

(a)

(b)

Figure 5.16 (a) Bullet piece separated near cannellure of .38 homemade pistol; (b) separate bullet piece hole on the target.

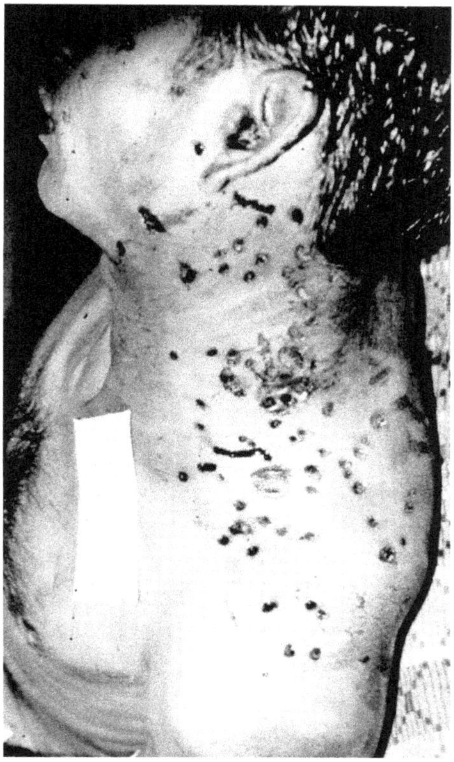

Figure 5.17 Incomplete pellet dispersion.

5.6 Projectile–Tissue Interactions and the Wound Track

The nature of tissue and organ disruption is the most important part of medico-legal examination in shooting incidents. The wound track determines the course of the projectile. This leads to the recovery of the lodged projectile. It identifies the entry–exit wound track in the body and signifies the probable direction of fire. It also aids in assessing the relative assailant–victim position whether at the same, higher, or lower level, etc. The presence of firearm discharge inside the wound track indicates a contact shot. The presence of wads indicates a close-range shotgun fire. It suggests types of firearm, and so on. The mechanics of firearm injuries and the procedure adopted for the medico-legal examination of firearm injuries are well known and are available in text books on the subject, related journals, magazines, and web sites. This forms part of teaching in medical science courses, particularly the specialized field of forensic medicine.

The subject of wound ballistics, though not a new field, lacks adequate data on wound profiles of unusual firearms. Literature on the subject is meager. It is usually a difficult task to make a reasonable assessment of wounding effectiveness of bullets that are fired from illegally made, nonstandard firearms. For assessing the wounding effect of unusual firearms, the tissue–projectile interaction and mechanics of wounding by fired bullets is briefly summarized.

When a projectile enters a body, it crushes the tissues in its path of travel and impels the surrounding tissues. The penetrating projectile creates a cavity of crushed tissues. This cavity signifies the projectile track, and is known as a *permanent cavity*.

The impelled tissues that hurl away from the passage of the projectile compress the surrounding tissues radially. This radial energy, transferred from the bullet, temporarily creates a cavity that surrounds the crushed hole of the penetrating projectile. It finally collapses with the wound track. This cavity lasts only for a few milliseconds and, thus, is called a *temporary cavity*, and is larger than the diameter of the penetrating projectile. It may be many times larger than the projectile diameter. It depends on the transferred energy displacing the surrounding tissues, the elasticity, and cohesiveness of the impelled tissues. The majority of the tissues are elastic, such as lung, bowel wall, skeletal muscle, etc. The severity of the wound depends on the tissue crush due to the penetrating projectile, the stretch, and disruption of the stretching tissues throughout its track. There is very little radial stretch in cases of subsonic velocity projectiles. Therefore, injuries caused by subsonic velocity projectiles are cleaner, especially if it is a very low subsonic velocity creating very little or no radial expansion. Wound profiles of a variety of high and low velocity projectiles on simulated gelatin block targets have been studied and analyzed. Wound profiles and casualty criteria of unusual firearms that need more explanation are detailed in Section 5.8.

5.7 Exit Holes and Unusual Firearms

Exit holes are characterized by everted margins and absence of close-range phenomena. The misconception also prevails that an exit hole is always larger than the corresponding entry hole. It is not always true. An exit hole may be larger or smaller compared to an entry hole. There also may be a mere split of the skin.

1. Exit holes depend on the positioning of the exiting bullet. It may create a circular or irregular hole depending on whether the nose of the exiting bullet is pointing onward or is placed broad side on. A spin-stabilized bullet may emerge out sideways creating a large wound of exit if it tumbles inside the body.

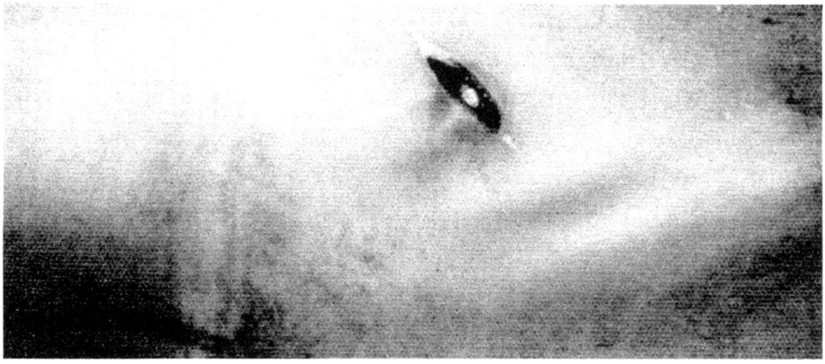

Figure 5.18 Protruding exiting bullet.

2. Exit holes depend on elasticity and density of the tissue they encounters while exiting. If the bullet is stopped inside the body just before exiting, it may split the soft tissue. The front portion of the exiting bullet may protrude through the split (Figure 5.18).
3. The penetrating, tumbling bullet, if experiencing yaw, may change the direction and striking frontal area of the moving bullet. It may move nose pointing onward and create a circular exit hole. While experimenting with .32 smoothbore, improvised revolvers on a gelatin block, Jauhari et al. observed that most of the bullets created circular exit holes, which formed elongated entry holes.

   Thus, bullets fired from unusual firearms creating an irregular, large entry hole may create a circular hole on exiting the body, if it yaws inside the body.
4. A bullet may fragment during its travel inside the body. The fragmented bullets may create separate exit holes.
5. A bullet may strike bone and break into pieces. The bone splinters act as secondary missiles and create multiple exit holes.
6. Tandem bullets separating inside the body create separate exit holes. The exit holes may be large or small depending on whether exiting sideways or nose pointing onward.
7. Soft-nose and hollow-point, expanding bullets mushroom inside the body. They create large exit wounds, if not fragmented. Fragmented bullets may create separate exit holes.
8. There may be multiple exit holes corresponding to dispersed buckshot entry holes. The dispersion of pellets inside the body also may create multiple exit holes without communicating entry holes. Thus, it will be erroneous to assess the range from dispersion of pellets inside the body creating multiple exit holes.
9. Self-inflected pellet injuries create deceptive margins. The margins of self-created holes are everted, signifying it to be an exit hole. In an attempt to plead self-defense, the accused created a skin-deep, small

hole with a thick needle. An unfired pellet of .177 inch was forcibly inserted in the hole by ramming. On taking out the ram rod, the margins of the hole got everted. Thus, planting of small pellet in a self-made hole would give rise to everted edges instead of inverted edges of an entry hole. The recovery of the pellet from inside the hole coupled with everted margins establishes that the injury is self-inflicted, and is not a fired pellet injury due to a distant shotgun fire.

5.8 Wounding Effect of Fired Bullets of Unusual Firearms

One of the important issues an expert is often confronted with is in forming an opinion on the wounding capability of a fired bullet at various ranges. This calls for identifying casualty criteria. Casualty criteria have been proposed in a varied manner by wound ballistics researchers and field autopsy surgeons. Based on exhaustive experiments with a variety of firearm–ammunition combinations, prevailing myths and misconceptions have been highlighted. They provide necessary data to assess the wounding effectiveness of a projectile fired from a regular rifled or smoothbore firearm using appropriate ammunition.

The assessment of wounding effectiveness becomes problematic if it is a nonspinning projectile fired from an illegally made, nonstandard, unusual firearm. It is obviously because of a wide variation in constructional features, designs, and performance of the same caliber unusual firearms using similar ammunition. The ballistics of unusual firearms varies not only with same caliber firearm–ammunition combinations, but also from round-to-round in the same firearm using similar ammunition. Consequently, the wound profiles may vary considerably from one round to the other in the same firearm. In view of this, experimental data relating to casualty criteria of unusual firearms are lacking. In the absence of adequate experimental data, opinion on wounding effectiveness is either noncommittal or a mere guess, which may, at times, be wrong and misleading. A caution is needed while deposing on the issue during cross examination. Admittedly, the opinion must have scientific bases.

For an objective assessment of causation of casualty by unusual firearms, the only recourse is to identify the minimal basic experimental data that are essential and are available or easily obtainable. This coupled with theoretical considerations and plausible reasoning may prove helpful in identifying casualty criteria of nonspinning projectiles.

The factors that influence the severity of a wound include the wounding potential of the striking bullet and the tissues it encounters inside the body. The bullet acquires wounding potential by virtue of its mass, striking velocity, shape and size, orientation at impact, and its disruptive capability of damage to the tissue that comes in its way inside the body. Therefore, to assess the casualty criteria of nonspinning bullets fired from unusual firearms, evaluation of following issues is needed.

1. Determination of striking velocity of nonspinning bullet at impact
2. Area of presentation/orientation of striking nonspinning bullet at impact
3. Wounding capability of nonspinning bullet causing tissue destruction

5.8.1 Determination of Striking Velocity

Striking velocity is the remaining velocity of the projectile at impact. The muzzle velocity of a projectile and its ability to overcome air resistance determine the remaining velocity at various ranges. The index that denotes the ability of a spinning bullet to overcome air resistance is known as ballistic coefficient (BC). After determining the muzzle velocity and BC of a bullet, the remaining velocity of the bullet is calculated by adopting appropriate equation of motion. The striking velocity of a bullet at various ranges, therefore, can be ascertained by knowing the muzzle velocity and ballistic coefficient.

5.8.1.1 Muzzle Velocity

Muzzle velocities of bullets fired from rifled firearms are subsonic and supersonic depending on the type of firearm and cartridge used. Military and sporting rifles are high-velocity firearms. Handguns are low-velocity firearms, mostly subsonic and low subsonic. The muzzle velocity of the firearm–cartridge combination is determined experimentally. Various workers in the field have measured muzzle velocities of a variety of regular-branded, rifled firearms. They are documented in books, ballistic tables, web pages, and commercially available software. However, the available data are inapplicable in cases involving illegally made, substandard firearms meant to fire revolver, pistol, and rifle cartridges. For an objective assessment of the wounding effectiveness of bullets fired from such a firearm, muzzle velocity must be known. It has to be determined experimentally. Nag et al. experimentally measured muzzle velocities of a variety of representative country-made, smoothbore firearms chambered for pistol, revolver, and rifle cartridges usually encountered in crimes in India. The firearms chosen for the study were .22, .32, .38, 9 mm, and .303 caliber. The same caliber firearms varied in their constructional features, such as barrel length, bore diameter, chamber diameter, etc. The muzzle velocities of 30 country-made firearms were determined experimentally by electronic chronograph. The observed muzzle velocities were far less compared to their counterpart regular rifled firearms using similar ammunition. They were low subsonic velocities, usually less than 500 feet per second irrespective of the caliber of the firearm and the type of ammunition used, whether high- or low-velocity cartridges. The observed muzzle velocities of 10 different country-made .303 pistols and guns were found to be 124, 259, 122, 132, 284, 259, 277, 181, 308, and 499 feet per second. These muzzle velocities are comparatively far less than 2,400 feet per second, usually achieved by .303 service rifles firing similar ammunition.

Jauhari et al., while studying wound ballistics of an improvised smoothbore .38 revolver, also observed that muzzle velocities of the .38 improvised revolver were of low subsonic velocity. The observed muzzle velocities of 10 .38 K.F. cartridges, when fired from the .38 improvised revolver, were found to be 253, 267, 238, 208, 327, 312, 274, 310, 323, and 253 feet per second.

The author, while experimenting with a variety of smoothbore unusual firearms, has also observed the muzzle velocities to be subsonic, generally, low subsonic.

These experimental observations reveal that illegally made, smoothbore pistols, guns, and revolvers develop subsonic velocity irrespective of the firearm and rifled ammunition combination. Based on these experiments, a rational assumption can safely be made that illegally made, smoothbore homemade, converted, and improvised firearms are low-velocity firearms irrespective of the rifled ammunition used, whether meant to develop high velocity or not. This clearly signifies that wounding effectiveness of illegally made, smoothbore firearms is expected to be similar to low-velocity revolvers and pistols (handguns). This eliminates casualty criteria that are characteristic of high-velocity projectiles.

5.8.1.2 Ballistic Coefficient

The ballistic coefficient (BC) is an index of the ability of a spinning bullet to overcome air resistance. It can be determined mathematically by the expression $BC = W/nd^2$ where W, n, and d, are weight, diameter, and coefficient of shape, respectively. This expression is not applicable to illegally made, unrifled firearms, obviously because there is no provision of rifling in unusual firearms resulting in nonspinning fired bullets.

Cylindro-conical bullets fired from smoothbore unusual firearms, being nonspinning, are unstable projectiles. The unstable bullet tumbles and continuously changes its frontal area. This results in varying ballistic coefficients throughout its flight in air. The continuously changing ballistic coefficient of a bullet is difficult to determine experimentally. Therefore, instead of using standard values based on form factor and sectional density, an average ballistic coefficient for the entire flight for each bullet has to be determined.

An average ballistic coefficient of a tumbling bullet can be estimated by using the Cummings approximation. It states that ballistic coefficient of a

Table 5.1 Average Ballistic Coefficient of Nonspinning Bullets of Unusual Firearms

Ammunition	Ballistic Coefficient
.303 K.F Bde NK.7	0.03490
.38 Ball mark 12	0.03440
.315 KF Soft Nose	0.04330
.32 KYNOCH Auto	0.02999
.45 KF Revolver	0.038820
7.62 mm KF	0.02285
.32 KF LR	0.03376

tumbling bullet is approximately equal to a sphere of same weight and surface area after neglecting the spin factor. The ballistic coefficient of a sphere can be determined easily by using the mathematical expression $C = W/2.3d^2$, where W denotes the weight in pounds and d the diameter in inches. The weight of the equivalent sphere is that of the bullet. Therefore, it is only the diameter of the equivalent sphere that has to be determined to ascertain the average ballistic coefficient of a tumbling bullet.

Because bullets fired from smoothbore, unusual firearms do not impart spin, the Cummings approximation for determining the average ballistic coefficient of bullets can be used with advantage. The surface area and weight of bullets are determined. The sphere of equivalent surface area and weight determines the required diameter. Knowing the weight of the sphere and its diameter, the average ballistic coefficient of nonspinning bullets can be calculated. The average ballistic coefficients of commonly used bullets of .32, .38, 9 mm, 7.62 mm, 8 mm, and .303 caliber have been calculated. They are detailed in Table 5.1.

As expected, they are far less compared to their values, based on form factor and sectional density that are documented and available in ballistic tables.

5.8.1.3 *Remaining Velocity*

Having known ballistic coefficient and muzzle velocities of tumbling bullets, the remaining velocity at any desired distance can be determined by adopting appropriate equation of motion. The McShane et al. equation of motion of trajectory of a projectile fired horizontally at subsonic velocity is applicable. Since illegally made firearms achieve subsonic velocity, the solution based on the normal equation of motion of McShane et al. is valid and can be conveniently adopted.

Using these equations, remaining velocity, time, angle of attack, and drop below line of fire can be calculated for a given initial velocity at any distance.

$$t = \frac{C}{AV_0}\left(e^{\frac{AX}{C}} - 1\right) \tag{5.1}$$

$$V_R = \frac{CV_0}{C + AV_0 t} \tag{5.2}$$

$$\tan\theta = -gt\left[\frac{1}{V_0} + \frac{At}{2C}\right] \tag{5.3}$$

$$D = -1/2\,gt^2\left[1/2 + \left\{\frac{V_0}{V_R} - 1\right\}^{-1} - \left\{\frac{V_0}{V_R} - 1\right\}^{-2} l_n\left(\frac{V_0}{V_R}\right)\right] \tag{5.4}$$

5.8.2 Orientation/Area of Presentation of Nonspinning Bullets at Impact

Nonspinning bullets are unstable projectiles. They tumble during their entire flight in air, and continuously change their front area. Therefore, they usually strike sideways or at an angle making elongated holes. It is seldom that they fly in the direction of fire and strike nose onward. The experimental observations, discussed above (section 5.1), also reflect that the shape and size of bullet holes are almost always elongated and irregular.

Similar observations were made by Jauhari et al. while studying wound ballistics of an improvised .38 smoothbore revolver by firing 10 shots into a gelatin block. Out of 10 shots, they observed that 9 entry holes were elongated and their dimensions varied widely.

5.8.3 Wounding Capability of Nonspinning Bullets of Unusual Firearms

Knowing the likely influence of the aforementioned variables, it is possible to evaluate which weighs most in assessing the casualty criteria of unusual firearms.

The above experimental observations and theoretical considerations reveal the following:

- Unusual firearms develop subsonic velocities irrespective of the type of ammunition used. Their velocities are usually low subsonic. Therefore, their wound profiles are likely to be similar to those of low-powered handguns having little or no lateral expansion of the wound track. With the low subsonic velocity of less than 300 to 400 feet per second, usually achieved in unusual firearms, no lateral expansion is expected. As such, there is no stretching of tissues surrounding the wound track. Therefore, neither is temporary cavity formed nor is any energy lost on this count. It is apparent that the penetrating projectile, in such cases, solely utilizes its available kinetic energy to crush the tissues that come in the way.

- The other important parameter that influences the wounding capability is the constructional features of the projectile, yaw, and its striking orientation. The orientations of striking bullets that are nonspinning almost always make sideways entry into the body. The unstable tumbling bullets make elongated holes, irrespective of the type of ammunition, distance, and direction of fire. Therefore, constructional features and yaw do not play any significant role and may be ignored.
- Associated with high-velocity projectiles, shock wave pressure also is generated. It may compress the surrounding tissues that lay ahead of the moving projectile. As most of the handguns are low-velocity firearms, this factor may not be considered relevant. This is true as well with unusual firearms that are essentially low subsonic velocity firearms irrespective of the type of the ammunition used, whether low- or high-velocity. Therefore, the shock wave factor can safely be ignored in the wounding mechanism of unusual firearms.

A combined reading of the aforesaid review clearly reflects that the only dominant factor for assessing the wounding effect of nonspinning bullets is the striking kinetic energy.

The threshold energy to cause a disabling wound or to cause a human casualty is difficult to estimate. The criterium of 58 foot pounds, used in World War II, though arbitrary, may be taken as the guiding reference in assessing the relative wounding effect of nonspinning bullets. The kinetic energy of tumbling bullets at any distance can be determined by adopting the above-mentioned ballistic coefficient data and the McShane equation of motion. The computed data serves as a ready reckoner for evaluation of the variety of trajectory-related problems of forensic interest, in such cases. A modified ballistic table can easily be computed for possible muzzle velocities and distances for all of those bullets that are usually encountered in cases involving illegally made, smoothbore firearms.

The one computed by the author is for frequently used rifled ammunition in smoothbore unusual firearms. They are .32, 9 mm, .38, and .45 handgun bullets and .303, .315, and 7.62 mm caliber rifle bullets. The subsonic velocities chosen for the study are at intervals of 50 feet per second, from

800 down to 100 feet per second. Thus, in all, for each bullet, 15 different muzzle velocities ranging from 100 to 800 feet per second have been used for calculating the remaining velocities at impact at various ranges. Likewise, 15 possible ranges from 20 to 300 feet having an interval of 20 feet have been considered appropriate for the table. The ballistic table can be used to ascertain the wounding capability of firearm–ammunition combinations at various ranges by experimentally determining the approximate muzzle velocity. In addition to wounding potential at various ranges, the maximum possible range can also be ascertained from the values of a drop in the table. For a fairly approximate estimate, it is assumed that the firearm is kept at a height of about 4 to 5 feet from the ground and is fired almost horizontally. The table reveals that the .303, .38, .315, .45, 7.62 mm, .32, 9 mm, and .45 bullets, having assumed velocity of 400 feet per second, if fired from a distance of 200 feet, would drop 5.02, 5.04, 4.79, 4.90, 5.72, 5, 5.14, 5, and 4.87 feet, respectively, below the line of fire. Thus, for the assumed height of the firearm above the level of the ground, if taken to be between 4 to 5 feet, the maximum range up to which these projectiles can travel is about 200 feet except for the 7.62 mm bullet, which would drop about 6 feet.

Their respective energies have been found to be 32, 32.5, 52.06, 52.23, 18.96, 17.64, 16.71, 12.97, 47.40 foot pounds, respectively. None of the bullets is likely to cause disabling wounds, if the 58 foot pounds criterium is taken.

By using the computed table, the wounding potential at various ranges, effective range, and maximum range can be assessed by ascertaining the average muzzle velocity of the bullet fired from the questioned unusual firearm.

Additional Reading 6

6.1 Firearm Discharge and Time of Firing

The combustion products of firearm discharge are both gaseous and solid compounds. The combustion products are retained inside the cartridge and the barrel during the travel of the projectile until it leaves the barrel. The nature and quantity of discharge residues depends upon the firearm–ammunition combination and on other allied factors. Whereas detection of discharge residues provides evidence of firing, its time-variant, quantitative estimation forms the basis of ascertaining the probable time lapse after firing.

6.1.1 Evidence of Firing and Unusual Firearms

In the absence of fired cartridges and projectiles, sometimes it is necessary to determine whether the questioned firearm had been fired. The presence of discharge residues inside the barrel and fired cartridge provides evidence of firing. Traditional methods of detection of anions of combustion products by barrel wash and cotton swabs are well known. The presence of discharge residues simply signifies that the firearm had been fired sometime before it was seized. It virtually is of no forensic significance. It is commonly believed that legally owned firearms must have been fired at one time or another. It is especially so for legally manufactured firearms because they are subjected to proof firing before leaving the factory to ensuring safety of the end user.

Furthermore, the anions of combustion products, being water soluble, can be removed easily by thorough barrel washing or by repeatedly pushing cotton plugs. Therefore, the absence of combustion products does not lead one to conclude that the firearm was not used for firing. Thus, the opinion that the firearm had been fired before is of no practical utility.

However, it assumes forensic significance in cases involving unusual firearms, especially converted, improvised, and locally made. In the absence of cartridge and projectile, the defense often argues that the seized firearm is a nonfunctional dummy and had never been used for firing. The usual procedure of detecting firearm discharge cannot be employed if the barrel is thoroughly cleaned after firing. Most of the anions of the combustion products of the propellant, being water soluble, are removed by repeated barrel wash. In such a situation, residues other than combustion products are to be utilized for ascertaining whether the firearm had been used for firing. Sinha et al. utilized projectile traces that were left behind due to rubbing against the surface irregularities of the barrel. Projectile traces, being metallic, are retained inside the barrel, despite thorough cleaning. Metal vapors also contribute to the available metallic residues in the barrel. However, formation of metal vapor is usually inadequate or nonexistent in most of the illegally made, substandard, short-barreled contraptions because of comparatively very low temperature and pressure. Experiments with cleaned barrels revealed traces of lead and copper from firing of unjacketed and jacketed bullets. Their presence can be detected by adopting the usual chemical tests. A cotton plug moistened with a few drops of 25% acetic acid is pushed through the barrel. Then the acid cotton swabs are chemically tested for the presence of lead and copper.

The then commonly used test for lead includes a few drops of .02% freshly prepared solution of sodium rhodizonate added to the swabs taken from the barrels. The development of a pink color of lead rhodizonate signifies the presence of lead.

Test for copper (cu) includes a few drops of alcoholic solution of rubeanic acid added to the swabs taken from the barrels. A few drops of an ammonia solution are then added to the swabs treated with rubeanic acid. Development of an olive green color in an ammonia medium indicates the presence of copper. Control tests should invariably be carried out by taking acetic acid swabs from the upper portion of the barrel. It is desirable, when confronted with such a situation, to adopt a usual procedure of detection of combustion products before testing for projectile traces.

Jauhari also has reported a case in which the defense contended that guns recovered from a place of worship were dummy guns alleged to be an object of worship and had never been fired. They were regular, old muzzle loading guns. Anions usually detected after firing were found present in their barrels. The findings nullified the defense plea and supported the prosecution contention that the guns had been fired.

Besides firearm, one also may be confronted with such a situation concerned with cartridges alleged to be fired from illegally made firearms. In a shooting incident, a 12-bore empty was recovered from the victim's house. The firearm seized from the suspect was a 12-bore homemade pistol. The empty and the homemade pistol were sent to the laboratory for examination and opinion. Attempts were made to fire test cartridges from the questioned 12-bore homemade pistol for routine examination and comparison of marks. Nearly 20 attempts were made to fire cartridges from the pistol, but to no avail. All attempts resulted in misfires. Thus, test cartridges could not be fired from the questioned homemade pistol despite all efforts. Under the circumstances, the firing pin marks available on missed test cartridges were compared with the firing pin marks of the evidence empty. They were found similar in their individual characteristics. In view of repeated misfires, a careful examination of the questioned pistol was made. It revealed that the main spring actuating the hammer was very weak. This resulted in ineffective protrusion of a firing pin hit on the percussion cap, which caused misfires. The questioned pistol was found to be not in proper working order. Under the circumstances, despite similar firing pin impressions, it was considered necessary to ascertain whether the empty was indeed a fired one. Thus, evidence of firing of the evidence cartridge was the main issue that needed thorough probing in the case. The inside of the evidence cartridge was examined for the presence of discharge residues. On examination, it was found that the inside of the empty did not carry firearm discharge residues. This would not be possible had the cartridge been fired from a firearm. Thus, despite similar firing pin marks, it could be inferred that the evidence empty was not a fired cartridge case. It was found that the misfired evidence cartridge, bearing the firing pin marks of the pistol, was made empty after the removal of the shot charge, wads, and propellants. Based on these findings, it was decided that the evidence empty cartridge bears the firing pin marks of the questioned homemade pistol, but the same has not been fired from the pistol in question. This opinion corroborated missing pellets and wads near the alleged place of shooting—the victim's house.

Therefore, it is apparent that there may be occasions when one is confronted with the evaluation of the basic issue of evidence of firing in cases involving illegally made, unusual firearms, especially homemade and converted firearms.

6.1.2 Time of Firing

An estimate of time lapse since a firearm was last fired provides useful corroborative evidence in reconstructing the shooting incident. In the past, efforts have been made to correlate the time lapse with the chemical changes of the firearm discharge residues. Both qualitative and quantitative variation of the combustion products with the passage of time have been studied by examining barrel washings and dry swabs pushed through the barrel. Such examinations, however, did not yield satisfactory results because, besides the time factor, chemical changes of the discharge residues were found to be significantly influenced by the atmospheric conditions. It also was difficult to extract the total quantity of combustion products by dry or wet methods for correct quantitative estimation. Various other phenomena, such as presence of carbon monoxide, mercury vapor, and pollen grains, have been utilized as well by various personnel to ascertain the time of firing. Their limitations in correlating the time lapse are well known.

The projectile and the discharge ejecta leave the barrel after the volatile discharge starts escaping from both the cartridge and the barrel. The escape of volatile gases decreases with the time lapse. It depends on the quantity of volatile gases occupying the constant volume, the thermal conditions, the combined effect of the partial pressures of various gases, van der Waals forces, the molecular forces acting between the molecules of the various gases produced during firing, and the surrounding atmospheric conditions. The phenomenon of the escaped gases has been observed for a sufficiently long time. Their rate of escape is nearly similar for same firearm–ammunition combination. Therefore, the quantity of escaped gases per unit time can be considered as a potential time variant factor. This forms the basis of estimation of time lapse since a cartridge or a firearm was last fired.

6.1.2.1 *Time of Firing of Firearm*

The rate of escape of discharge gases from the firearm is expected to vary significantly with the number of firings. It depends on the upkeep of the firearm, before and after the commission of crime until its recovery, as well as the atmospheric conditions in between. These variable factors affecting the escape of gases can be minimized if:

- the firearm is recovered in undisturbed condition;
- the time lapse between crime and recovery of weapon is within few hours;
- there is no subsequent firing after the questioned fire;
- the breech is neither cleaned nor opened for unloading or loading of a fresh cartridge; and
- there is no likely extreme variation in temperature and humidity due to storm, heavy rain, snow, etc.

These variables are minimized if the firearm is used in committing suicide. The incident of firing in such cases, very often attracts the notice of the victim's relatives and neighbors. The firing incident is brought to the notice of the enforcement agencies within a very short time, usually within a few hours. The involved firearm, therefore, is expected to be recovered in an undisturbed condition. The number of fired rounds in a suicide is also expected to be only one.

The commonly used firearms for committing suicide are pistols and revolvers. It is either personally belonging to the victim or is made available from friends and relations. It is invariably a licensed firearm and, generally, is kept in cleaned condition. If it is a revolver, the fired cartridge case also is recovered in the chamber at a 12 o'clock position. Therefore, under normal circumstances, one would expect recovery of the revolver in undisturbed condition along with the fired cartridge in the chamber. This also ensures a free escape of volatile gases from the barrel, a prerequisite for correlating rate of escape with the time lapse after firing. The variation in weather condition (temperature, pressure, humidity, etc.) also is likely to be insignificant during the short time interval between the firing incident and the recovery of the firearm. In view of the above, the aforementioned variables are evidently minimized in suicide cases. Hence, estimation of quantity of escaped gases per unit time may prove helpful in assessing the probable time of firing, thereby corroborating or eliminating the suspected suicide.

The quantity of escaped gases per unit time has been determined indirectly by simple chemical spot tests. The volatile gases emanating from the discharge of a smokeless propellant contain nitro compounds. It can be detected by diazotization and coupling reaction. The then commonly used reagents α-naphthylamine and sulfanilic acid in acetic acid have been used for diazotization and coupling reaction. The reagent develops a pink color showing nitrite ions of the volatile gases that are emerging from the barrel. The rate of escape of gases per unit time can be determined by ascertaining the time taken to develop color with the escaping gases. The rate of gaseous escape is correlated with the time lapse after firing.

To study the practical viability, the author conducted experiments with regular branded revolvers as well as illegally manufactured revolvers. Experimental details and findings are briefly described for assessing the utility of the test in actual cases and its limitations.

One of the illegally manufactured revolvers chosen for the study was oversized, having a high cartridge head space, and the other was undersized. The barrel lengths of both the improvised revolvers were 4 inches and their muzzle diameters were .34 and .27 inches respectively. Among the branded revolvers, two were Smith and Wesson having a 3-inch barrel length. The other was a 4-inch barrel, German make revolver. The cartridges chosen for experimental firing were from an Indian ordnance factory, .32 K.F. S&W L.R. cartridges.

The fired empty, after firing from each revolver, was allowed to remain inside the cylinder for uninterrupted escape of volatile gases. Time, date of firing, room temperature, and weather conditions (sunny, cloudy, or rainy) were noted in respect to each revolver. The escaping gases were subjected to chemical tests for detection of nitrite ion after regular intervals: 6 hours after firing and every 24 hours thereafter up to 10 days. The then commonly used reagent solutions were prepared fresh at each interval.

1. 0.03 g of α-naphthylamine is boiled for a few minutes in 100 cm^3 of water and mixed with 30 cm^3 of glacial acetic acid.
2. 1 gm of sulfanilic acid is dissolved by warming in 100 cm^3 of 30% acetic acid.

The procedure adopted for chemical test was as under:

> Each revolver was placed on a suitable stand such that the muzzle of the barrel pointed upwards. A small piece of plastic of suitable size having a small hole at the center was placed over the muzzle. A small piece of filter paper was placed over the hole such that it did not touch any part of the muzzle. A drop of the mixed reagent solution (1) and (2) was placed over the part of the filter paper that covered the hole. The escaping gases on reaction with the mixed reagent solution developed a pink color on the filter paper. For uniformity and proper assessment instead of a color chart, the time interval between the dropped mixed reagent solution and the appearance of pink color was noted. This is referred as time taken to develop color, hereafter. The room temperature and the general weather conditions (cloudy, sunny, or rainy) also were noted. These observations are detailed in Table 6.1.

The significant revelations are summarized as under:

1. Time taken to develop color tends to increase with the time lapse after firing, but the increase is not uniformly related to time interval. There are overlapping observations as well.
2. Illegally made, undersized revolvers behaved very similar to regular branded revolvers.
3. Illegally made, oversized revolvers having high cartridge space behaved differently. The time to develop color regularly increases with the time interval without overlapping.
4. After a lapse of up to six hours of firing, the time taken to develop color is well within one minute, irrespective of the type of revolver whether legally or illegally made.
5. After 10 days of firing, the time taken to develop color for illegally made and regular revolvers is more than seven minutes and three to four minutes, respectively.
6. Linear relationship cannot be established for all possible time intervals. It, therefore, may be essential to have a suitable choice of interval for possible correlations with time of firing under interpretable limits.

Control tests were performed with all the revolvers after thoroughly cleaning the barrels. They were subjected to chemical tests with the mixed reagent solutions by adopting the above procedure. After about 40 to 50 minutes, pink color developed in all the cases due to auto oxidation.

These observations provide valuable clues for elimination or corroboration of firing within a short interval of a few hours or so. Different criteria are

Table 6.1 Time Taken to Develop Color in Minutes and Seconds and Weather Condition at Each Interval

Time Lapse after Firing (hours/days)	A S&W Revolver B.L.—3 sec.	B German Revolver B.L.—4 sec.	C S&W Revolver B.L.—3 sec.	D Improvised Revolver B.L.—4 sec. MD—.34 sec.	E Improvised Revolver B.L.—.4 sec. MD—27 sec.	Temperature & Weather (sunny, cloudy, or rainy)
6 hours	53 sec.	50 sec.	43 sec.	47 sec.	52 sec.	62°F sunny & fair
1 day	1 min/39 sec	1 min/15 sec	1 min/8 sec	1 min/20 sec	1 min/20 sec	60°F sunny
2 days	2 min/12 sec	2 min/19 sec	2 min/30 sec	2 min/5 sec	1 min/37 sec	60°F sunny
3 days	2 min/25 sec	1 min/44 sec	1 min/46 sec	2 min/40 sec	1 min/55 sec	60°F sunny
4 days	2 min/25 sec	1 min/37 sec	2 min/15 sec	3 min/13 sec	2 min/30 sec	60°F sunny
5 days	2 min/31 sec	1 min/29 sec	1 min/57 sec	3 min/56 sec	3 min/24 sec	60°F sunny
6 days	2 min/38 sec	1 min/39 sec	2 min/14 sec	3 min/53 sec	2 min/17 sec	60°F sunny
7 days	2 min/37 sec	2 min/19 sec	2 min/40 sec	4 min/13 sec	2 min/22 sec	60°F sunny
8 days	2 min/58 sec	3 min/23 sec	2 min/57 sec	5 min/5 sec	3 min/56 sec	61°F sunny
9 days	3 min/10 sec	2 min/30 sec	3 min/19 sec	5 min/55 sec	4 min/15 sec	62°F sunny
10 days	3 min/34 sec	3 min/4 sec	4 min/17 sec	7 min/15 sec	3 min/45 sec	63°F sunny

adopted for elimination and corroboration under certain limits. Duration of less than one minute to develop color can be correlated with the time lapse of up to six hours of firing of the revolver, irrespective of the type, whether regular or improvised. On the other hand, the firing of the revolver within a day or so can safely be eliminated if the time taken to develop color exceeds the upper limit of three minutes or so. Due weightage can be given on the findings, if variation of weather conditions between the examination of the revolver and the shooting incident is not very significant and the firearm is recovered in an undisturbed condition, as is expected in suicide cases.

To study the variability of the method, experiments were repeated after two years with the same firearm–ammunition combination, using freshly prepared reagents. It was observed that the time taken to develop color was almost consistent only for a short interval of firing, especially when the temperature and general weather conditions were nearly similar, a necessary condition for evaluating time of firing in suicide cases.

The above procedure may be adopted in actual cases. The seized revolver along with the empty cartridge inside the chamber is subjected to chemical tests by adopting the above procedure. The time taken to develop color by freshly prepared reagent solution is noted. Thereafter, the empty cartridge is removed and the barrel is cleaned. Experimental firing is conducted with the revolver using ammunition of the same make and, if possible, of the same lot and batch. The time taken to develop color, after every six hours of time lapse, is noted. These readings are compared with the time that was noted before experimental firing, for possible correlation. In most of the cases, elimination or corroboration may be possible. They can be interpreted appropriately for elimination or corroboration of suicide cases with reference to temperature and weather conditions under which the experiments are performed. Admittedly, meaningful results are obtainable only for less than a day, both for corroboration or elimination.

If the suicide weapon is an automatic pistol, the empty is ejected and found near the shooting incident. The pistol is recovered along with a live cartridge inside the chamber in the cocked position. If the evidence cartridge is the last round of the magazine, the pistol is recovered without a live cartridge in the chamber. In addition to an empty chamber, the breech may be found opened, if a breech open safety is provided. If it is an illegally made, cheap pistol, the empty may not be ejected and get jammed; not a very uncommon event. If the ammunition is old, the empty may sometimes be jammed as well.

Thus, unlike revolvers, the quantity of gases and the occupied volume may vary even with the same firearm–ammunition combination and, thus, also the rate of gaseous escape per unit time. Therefore, it is desirable that, instead of the automatic pistol, the ejected empty occupying the constant volume of volatile gases should be utilized for determining the time lapse after firing. The rate of gaseous escape in an empty can conveniently be ascertained by adopting the above procedure.

6.1.2.2 Time of Firing of Fired Cartridge

The adsorption of discharge residues inside the fired cartridge depends on the construction material of the cartridge case. The constructional materials are varied. The adsorption in shotgun paper cartridge cases is expected to be comparatively more than brass, plastic, and other construction metals. The quantity and rate of gaseous escape also vary accordingly.

The author, in his published paper on Time of Firing of shot shells, made an exhaustive study of 12-bore fired cartridges to correlate the time lapse with the escaped gases. The cartridges chosen for the study were commonly used, 12-bore 2½-inch (6.35 mm) Indian ordnance factory manufactured, K.F special paper cartridges. The shotgun, used for experimentation was a 12–bore, single barrel breech loading (SBBL) gun. The intervals chosen for the study were after every 6 hours up to 24 hours and, thereafter, after every 24 hours up to 10 days. The barrel of the gun was cleaned after each firing. The time and date of firing were noted on each of them. They were kept apart, about 2 meters from each other. To ensure an effective and free escape of gases, their mouths were kept pointed upward. The escaping gases containing nitro compound, were detected by using aforementioned reagents: α-napthylamine in acetic acid and sulphanilic acid in acetic acid. Freshly prepared reagent solutions were used for development of color by diazotization and coupling reaction.

The fired empties were kept in vertical position, keeping the base downward. A small plastic piece was placed on the mouth of the fired empties. The plastic piece had a small hole at the center. A small piece of filter paper was placed over the plastic piece covering the central hole, but without touching the fired empty. A drop of the freshly prepared mixed reagent solution was placed over the filter paper covering the central hole. The time taken to develop pink color by gases escaping through the hole was noted. This determined the relative rate of gaseous escape at different times. A fresh drop of the same reagent solution was added after approximately every 8 to 10 min, if it dried up. The room temperature and the general condition of weather were noted.

Control tests were performed on unfired cartridges. Their wads and shots were removed. Two types of unfired cartridges were used for control tests. In one, the unburned powder also was removed. The other contained only unburned powder without wads and shots. Control tests were carried out by adopting the above procedure. A faint pink color appeared after 40 to 45 minutes due to auto-oxidation.

These observations revealed the following:

1. The rate of escape of gases is almost similar to firing of a revolver for short intervals of up to six hours. Duration of less than one minute to develop color can be correlated with the time lapse of up to six hours of firing.
2. The quantity of escape of gases is far less compared to a fired revolver. The time duration to develop color after 10 days of firing is 30 to 35 minutes in 12-bore fired cartridges compared to only 3 to 7 minutes.
3. The time duration to develop color tends to increase with the time lapse after firing.

The increase, however, is not uniform. Besides insignificant increase in certain intervals, there are overlapping observations as well. A choice of a suitable time interval may prove helpful to eliminate overlapping. It must be such that the minimum of the interval is distinctly different from the maximum of the preceding interval. In the present case, the suitable time intervals are within 24 hours, 2 to 5 days, and 6 to 10 days. These intervals differentiate a firing of 24 hours with a firing of 2 to 5 days, which, in turn, can be differentiated from a fire of 6 to 10 days. The suitable time intervals may be different with different firearm–ammunition combinations. It may be determined experimentally in each case.

It has been observed on experiments with other shotguns that time duration of up to about 3 minutes to develop color indicates a firing within 24 hours, irrespective of the firearm and the type and make of a 12-bore paper cartridge used, especially when the weather condition is nearly similar. However, it is desirable that the results be verified before arriving at any conclusion.

The applicability of the method also was studied with single-base powder and other types of firearms. It has been found that single-base propellants loaded in 7.62 mm Indian ordnance factory K.F. rifle cartridges also give off nitrite ions on firing. It was possible to correlate the time lapse by studying the rate of gaseous escape when a single-base 7.62 mm cartridge was fired from a 7.62 mm rifle (SLR).

6.2 Unusual Rifling Marks on Jacket Pieces and Lead Core

Bullets fired from high-powered rifled firearms, very often, fragment inside the body or on impact with other objects. The nature and extent of fragmentation depends upon the striking energy, the path traveled, and the target.

During the process, the lead core may be separated from the jacket. It may be a partial or a complete separation. The separated lead core part may be fragmented further. Likewise, the jacket also may be fragmented. The brunt of the impact, in such cases, is on the jacket itself resulting in formation of additional rubbing and impact marks on the available rifling marks on the jacket. Rifling marks may be masked, obliterated, or interfered with and may not be retrievable. Sometimes, even elimination on the basis of class characteristics may not be possible. The opinion in such cases is noncommittal. Essentially, important forensic evidence is lost.

It is apparent that jacket/jacket pieces may be identified only if the rifling marks are retrieved. It needs to be explored in other areas that are likely to carry rifling marks and remain unaffected by the impact. It is the undersurface of the jacket/jacket pieces that are usually not affected. The markings, if any, on the undersurface of the jacket are likely to remain intact. Sinha et al. observed that deeper engravings of rifling marks invariably leave their impressions on the undersurface of the jacket. The portion of the lead core, in contact with the undersurface of the jacket, also is likely to carry an impression of deeper engravings. Significant influence of impact and rubbing on the undersurface of the jacket or on the lead core is unlikely unless they also strike with other objects or the rubbing or impact marks are deeper than rifling marks. Before an attempt is made to examine and compare the retained marking, it must be known whether the impressions are a negative or positive profile of the rifling engravings. It clearly can be evaluated from the engraved rifling surface. Because rifling engravings are on the outer jacket surface, the underjacket surface bears its negative profile. In contradiction, deep rifling engravings imprint their replica on the soft lead core that is the subsequent layer in contact with the jacket. Consequently, the marks, if imprinted on the lead core, are the positive profile of the rifling engravings on the upperjacket surface. Therefore, whereas marks on the underjacket surface involve positive–negative comparison, the lead core involves comparison of rifling marks similar to those on fired bullets.

Because rifling marks on the underjacket surface involve a positive–negative comparison, the right-handed rifling appears as left-handed and vice versa. Similarly, lands appear as grooves and striations are at 180 degrees phase difference (Figure 6.1).

Engravings are often sufficient for the identification of class characteristics (width of rifling, angle and direction of fire, etc.). Sometimes, the marks may be sufficient to permit positive identification in respect of suspect firearms. By adopting a positive–negative comparison of the rifling marks on the test bullets with the markings on the underjacket surface, positive linkage is possible if marks are sufficient.

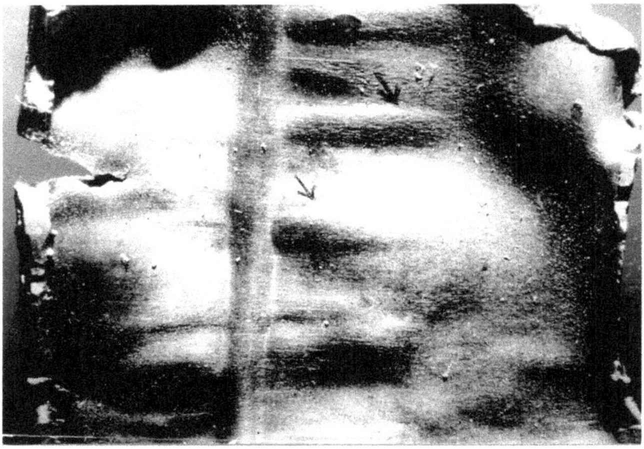

Figure 6.1 Class characteristic rifling marks on undersurface of jacket. The raised portion corresponds to groove of fired bullet.

If the lead core bears rifling marks, they can be examined and compared with the rifling marks on test bullets in the usual way. Individual characteristic striations, if sufficient, on the lead core also can be utilized for linkage with the suspect firearm (Figure 6.2(a)(b)).

In the absence of jacket pieces, presence of even-class characteristic rifling marks on irregular lead pieces provides valuable clues in establishing the involvement of a rifled firearm and also may lead to ascertain probable bullet/firearm caliber.

In a criminal case, a badly mutilated lead core of a fired jacketed bullet was recovered. There were two suspect rifles. One of them was a 7.62 mm SLR and the other was an 8 mm/.315 sporting rifle. The evidence lead core piece had clearly demarcated land and groove impressions. On the basis of width of lands and grooves imprinted on the lead core piece, it was possible to eliminate one of the two rifles. The individual characteristic marks, if sufficient, also can be identified with test-fired bullet (Figure 6.3 and Figure 6.4).

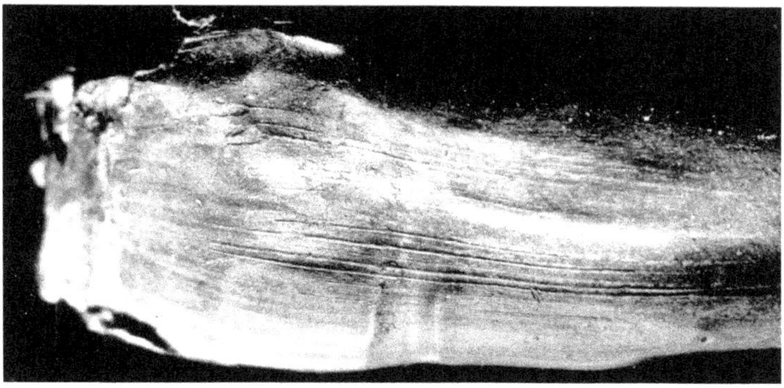

(a)

(b)

Figure 6.2 (a) Individual characteristic rifling marks on lead core; (b) matching of individual characteristic rifling marks on lead core with the corresponding marks on undersurface of jacket.

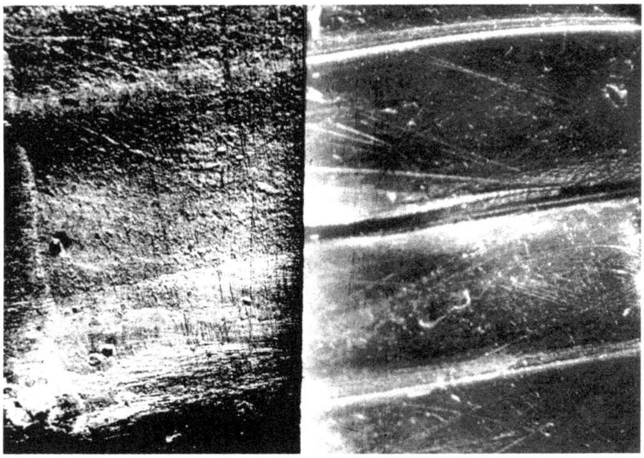

Figure 6.3 Class characteristic marks on lead core with the test bullet.

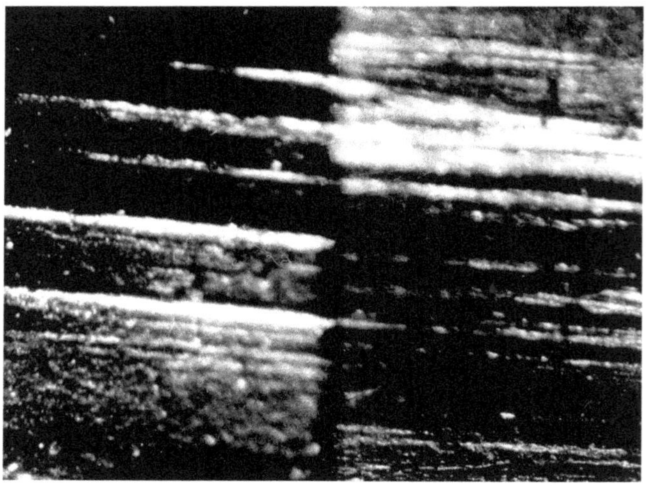

Figure 6.4 Striations matching of the individual characteristic marks on the lead core with the test bullet.

Related References and Readings

Bayer, J. (ed). 1962. *Wound ballistics.* Washington, DC: Office of the Surgeon General, Department of Army.

Burrard, G. 1951. *The identification of firearms and forensic ballistics.* London: Herbert Jenkins.

Burrard, G. 1952, 1955, 1959. *The modern shotgun,* vol. I, II, III. London: Herbert Jenkins.

Chenow, R. 1977. A smooth bore auto pistol. *AFTE Journal* 9(2): 154-156.

Cole, M. D., N. Ross, and J. W. Thorpe. 1992. Gunshot residue and bullet wipe detection using a single lift technique. *AFTE Journal* 24: 254.

Cummings, C. S. 1953. *Everyday ballistics.* New York: Stackpole and Heck.

Di Mio, M. D., and Vincent, J. M. 1985. *Gunshot wounds. Practical aspects of firearms, Ballistics and forensic techniques.* New York: Elsevier.

Fackler, M. L. 1988. Wound ballistics: A review of common misconception. *The Journal of American Medical Association* 259(18): 2730–2736.

Hatcher. J. S., F. J. Jury, and J. Weller. 1957. Firearms investigation identification and evidence. Harrisburg, PA: The Stackpole Company.

Heard, B. J. 2008. *Handbook of firearms and ballistics: Examining and interpreting forensic evidence.* Hoboken, NJ: John Wiley & Sons.

http://www.paranynj.org/Security/Weapons/CellGun.htm

Jauhari, M., and P. Mahanta. 1978. Wound ballistics of an improvised revolver. *Indian Academy of Forensic Science* 17(1): 11–19.

Jauhari, M. 1980. *Identification of firearms, ammunition and firearm injuries.* New Delhi, India: Bureau of Police Research and Development.

Jauhari, M., S. M. Chatterji, and A. Sen. 1983. Trajectory of shotgun wadding *Journal of Forensic Science International* 22: 123–130.

Mathews, J. H. 1962. *Firearms identification,* vol. I. Madison, WI: University of Wisconsin Press; vol. III, Springfield, IL: Charles C Thomas.

Matto, B. N., and A. K. Wani. 1969. Casualty criteria for wounds from firearm with reference to shot penetration. *Journal of Forensic Sciences* 14: 120.

McShane, E. J., J. L. Kelley, and F. V. Reno. 1953. *Exterior ballistics.* Denver, CO: The University of Denver Press.

Modi, J. K., C. Nigam, and K. Kumar. 1984. Improvised firearms versus regular firearms. *Forensic Science International* 26: 199–205.

Nag, N. K., S. Ganguly, and S. Rudra. 1979. The character and characteristic of country made firearms: A study. Paper presented at the Proceedings of the Forensic Science Society Autumn Symposium, Chandigarh, India, pp. 19–26 .

Royse, D. 1995. Identification made on a bullet fired from an unrifled pistol. *AFTE Journal* 27(3): 197–199.

Sinha, J. K. 1967. Distance of firing beyond powder range. *Journal of the Indian Academy of Forensic Sciences* 6(2): 34.

Sinha, J. K. 1975. Chamber marks. *Archives fur Kriminology, Germany* 155(1&2): 39-45.–

Sinha, J. K. 1976. Time of firing shot shells. *Journal of Forensic Sciences* 15: 171–175.

Sinha, J. K. 1981. Wad identification. Paper presented at the scientific meeting of Indian Academy of Forensic Sciences.

Sinha, J. K. 1981. Tampered unserviceable firearm and cartridge identification. Paper presented at the scientific meeting of Indian Academy of Forensic Sciences.

Sinha, J. K. 1983. Scientific techniques for committing crimes. *Indian Police Journal Vigyan (science), Bureau of Police Research and Development* 2(3): 50–53.

Sinha, J. K. 1984. Identification of broken gun. *Indian Police Journal of Vigyan (science), Bureau of Police Research and Development* 10: 20–23.

Sinha, J. K. 1984. Range estimation limits from presence or absence of overshot wads. *Indian Police Journal, Bureau of Police Research and Development* (3): 25.

Sinha, J. K. 1984. Identification of unavailable or destroyed gun. *Indian Police Journal, Bureau of Police Research and Development* 31(4): 49–50.

Sinha, J. K. 1985. Test breech marks by low pressure test rounds. Paper presented at All India Forensic Science Conference, Madras.

Sinha, J. K. 1985. Cartridge identification by chamber marks without test firing. *Journal of International Criminal Police Review*, France, 131–133.

Sinha, J. K. 1985. Test extractor marks under low pressure on shotgun cartridges. *Journal of Forensic Science International* 27: 131–133.

Sinha, J. K. 1986. Identification of projectiles (bullets, pellets and wads) fired through locally made illegal firearms. PhD thesis, Punjabi University, India.

Sinha, J. K. 1989. Forensic significance of projected fired cartridge pieces. Paper presented at the National Seminar on Identification in Forensic Science.

Sinha, J. K. 1989. Bullets appearing like unfired whether fired or not. Paper presented at the 11th International Symposium on Ballistics, Brussels, Belgium.

Sinha, J. K. 1993. Wounding effect of bullets fired from smoothbore homemade/improvised firearms and modified ballistic table. Paper presented at the 13th Meeting of the International Association of Forensic Sciences, Dusseldorf, Germany.

Sinha, J. K. 1994. Unusual improvisation of factory made firearms and likely misleading investigation. *CBI Bulletin* 2(4): 23–24.

Sinha, J. K., and G. J. Misra. 1971. Detection of powder particles at the crime scene. *Journal of Forensic Sciences 16(1): 109–111.*

Sinha, J. K., and G.J. Misra. 1972. Shot size from fired shell. *Indian Police Journal, Bureau of Police Research and Development* 2(1): 20–22 .

Sinha, J. K., and M. L. Kshettry.1972. Pellet identification. *Journal of Criminal Law, Criminology and Police Science* 63(1): 134–136.

Sinha, J. K., and M. L. Kshettry.1972. Unusual chamber marks. *Journal of International Criminal Police Review, Interpol.* 173–174.

Sinha, J. K., and G. J. Misra. 1975. Projectile traces. *Journal of International Criminal Police Review, Interpol* 150–151.

Sinha, J. K., and L.A. Kumar. 1978. Deceptive striations on fired cartridges. *Identification News* XXVIII(10): 3.

Sinha, J. K., and L. A. Kumar. 1981. Unusual variation in breech marks. Paper presented at the scientific meeting of Indian Academy of Forensic Sciences.

Sinha, J. K., and C. N. Bhattacharyya. 1983. Mismatched ammunition. *Journal of Criminology and Criminalistics,* 3.

Sinha, J. K., and C. N. Bhattacharyya. 1985. Time of firing of revolver in suicide cases. Paper presented at all India Forensic Science Conference, Madras.

Sinha, J. K., and C. N. Bhattacharya. 1989. Identification of tandem bullets. *Journal of Medicine, Science and Law* 29(3): 249–250.

Sinha, J. K., V. K. Mehrotra, and L. A. Kumar. 1974. Bullet identification by nonstriated land and groove marks of abnormally undersize barrels. *Forensic Science International* 4(4): 43–45.

Sinha, J. K., V. K. Mehrotra, and L.A. Kumar. 1975. Plantation of fired cartridges. Paper presented at the Indian Forensic Science Conference, Ahmedabad.

Sinha, J. K., V. K. Mehrotra, and L. A. Kumar. 1976. Flight of wads and their forensic significance. *Journal of Indian Academy of Forensic Sciences* 15(2): 46–47.

Sinha, J. K., V. K. Mehrotra, and L. A. Kumar. 1976. Direct breech face comparison. *Journal of Police Science and Administration* 4(3): 261–263.

Sinha, J. K., V. K. Mehrotra, and L. A. Kumar. 1976. Misleading firing pin impressions. *Identification News,* XXVI(4): 16.

Sinha, J. K., V. K. Mehrotra, and L. A. Kumar. 1976. Identification of shooter at the crime scene. *Indian* Police *Journal, Bureau of Police .Research and Development,* 14.

Sinha, J. K., V. K. Mehrotra, and L. A. Kumar. 1977. Unusual rifling marks for identifying lead core and non-identifiable jacket pieces. *Forensic Science International* (9): 139–144 .

Waghmare, N. P., R. Suresh, P. Puri, et al. 2012. Modern trend of country made /improvised pistols used in the capital of India. *Journal of Forensic Research* S1: 003.

Warlow, T. 2011. *Firearms, the law, and forensic ballistics.* Boca Raton, FL: Taylor & Francis.

Whelen, T. 1946. *Small arms design and ballistics,* vol. I & II. Georgetown, NC: Small-Arms Technical Publishing Company (Samworth Books).

Wolten, G. M., and R. S. Nesbit. 1980. On the mechanism of gunshot residue particle formation. *Journal of Forensic Sciences* 25: 533.

Index

A

abraded collar, 135, 138, 146
absence of striations, 83, 108–109, *see also* Striations
absence/presence, close-range phenomena
  blackening, 132
  bullet chips, 133, 135
  burning, 131
  contact shots, 135
  gunshot residue particles, 135
  metal vapor smudging, 133
  overview, 130–131
  powder tattooing, 132–133
  projectile scrapings, 133, 135
  scorching, 131–132
adapters, 68, 98
air-cushion wads
  barrel marks, 119
  chamber marks, 121
  flight of cushion/sealing wads, 116
  mathematical formulism, 117
  spread of pellets, 95–96
ambiguous and deceptive marks evaluation
  breech scrape marks, 37–38
  partial sliding marks, 37–38
  striations due to cartridge tampering, 36–37
  striations on primer, 33–36
angular slant, 61–62
assessment
  absence of striations, 83
  bullets appearing as unfired, 79–81
  bullets without striations, 78
  chamber alignment, 81–83
  continuous striations, 77, 81
  discontinuous striations, 77–78, 81
  faint striation patches, 78
  insignificant striation patches, 78
  longitudinal joints/protrusions from barrel marks, 83
  multiple striation patches, 83
  single striation patch, 78, 81–82
  smoothbore firearms using rifled ammunition, 77–83
asymmetrical bullets, 125
automatic firearms
  ejector marks, 57
  self-inflicted injuries, 168

B

backward projection, closing disk, 114
ballistic coefficient, 155, 156–157
barrel dimension
  choke, 97–98
  length, 98–100
barrel lengths
  irrespective of ammunition, 12–13
  misleading range determination, 99–100
  overview, 98–99
barrel marks
  on fired shot/pellets l, 101
  on wads, 119–120
barrel shape and size, varying
  barrel shape, 10
  bore dimension, 10, 12
  breech diameter, 12
  muzzle diameter, 12
  overview, 9–10
bent bullets, 128
Beretta guns, 5
blackening
  absence, 149
  bullet periphery, 138–141
  entry wound, 147
  overview, 132
bolt action rifles, 39
bore/caliber designation
  overview, 20
  relative bullet-bore diameter designation, 20–21
  relative wad-bore diameter designation, 21

bore dimensions
  barrel shape and size, 10, 12
  misleading range determinations, 99–100
bottlenecked characteristics
  chamber marks, low-pressure rounds, 47
  chamber shape and size, 42–43
branded legal firearms
  global origination, 5
  modification, 3–4
breech-cartridge comparison, 40
breech diameter, 12
breech edge marks, 33
breech examination, 38–41
breech face marks
  deceptive and ambiguous marks evaluation, 33–38
  examination of breech, 38–41
  modified procedures for reproduction, 27–33
  overview, 24–27
breech impressions without firing, 31–32
breech marks, 52
breech scrape marks
  ambiguous and deceptive marks evaluation, 37–38
  striated breech comparison, 40–41
breech thickness, irrespective of ammunition, 13
buckshot/LG/SG
  barrel marks, 101
  number of fires, misleading conclusions, 106–107
  reloaded short size, 110–112
bullets
  appearing as unfired, 79–81
  bore size, without striations, 78
  chips, 133, 135
  fragments, 62, 149
  tandem, 148–149
  without striations, 78
burning, 131

C

caliber
  designation, 20–21
  overview, 143–144
cartridge-cartridge comparisons, 39
cartridge headspace (CHS), 16, 29–30
cartridges
  breech scrape marks, 37
  partial sliding marks, 37
  replaced firing pin, 52
  splits and unusual chamber marks on fired wads, 120–122
  time of firing, 169–170
castings
  barrel marks, 102
  chamber marks without firing, 45–46
chamber-bore joint marks, 43–44
chamber dimensions, 99–100
chamber length, 15–16
chamber marks
  chamber-bore joint marks, 43–44
  low-pressure test rounds, 47
  modified procedure for reproducing, 44–47
  overview, 41–42
  shape, 42–43
  size, 42–43
  without firing, 45–46
chambers, shape and size
  chamber length, 15–16
  irregular bottlenecked chamber, 16
  overview, 13–14
  relative chamber-bore alignment, 15
  relative chamber-bore diameter, 15
chemical examination, 79
choke, 97–98, 102
CHS, *see* Cartridge headspace (CHS)
circular holes, 145–146, *see also* Keyholes
circular wounds, 146
class characteristic parameters
  chambers, shape and size, 14
  irregular bottlenecked chamber, 16
  oversized smoothbore barrel marks, 71–73
  rifling marks, 161
  smoothbore firearms using rifled ammunition, 76–83
  undersized smoothbore barrel marks, 70–71
  variable smoothbore barrel marks, 74–76
classification system, 20–21
claw-type extractor, 56
close-range phenomena
  blackening, 132
  bullet chips, 133, 135
  burning, 131
  contact shots, 135
  gunshot residue particles, 135
  metal vapor smudging, 133

overview, 130–131
powder tattooing, 132–133
projectile scrapings, 133, 135
scorching, 131–132
coaxial bullet-bore, 70
coaxial bullets, 73
cocking operations, 18
Colt guns, 5
constructional features, 1–2
chamber length, 13
classification system, 20–21
contact shots, 135
continuous striations, 77, 81, *see also* Striations
convergent striation, 39
copies of branded firearms, 4–5
copper, tests for, 162
crime and crime cases
blackening/blackened bullet periphery, 141
breech examination, 41
breech impressions without firing, 31–32
breech marks, 28, 38
DBBL gun, 51
dispersion of wad, 113–114
ejector marks, 58
extractor marks, low-pressure round, 56–57
firing pin arrangement, 18
firing pin marks without test firing, 54
illegal firearms in, 1–3
jacketed bullets and lead core, 172
lead bullets, 64
modified LLAMA auto pistol, 4
multifiring pin hits evaluation, 49–51
obsolete shotgun/sporting rifle, 4, 66
place of worship, 162–163
replaced firing pin, 52–53
SBBL gun, 58
slightly oversized rifled barrels, 66
striations on primer, 34
tampered firearms, 30–31
Cummings approximation, 116–117, 156
cupped shotgun cartridge, spread of pellets, 97
curved keyholes, 144–145, *see also* Keyholes
cylindro-conical bullets, 156

D

Danao (Bohol province), 4
Danao City (Cebu), 5
Darra (Pakistan/Afghanistan border)
branded legal firearm copies, 4–5
breech marks, 28
lead bullets, 64
data bank, rifling specifications
inappropriate/irregular rifling, 67
lead bullets, redundancy, 63
overview, 62
DBBL (double barrel breech loading) gun
breech impressions without firing, 31–32
choke, barrel dimensions, 98
ejector marks, 57
multifiring pin hits evaluation, 50–51
deceptive and ambiguous marks evaluation, *see also* Misleading conclusions
breech scrape marks, 37–38
partial sliding marks, 37–38
striations due to cartridge tampering, 36–37
striations on primer, 33–36
direction of fire
homemade firearms, 19
overview, 146–150
dirt collar, 135, 138
discharge gases, 164–165
discontinuous striations
bore size from barrel marks, 77–78
chamber alignment from barrel marks, 81
dispersion of pellets
barrel dimension, 97–100
fired shot charge, 95–100
overview, 95
wad type, 95–97
dispersion of wads
fired shot charge, 112–118
overview, 112–113
dissimilar marks
fired wads, 121
firing pin periphery marks, 53–54
misleading conclusions, 54–55
multifiring pin hits evaluation, 49
double barrel breech loading gun, *see* DBLL gun
double firing pin impressions, 50
doubtful recovery, defense plea, 32

E

edge marks, 58
EDXA, *see* Energy-dispersive x-ray analysis
elasticity, 9

elemental analysis, 80–81
energy-dispersive x-ray analysis (EDXA), 80–81
entry wounds, 146–150
escape of discharge gases, 164–165
evidence of firing, 161–163, *see also* Medico-legal evidence
excessively oversized bore firearms, 88
excessively oversized rifled bore, 67
exit holes, 152–154
extractor and ejector marks
  low-pressure round, extractor marks, 56–57
  overview, 55–56
  tampered firearms, ejector marks, 57–58
extraneous marks
  misaligned revolving cylinder, 27–28
  striations on primer, 36

F

faint striation patches, 78
firearms, discharge
  evidence of firing, 161–163
  firearms, 164–169
  fired cartridges, 169–170
  overview, 161, 163–164
  time of firing, 163–170
firearms, type, 143, 144–146
fired bullets
  assessment, 77–83
  bore size from barrel marks, 77–81
  chamber alignment from barrel marks, 81–83
  class characteristic parameters, 76–83
  identification of, from smoothbore firearm, 83–92
  inappropriate/irregular rifling, 67
  inappropriate modified chamber, 67
  inappropriate rifled bore barrel marks, 63–68
  longitudinal joints/protrusions from barrel marks, 83
  mismatch rifled firearms, 68
  mixed-sized, smoothbore firearms, 91–92
  nature of barrel marks, 70–76
  new parameters, 76–83
  over-bore size rifled barrels, 65–67
  oversized smoothbore barrel marks, 71–73
  oversized smoothbore firearms, 87–91
  overview, 61–63
  smoothbore firearms using rifled ammunition, 69–92
  summary, 89, 91
  under-bore size rifled barrels, 63–65
  undersized smoothbore barrel marks, 70–71
  undersized smoothbore firearms, 84–87
  variable smoothbore barrel marks, 74–76
fired cartridges
  breech face marks, 24–41
  chamber-bore joint marks, 43–44
  chamber marks, 41–47
  deceptive and ambiguous marks evaluation, 33–38
  examination of breech, 38–41
  extractor and ejector marks, 55–58
  firing pin marks, 47–54
  low-pressure round, extractor marks, 56–57
  modified procedures for reproducing, 27–33, 44–47
  multifiring pin hits evaluation, 48–51
  overview, 23–24
  shape, 42–43
  size, 42–43
  summary, 59
  tampered firearms, ejector marks, 57–58
  tampered firing pin, 51–54
  tampering with, 36–37
  time of firing, 169–170
fired shot charge
  barrel dimension, 97–100
  barrel marks, 101, 119–120
  cartridge splits, 120–122
  chamber marks on fired wads, 120–122
  dispersion of pellets and wads, 95–100, 112–118
  identification of barrel marks, 101–105
  lack of striations, 108–109
  linkage, fired pellets with suspect firearm, 101–105
  misleading conclusion, 105–108
  number of fires from fired pellets, 105–108
  overview, 93–95
  pellets without striations, 108–109
  possible misleading range determination, 95–100
  reconstruction of shooting incidents, 112–118

reloaded shot size from fired shell, 110–112
reproducibility of barrel marks, 101–105
suspect firearm, linkage, 101–105
type of wads, 95–97
wads, 95–97, 112–118
firing pin and pin marks
arrangement, 18
multifiring pin hits evaluation, 48–51
overview, 47–48
periphery marks, 53–54
tampered firing pin, 51–54
without test firing, 54
flattened buckshot, *see also* Lead
breech impressions without firing, 31
extractor marks, low-pressure round, 56
firing pin marks without test firing, 54
flight
closing disks, 114, 116
cushion/sealing wads, 116–118
mathematical formulism, 116–117
plastic wads, 117–118
wads at crime scene, 116–118
flyers, 96
forensic investigations, fired bullets
assessment, 77–83
bore size from barrel marks, 77–81
chamber alignment from barrel marks, 81–83
class characteristic parameters, 76–83
identification of, from smoothbore firearm, 83–92
inappropriate/irregular rifling, 67
inappropriate modified chamber, 67
inappropriate rifled bore barrel marks, 63–68
longitudinal joints/protrusions from barrel marks, 83
mismatch rifled firearms, 68
mixed-sized, smoothbore firearms, 91–92
nature of barrel marks, 70–76
new parameters, 76–83
over-bore size rifled barrels, 65–67
oversized smoothbore barrel marks, 71–73
oversized smoothbore firearms, 87–91
overview, 61–63
smoothbore firearms using rifled ammunition, 69–92
summary, 89, 91
under-bore size rifled barrels, 63–65
undersized smoothbore barrel marks, 70–71
undersized smoothbore firearms, 84–87
variable smoothbore barrel marks, 74–76
forensic investigations, fired cartridges
breech face marks, 24–41
chamber-bore joint marks, 43–44
chamber marks, 41–47
deceptive and ambiguous marks evaluation, 33–38
examination of breech, 38–41
extractor and ejector marks, 55–58
firing pin marks, 47–54
low-pressure round, extractor marks, 56–57
modified procedure for reproducing, 44–47
modified procedures for reproduction, 27–33
multifiring pin hits evaluation, 48–51
overview, 23–24
shape, 42–43
size, 42–43
summary, 59
tampered firearms, ejector marks, 57–58
tampered firing pin, 51–54
forensic investigations, fired shot charge
barrel dimension, 97–100
barrel marks, 101, 119–120
cartridge splits, 120–122
chamber marks on fired wads, 120–122
dispersion of pellets and wads, 95–100, 112–118
identification of barrel marks, 101–105
lack of striations, 108–109
linkage, fired pellets with suspect firearm, 101–105
misleading conclusion, 105–108
number of fires from fired pellets, 105–108
overview, 93–95
pellets without striations, 108–109
possible misleading range determination, 95–100
reconstruction of shooting incidents, 112–118
reloaded shot size from fired shell, 110–112
reproducibility of barrel marks, 101–105
suspect firearm, linkage, 101–105
type of wads, 95–97
wads, 95–97, 112–118
fragments, bullets, 62, 149

G

game hunters, 93
gangs, 2
gradients, 16
grooves, *see also* Lands
- bullets, 61
- inappropriate/irregular rifling, 67
- irregular rifling, 9
- jacketed bullets and lead core, 172
- number of, 62
- undersized smoothbore firearms, 84

gunshot residue particles (GSR)
- bullets appearing as unfired, 80
- presence/absence, close-range phenomena, 135

H

homemade firearms
- barrel length, 99
- bore dimension, varying, 12
- bottlenecked cartridges, 47
- cartridge headspace, 16
- chamber marks, low-pressure rounds, 47
- chambers, shape and size, 13–14
- characteristics, 7
- constructional features, 7
- ease of making, 2–3
- extractor and ejector marks, 55
- irregular barrel shape, 9
- irregular bottlenecked chamber, 16
- locking arrangement, 19
- pellet spread, 100
- relative chamber-bore alignment, 15
- relative chamber-bore diameter, 15
- replaced firing pin, 53
- tapered barrel shape, 9
- trigger pull, 19
- true cylindrical barrel shape, 9
- variable, unrifled bore and bullet holes, 129

I

identification of, from smoothbore firearm
- oversized smoothbore firearms, 87–91
- overview, 83–84
- summary, 89, 91
- undersized smoothbore firearms, 84–87

illegal firearms
- in crime, 2–3
- making/manufacture, 3–7

inappropriate constructional features
- barrel lengths irrespective of ammunition, 12–13
- barrel shape and size, varying, 9–10
- breech thickness, irrespective of ammunition, 13
- chambers, shape and size, 13–16
- irregular rifling, 9
- misaligned revolving cylinder, 27–28
- modified procedures for reproduction, 27–28
- muzzle thickness, irrespective of ammunition, 13
- overview, 7

inappropriate/irregular rifling, 67
inappropriate modified chamber, 67
inappropriate rifled bore barrel marks
- inappropriate/irregular rifling, 67
- inappropriate modified chamber, 67
- mismatch rifled firearms, 68
- over-bore size rifled barrels, 65–67
- overview, 63
- under-bore size rifled barrels, 63–65
  - jacketed bullets, 64–65

individual characteristic parameters, 161
inner periphery, 33
insignificant striation patches, 78
inverted margins, 146
irregular barrel shape, 9
irregular bottlenecked chamber, 16
irregular rifling, 9

J

jacketed bullets
- gunshot residue particles, 135
- under-bore size rifled barrels, 64–65

jacket pieces, rifling marks, 170–174

K

Katta, 5
keyholes
- bent bullets, 128
- caliber of bullet, 147
- direction of fire, 147
- high caliber height ratio, 143–144
- oversized, unrifled bore, 128
- type of firearm, 144–145
- undersized, unrifled bore, 126–127
- variable, unrifled bore and bullet holes, 129

L

lands, *see also* Grooves
inappropriate/irregular rifling, 67
jacketed bullets and lead core, 172
number of, 62
overview, 61
laws, possession of firearms, 2
lead, *see also* Flattened buckshot
barrel marks, 103
breech impressions without firing, 31
bullets, under-bore size rifled barrels, 63–64
chamber marks, low-pressure rounds, 47
core, rifling marks, 170–174
oversized smoothbore firearms, 87–91
reloaded short size, 111
tests for, 162
lead rhodizonate, 111
legal evidence, *see* Medico-legal evidence
linkage, fired pellets with suspect firearm
barrel marks on fired shot/pellets, 101
overview, 101
reproducibility and identification of barrel marks, 101–105
live cartridges
extractor marks, low-pressure round, 57
firing pin marks, 48
rough handling, 33
sliding chamber marks, 41–42
LLAMA auto pistol
low-pressure test rounds, 30
modification, 4
locking arrangement, 19
loose chambers
relative chamber-bore alignment, 15
relative chamber-bore diameter, 15
undersized smoothbore firearms, 84, 87
low-pressure rounds
chamber marks, 45, 47
extractor marks, 56–57
tampered firearms, 29–31
lubricating felt/fiber wad, spread of pellets, 96

M

making/manufacture, illegal firearms
copies of branded firearms, 4–5
homemade firearms, 7
illegally modified, legal firearms, 3–4
overview, 3
substandard branded firearms, 4–5
margins, 146, 153–154
mathematical formulism, 116–117
McShane equation, 157
McShane solution, 116–117
medico-legal evidence
abraded collar, 135, 138
bent bullets, 128
blackening, 132, 138–141
bullet chips, 133, 135
burning, 131
caliber of bullet, 143–144
circular holes, 145–146
close-range phenomena, 130–135
contact shots, 135
curved keyhole, 144–145
direction of fire, 146–150
dirt collar, 135, 138
entry wound, 146–150
exit holes, 152–154
firearm type, 143, 144–146
gunshot residue particles, 135
keyhole, 144–145
metal vapor smudging, 133
nonspinning bullets, 158–160
orientation/area of presentation, 158
oval holes, 145–146
oversized, unrifled bore, 128
overview, 123
powder particles, 141–143
powder tattooing, 132–133
projectile scrapings, 133, 135
projectile-tissue interactions and wound track, 151–152
rifled firearms, 129–130
scorching, 131–132
shape and size of bullet hole, 123–130
smudging, metal vapor, 133
undersized, unrifled bore, 125–127
unrifled bore using rifled ammunition, 124–129
variable unrifled bore and bullet holes, 128–129
visual examination, 138
wounding effect, fired bullets, 154–160
wound track, 151–152
metal vapor smudging, 133
militant groups, 2
misalignment
chamber, 84
revolving cylinder, 27–28

misfired cartridges, 48
misleading conclusions
  breech marks, 28
  gradients, 16
  number of fires from fired pellets, 105–108
  partial sliding marks, 37
  range determination, 99–100
  striations on primer, 34
mismatch rifled firearms, 68
mixed-sized, smoothbore firearms, 91–92
modified procedures
  breech marks, 27–33
  chamber marks, 44–46
  chamber marks, low-pressure rounds, 47
  inappropriate constructional features, 27–28
  overview, 27, 44–45
  tampered firearms, 28–33
multifiring pin hits, 48–51
multiple striation patches, 83
Munger (India), 5
muzzles
  diameter, varying, 12
  imprint, 147
  thickness, irrespective of ammunition, 13
  velocity determination, 155–156

N

nature of barrel marks, 70–76
new class characteristic parameters, 76–83
nitrate presence, 109, 142
"no gun" cases
  fired wads, 122
  inappropriate/irregular rifling, 67
  laboratory findings, 62
  lack of markings, 4
  new class characteristic parameters, 76–77
  shot charge range estimation, 94
noncoaxial bullet-bore
  relative chamber-bore alignment, 15
  undersized smoothbore barrel marks, 70–71
noncoaxial bullets, 73
nonspinning bullets, 158–160
nonstriated characteristic mark, 40
nontapered bore firearms, 75–76

O

obsolete shotgun/sporting rifle
  improvisation, 4
  slightly oversized rifled barrels, 66
oiled tests rounds
  breech marks, 28
  breech marks, modified procedures, 27
  partial sliding marks, 38
orientation/area of presentation, 158
oval holes, 145–146, *see also* Keyholes
over-bore size rifled barrels
  excessively oversized rifled bore, 67
  inappropriate rifled bore barrel marks, 65–67
  overview, 65
  slightly oversized rifled barrels, 65–67
overlapping striations, 92
oversized, unrifled bore, 128
oversized smoothbore barrel marks
  coaxial bullet, 73
  noncoaxial bullet, 73
  overview, 71–72
  smoothbore firearms using rifled ammunition, 71–73
oversized smoothbore firearms
  excessively oversized bore firearms, 88
  identification of, from smoothbore firearm, 87–91
  overview, 87–88
  very slightly oversized bore firearms, 89

P

Paltik, 5
partial sliding marks, 37–38
partly tampered gun and breech edge marks, 33
pellets, *see also* Fired shot charge
  number of fires, 105–108
  without striations appear as unfired, 108–109
perforated caps, 54
peripheral marks, 58
permanent cavity, 152
Philippines, 4, 5
physical examination, bullets, 79
pinkish color, 109, 166, 169
pistols/revolvers
  barrel lengths, 12–13
  "Saturday Night Specials," 3

place of worship, 162
plasticine
  chamber marks without firing, 46
  irregular rifling, 9
plastic wads
  flight of cushion/sealing wads, 117–118
  uncupped, single, 96–97
positive-negative comparisons, 39
powder particles, 141–143
powder pattern detection preparation, 142
powder tattooing
  absence, 149
  blackening/blackened bullet periphery, 139, 141
  close-range phenomena, 132
  entry wound, 147
  overview, 132–133
presence/absence, close-range phenomena
  blackening, 132
  bullet chips, 133, 135
  burning, 131
  contact shots, 135
  gunshot residue particles, 135
  metal vapor smudging, 133
  overview, 130–131
  powder tattooing, 132–133
  projectile scrapings, 133, 135
  scorching, 131–132
projectiles
  close-range phenomena, 133, 135
  movement, 12
  tissue interactions and wound track, 151–152
propellant combustion products, 79–80

R

range estimation
  dispersion of wad, 113–114
  misleading conclusions, 99–100
  "no gun" cases, 122
  shot charge, 94, 98–99
rate, escape of discharge gases, 164–165
reagent solution preparation, 142
relative bullet-bore diameter designation, 20–21
relative chamber-bore alignment, 15
relative chamber-bore diameter, 15
relative wad-bore diameter designation, 21
reloaded shot size from fired shell, 110–112
remaining velocity, 157–158
replaced firing pin, 52–53
reproducibility and identification of barrel marks, 101–105
revolvers, *see* Pistols/revolvers
rifles, barrel lengths, 12–13, *see also specific part*
"ring of fire," 3
Ruger guns, 5

S

"Saturday Night Specials," 3
SBBL (single barrel breech loading) gun
  breech examination, 41
  dispersion of wad, 113–114
  ejector marks, 57
  low-pressure test rounds, 30–31
  multifiring pin hits evaluation, 50
scanning electron microscope (SEM), 80
scorching, 131–132
scrape marks, firing pin, 47–48
screws, breech marks, 28
self-inflicted injuries
  automatic firearms, 168
  pellet wounds, 153–154
  timing of firing, 164–165
SEM, *see* Scanning electron microscope
semi-automatic firearms, 57
separated, dissimilar firing pin impressions, 49
shape, chamber marks, 42–43
shape and size of bullet hole
  bent bullets, 128
  oversized, unrifled bore, 128
  overview, 123–124
  rifled firearms, 129–130
  undersized, unrifled bore, 125–127
  unrifled bore using rifled ammunition, 124–129
  variable unrifled bore and bullet holes, 128–129
shot charge, *see* Fired shot charge
shotguns
  barrel lengths, 12–13
  chamber length, 15–16
  firing pin marks, 48
similar firing pin hit impressions, 49
singeing, 147, *see also* Scorching
single barrel breech loading gun, *see* SBBL gun

single striation patch
bore size from barrel marks, 78
chamber alignment from barrel marks, 81–82
size, chamber marks, 42–43
sliding barrel marks, 119
sliding breech marks
deceptive partial marks, 37
number of fires from fired pellets, 105
overview, 25
partial sliding marks, 38
striated breech comparison, 41
sliding chamber marks, 41–42
slightly oversized rifled barrels, 65–67
slugs, 102–104
Small Arms Company (India), 38
Smith and Wesson guns, 5, 165
smoothbore firearms using rifled ammunition
bore size from barrel marks, 77–81
chamber alignment from barrel marks, 81–83
nature of barrel marks, 70–76
new parameters, 76–83
oversized smoothbore barrel marks, 71–73
overview, 69–70
undersized smoothbore barrel marks, 70–71
variable smoothbore barrel marks, 74–76
spin
bullets, 61
irregular rifling, 9
shape and size, bullet hole, 123–124
sporting rifles, 68
startup gangs, 2
static breech marks
overview, 25
partial sliding marks, 38
striated breech comparison, 40–41
static chamber marks, 42–43
stray pellets, 96
striated breech comparison, 40–41
striations
absence, 83, 108–109
bore size from barrel marks, 77–81
cartridge tampering, 36–37
chamber alignment, 81–83
inappropriate/irregular rifling, 67
inappropriate modified chamber, 67
mixed-size smoothbore firearms, 91–92
oversized smoothbore barrel marks, 71–73
oversized smoothbore firearms, 87–91
pellets, 108–109
on primer, 33–36
undersized smoothbore barrel marks, 70–71
variable smoothbore barrel marks, 74–76
striking velocity determination
ballistic coefficient, 156–157
muzzle velocity, 155–156
overview, 155
remaining velocity, 157–158
substandard branded firearms, 4–5
suicide, *see* Self-inflicted injuries
suspect firearm linkage, 101–105

T

tampered firearms
breech impressions without firing, 31–32
ejector marks, 57–58
low-pressure test rounds, 29–31
overview, 28–29
partly tampered gun and breech edge marks, 33
tampered firing pin
firing pin marks without test firing, 54
firing pin periphery marks, 53–54
overview, 51–52
replaced firing pin, 52–53
tandem bullets, 148–149
tapered barrels
mixed-sized smoothbore firearms, 92
overview, 9
relative chamber-bore diameter, 15
variable smoothbore barrel marks, 74–75
temporary cavity, 152
tensile strength, 9
test papers preparation, 142
time of firing
firearms, 164–169
fired cartridges, 169–170
overview, 161, 163–164
toolmarks, destruction, *see* Tampered firearms
top break, hammerless shotguns, 48
trigger pull, 18–19
true cylindrical barrel shape
breech diameter, 12
overview, 9
pellet distribution, 98
relative chamber-bore diameter, 15

U

uncupped shotgun cartridge, spread of pellets
 air-cushion wad, 95–96
 lubricating felt/fiber wad, 96
 overview, 95
 uncupped single plastic wad, 96–97
 wads, 95–97
uncupped single plastic wad, 96–97
under-bore size longitudinal joints, 84
under-bore size rifled barrels
 inappropriate rifled bore barrel marks, 63–65
 jacketed bullets, 64–65
 lead bullets, 63–64
 overview, 63
undersized, unrifled bore, 125–127
undersized bore, non-aligned chamber, 84
undersized smoothbore barrel marks
 coaxial bullet-bore, 70
 noncoaxial bullet-bore, 70–71
 overview, 70
 smoothbore firearms using rifled ammunition, 70–71
 unusual surface joints, 71
undersized smoothbore firearms
 identification of, from smoothbore firearm, 84–87
 loose chamber, 84, 87
 misaligned chamber, 84
 overview, 84
 under-bore sized, longitudinal joints, 84
 undersized bore, non-aligned chamber, 84
unrifled bore using rifled ammunition
 bent bullets, 128
 oversized, unrifled bore, 128
 overview, 124
 undersized, unrifled bore, 125–127
 variable unrifled bore and bullet holes, 128–129
unusual barrel marks on wads, 119–120
unusual firearms
 barrel lengths irrespective of ammunition, 12–13
 barrel shape and size, varying, 9–10
 bore/caliber designation, 20–21
 breech thickness, irrespective of ammunition, 13
 caliber designation, 20–21
 cartridge headspace, 16
 chambers, shape and size, 13–16
 firing pin arrangement, 18
 illegal firearms, 2–7
 inappropriate constructional features, 7, 9–16
 irregular rifling, 9
 locking arrangement, 19
 making/manufacture, 3–7
 muzzle thickness, irrespective of ammunition, 13
 overview, 1–2
 trigger pull, 18–19
unusual surface joints, 71

V

variable smoothbore barrel marks
 nontapered bore firearms, 75–76
 overview, 74
 smoothbore firearms using rifled ammunition, 74–76
 tapered barrels, 74–75
variable unrifled bore and bullet holes, 128–129
velocity determination
 ballistic coefficient, 156–157
 muzzle velocity, 155–156
 overview, 155
 remaining velocity, 157–158
very slightly oversized bore firearms, 89
visual examination, 138

W

wads
 barrel marks, 103, 119–120
 cartridge splits and chamber marks, 120–122
 crime scene, 113–118
 cupped shotgun cartridge, 97
 dispersion, 95–97, 112–118
 entry wound, 149
 flight of closing disks, 114, 116
 flight of cushion/sealing wads, 116–118
 flight of wads, 118
 lubricating felt/fiber wads, 96
 overview, 95, 113–114
 plastic wads, 96–97, 117–118
 type, 95–97
 uncupped shotgun cartridge, 95–97

wall thickness, 13
Webley and Scott guns
    breech marks, 28
    copies, 4–5
    lead bullets, 64
Winchester cartridges, 36
Winchester Company, 36
worship, 162
wounding effect, fired bullets
    nonspinning bullets, 158–160
    orientation/area of presentation, 158
    overview, 154–155
    velocity determination, 155–158

Z

zigzag overlapping, 89

For Product Safety Concerns and Information please contact our EU representative GPSR@taylorandfrancis.com
Taylor & Francis Verlag GmbH, Kaufingerstraße 24, 80331 München, Germany

www.ingramcontent.com/pod-product-compliance
Ingram Content Group UK Ltd.
Pitfield, Milton Keynes, MK11 3LW, UK
UKHW011011180926
475701UK00004B/672

* 9 7 8 0 3 6 7 7 7 8 6 8 2 *